JOANNA _____ journal-
ist and an influential commentator on the British food chain. She
has won four Glenfiddich awards for her writing, including a
Glenfiddich Special Award for her first book, *The Food We Eat*, a
_____line Walker Media Award for 'Improving the Nation's Health
___ Means of Good Food', a Guild of Food Writers Award for *The
___d We Eat* and the *Good Housekeeping* Outstanding Contri-
b___ on to Food Award 2007. In 2004 she won the prestigious Derek
___per Award, one of BBC Radio 4's Food and Farming Awards.
___ has also written three other groundbreaking books, *How to
A___id GM Food*, *The Food Our Children Eat* and *Bad Food Britain*.
___ writes and broadcasts frequently on food issues.

Visit www.AuthorTracker.co.uk for exclusive information
on your favourite HarperCollins authors

From the reviews of *Shopped*:

'A___rave, important, eye-opening book . . . Joanna Blythman scrapes
___ the gloss to expose the chilling facts . . . She writes with calm,
cla__ty and wit, unafraid to point out that the emperor has no
clothes. Blythman has provided a compelling wake-up call. Now it
i___up to us to add our voices to hers, to vote with our shopping
___kets and take at least some of our business elsewhere'
PHILIPPA DAVENPORT, *Financial Times*

___llently documented and consciously fair . . . It does not rant,
___allows the catastrophe to unfold in slow and precise detail before
___r eyes'
ADAM NICOLSON, *Daily Telegraph*

___nvincing and damning picture, compellingly argued'
TOM FORT, *Sunday Telegraph*

'The facts [Blythman] sets out are stark and believable, the abuses she recounts are frightening, and the insight into how food reaches the consumer's plate is fascinating . . . A gripping read'
CRAIG SAMS, chair of the Soil Association and president of Green & Black's Chocolate

'Read Joanna Blythman's thought-provoking, witty and occasionally chilling voyage of discovery, and you'll never look at the contents of your supermarket trolley in the same way again'   *Herald*

'Shocking and galvanising . . . it is still possible to avert a future in which Tesco provides for all our needs from womb to tomb. Support alternatives to supermarkets wherever you can'   *Guardian*

'An emotive attack on our supermarket culture . . . a manifesto for another type of lifestyle. *Shopped* pricks a nerve. It's impossible to read it and not want to cut up your loyalty card'   *Sunday Herald*

'Devastating . . . it will change your shopping habits for good'
The Tablet

'Joanna Blythman has written a brilliant exposé of the supermarket culture pervading the country. It should be required reading in every household'   DOMINIC PRINCE, *Spectator*

'A bold and well-researched critique of supermarkets'
JOHN O'CONNELL, *Time Out*

'*Shopped* is Joanna Blythman's meticulously researched exposé of our favourite retailers. This is a book that will make you angry at just how far the supermarkets have misled us, seducing us with apparent convenience, choice and value whilst destroying our farming heritage and food culture'   *Food Magazine*

By the same author

The Food We Eat
The Food Our Children Eat
How to Avoid GM Food
Bad Food Britain

Shopped

THE SHOCKING POWER OF BRITISH SUPERMARKETS

Joanna Blythman

HARPER PERENNIAL
London, New York, Toronto and Sydney

Harper Perennial
An imprint of HarperCollins*Publishers*
77–85 Fulham Palace Road
Hammersmith
London W6 8JB

www.harperperennial.co.uk

This updated edition published by Harper Perennial 2007

Previously published in paperback by Harper Perennial 2005
(reprinted six times)
First published by Fourth Estate 2004

A catalogue record for this book
is available from the British Library

ISBN-13: 978-0-00-715804-1

Set in Sabon by
Rowland Phototypesetting Ltd, Bury St Edmunds, Suffolk

For Lynda and Nick

Contents

Acknowledgements

Literally hundreds of research sources have been used in this book, but I am particularly indebted to *The Grocer* magazine for its extensive news coverage and useful insights into the world of supermarketing. It has become compulsory Saturday morning reading. The Competition Commission's 2000 report on supermarkets and its 2003 report on the sale of Safeway were both invaluable sources of much remarkable but under-reported information. I have also benefited from a free press cuttings service of astonishing breadth and depth, thanks to the eagle eye of Janey Buchan.

Some friends and colleagues have given me tremendous support throughout the two years it took to research and write this book. Louise Haines is the finest editor any author could wish for. Without her regular prompts that it was time to get writing again, this book would never have seen the light of day. I wish I could tell my agent, Giles Gordon, how glad I am now that he finally twisted my arm into agreeing to write it, but sadly Giles died just as the manuscript was completed. He is sorely missed. Food writer Lynda Brown has been my close adviser throughout the project. Her sophisticated grasp of food issues combined with infinite patience made her the perfect sounding board when I was struggling with ideas. Her unswerving confidence in the book was a constant tonic. Sandra Bell of Friends of the Earth generously shared information and helped me in a number of ways, not least by reading the final manuscript. Professor Tim Lang of

City University also gave up his precious time to read and comment on the final text. Food writer Jo Ewart carried out some very efficient research on my behalf. Anne Askwith made a beautiful job of copy-editing the book.

All the following people put themselves out to help me in some way, mainly by offering or checking information, acting as guides or by agreeing to interviews: Chris Allen, Sue Clifford, Mary Contini, David Craig, Marguerite Cullen, Kath Dalmeny, Jonathan Eddy, Rex Goldsmith, Martin Goodfellow, Richard Haddock, Dave Hammond, Charlie Hicks, Peter Jacobs, Diane Lamb, Felicity Lawrence, David Lidgate, David McCrae, Iain Mellis, Sandra Nicholson, Moy Scott, Charles Secrett, Andrew Simms, Alistair Smith, John Thorley, Bill Vorley, Frances Ward, Judith Whateley, Andrew Whitley.

Finally, I want to thank the very long list of people who let me have their insights into how the supermarket system operates but who must remain anonymous for fear of repercussions. I hope I have managed to represent the full extent of their concerns.

Supermarket starters

Leafing through this book you might get the impression that it is written by a longstanding opponent and critic of supermarkets. It might surprise you to know that actually there was a time when I pushed my trolley around the supermarket just like the next person. In common with most food shoppers, I believed that supermarkets offered a welcome addition to traditional shopping outlets – butchers, fishmongers, grocers and so on – expanding the all-round food shopping choice. I thought, naively, that supermarkets were an 'as well as' not 'instead of' feature of the retail scene.

Then in 1992 I moved to Strasbourg in France. There I shopped like a typical French person. I used small shops and food markets routinely, making a trip out of town about once a month to stock up at the hypermarket on boring items such as cat food and dishwasher salt. Naturally, when I was there, I cherry-picked any attractive special offers. But I soon learnt that to a French person – or any other European for that matter – the British idea of buying everything you need in a once-a-week supermarket shopping blitz was alien, bizarre even. The French are quite clear that although supermarkets are handy for standard items, the best food is on sale elsewhere.

Returning to the UK in 1995, I found that I was bridling at the prospect of readjusting to the prevailing supermarket-shopping pattern. Indeed, I saw it with new eyes. Several useful independent local shops had closed down in the time I had been away and just up the road, where there used to be playing fields for schoolchildren, the dreariest of Tescos had sprung up. There it was, big, ugly and floodlit twenty-four hours a day, squatting behind a brash new roundabout in a sea of new roads and concrete parking spaces. Still, it was close and convenient (or so I thought), the obvious place to head for when the milk and toilet rolls ran out.

So I used it anyway, but it was only a matter of months before I realised that shopping there was stultifying any creative urge I had to cook because I simply couldn't find the sort of food I want to eat and feed to my family. In exasperation I started driving further to other supermarket chains, but I found myself having the same reaction. The penny dropped that what I was looking for was fresh, local, seasonal ingredients produced by a large number of small, diverse producers. What supermarkets excel at, on the other hand, is over-packaged, often over-processed, much-travelled ingredients that put two fingers up to the seasons and any notion of locality or geographical specificity.

I began to see what a spirit-crushing and alienating experience supermarket shopping actually was. How in UK chains, any given day of the year is just like every other day. How the experience of shopping in Salford is exactly like shopping in Southampton, Sheffield or Stirling. I realised that supermarket shopping was turning me into a robotic Stepford wife – minus the fixed smile. I bought the same repeat items and gritted my teeth as I made my way round the aisles on autopilot. I spent a fortune every time. My cupboards and fridge were constantly stuffed with food and yet somehow I could never think of anything to cook.

Slowly but surely I became deeply discontented with the quality of food that was on offer. I wasn't interested in 'Buy One Get One Free' offers on fizzy drinks and multi-packs of flavoured crisps, which seemed to be something of a supermarket speciality. I didn't buy much processed food and always bypassed the sprawling shelves loaded up with ready meals. I was looking for fresh, unprocessed food ingredients and I came to see that in this department UK supermarkets just didn't deliver. Ripe fruit? That's too much hassle for them so forget it. Properly hung meat? That takes too long and cuts profit margins, so forget that too. Decent bread without chemically hardened fats or GM enzymes? Nicely ripened cheese? Dream on. A chicken that has not stood in excrement in an overcrowded broiler shed? 'Well, we only get two boxes of free-range/organic chicken once a week and we've run out and even then it's only whole birds not chicken pieces . . .' Why? 'Because there's not enough demand for it.'

Eventually, I got fed up with being marginalised as a cranky customer with odd and unrepresentative eating habits. My patience ran out, and on 1 January 2002, I made a New Year resolution to support the independent food sector and stop shopping routinely in supermarkets. I started revisiting independent butchers, fishmongers, cheesemongers and greengrocers with increasing relish. I rediscovered vigorous coriander in fist-sized bunches, not a few limp and olive-coloured stalks in shiny plastic. My fish was lustrous and had a sparkle in its eye, unlike the matt, flaccid specimens on the supermarket slab. I was nudged into remembering how good beef was reddish-brown, marbled with creamy fat and tender, not bright red, lean and tough. I signed up for an organic vegetable box and really looked forward to Thursdays when it was delivered to my door, just for the sheer pleasure of seeing what was different and seasonal that week. Fortnightly farmers' markets became an unmissable event on Saturday mornings. I got to know the shopkeepers, stallholders and delivery men, and came to value my interaction with them. It's hard to build a relationship with a low-paid, mind-numbed checkout operator or a harassed shelf-stacker. Gradually, supermarkets became a residual shopping possibility for me, generally when I had completely run out of uninteresting and heavy items.

In no time at all it was as if a horrible black burden had been lifted off my shoulders. The day-in, day-out struggle to feed everyone seemed to abate. My urge to cook and my gastronomic creativity soared. The contents of my rubbish bin shrank as it no longer had to accommodate excessive quantities of unnecessary and unsustainable supermarket packaging. An unforeseen bonus was that far from spending more money, I was spending less. This was chiefly because the independents' prices were lower: supermarkets are surprisingly expensive places to shop for fresh, unprocessed meat, fish, fruit and vegetables. But it was also because I wasn't routinely over-buying and being snared into stocking up with products I did not need and probably would never get around to eating. In fact, we were spending less money on food but eating better and more healthily than before.

Then I got the idea of writing a book about supermarkets. I wanted to investigate why they were so incapable of supplying the kind of food that I, and a growing number of people, want to eat. I began to see how we consumers had unwittingly relinquished sovereignty over what we eat to a handful of large corporations that now control 80 per cent of the UK's shopping spend.

In effect, our shopping choices are now dictated by a few monopolistic retailers who, by wooing consumers with apparently low prices and lobbying subsequent governments not to interfere with their divine right to make money, have been allowed to develop an unhealthy grip over the nation's shopping basket. At the beginning of 2007, Tesco ate up almost 32 per cent of the UK's spend, giving it a scary degree of purchasing power over suppliers and considerable scope to redesign what we eat to suit its own objectives.

Let's be clear that large supermarket chains are companies whose aim is not, first and foremost, to meet society's interests. They aren't too concerned about being excellent grocers, or supplying the nation with good-quality, wholesome food, or supporting British farmers or treating Third World workers ethically or being kind to turkeys or helping working mothers to feed their children better – or any other goal of which many of us would approve. The leading supermarket chains are all making great play of how 'green' they are. Tesco says that it is going to publish the carbon footprint of each of its products while Sainsbury's, Asda and Waitrose have all pledged to reduce waste, amongst other measures. Some supermarket green claims sound better than they really are. Tesco has introduced degradable bags, but they are still made from plastic. These 'degradable' bags need sunlight in order to break down, and the majority will probably end up in landfill sites where they are more likely to break down into methane, a potent greenhouse gas.

UK supermarkets are definitely making efforts to green up their act, but when the National Consumer Council examined their performance in 2006 – looking at food transport, waste, sustainable sourcing and farming – it concluded that no supermarket rated well on all criteria. The truth is that supermarkets find it extremely difficult to 'go green' because environmental damage is part of the fabric of their business, thanks to transport-related carbon emissions, excessive packaging and their endless expansion plans. So they are happy to go along with ideas or demands that are generally progressive, such as stocking more organic food or installing solar panels, but only as long as it is in their commercial interest to do so. The crunch comes when doing the right thing – the ethical thing – would actually cost them money or interfere with their modus operandi. Then they are not so keen. The bottom line is that they are stock market-driven corporations whose overarching goal is to keep their shareholders happy. And the sad fact is that, in partnership with the food industry, they have debased our whole appreciation of food. It is no coincidence that the UK, the country with the worst food culture in Europe, the one with the most palpable obesity problem, is also the country most wedded to supermarket shopping.

When you read this book I hope you too will come to see that 'Big Food' and 'Big Retail' are really two sides of the same coin.

Big global food manufacturers need big supermarket chains to get their products on to the shelves and our big supermarkets need big food processors to churn out items such as chicken kievs glued together with additives to make their profits. It's an unholy alliance where supermarkets are effectively gatekeepers for a system of food production that is about putting profit before quality, the environment or public health.

Next time you are in a supermarket, take a look at what products are on prominent special offer on those lucrative shelf ends. You can bet your bottom dollar that the vast majority will be stacked high with everything the nation would be better off not eating. The business logic, of course, is faultless. Supermarkets make more money out of selling value-added processed junk than they do good food. There's a limit to how much they can charge for a potato, even well-scrubbed 'heirloom' varieties. But process a nondescript white spud into a pre-cooked, microwavable baked potato or 'child-friendly' potato shapes and the sky is the limit.

While consumers think that the supermarkets are there to serve us, they actually operate to a totally different agenda. Supermarkets sell us what it suits them to sell. They decide what makes them money and then they figure out ways of marketing it to us so that we want to buy it. Their stocks-in-trade are products sourced nationally or globally at their behest from an increasingly small number of large, but nevertheless captive, suppliers. In that process they are reshaping our food chain for the worse. The buying terms and prices that they impose on farmers reward and encourage intensive farming and militate against smaller, more quality-conscious producers. The supermarket system does not reward flavour or biodiversity, just volume and standardisation. You will doubtless have heard murmurings about how supermarkets treat their suppliers. Let me tell you that it is even worse than you might suspect. Nowadays supermarkets and suppliers have a feudal relationship with each other: they are lord and vassal.

The irony of the great supermarket revolution is that the concept they sold us, choice, has actually become a vehicle for denying us that. What 'choice' do we really have when all we have to choose between is a Tesco or an Asda, a Sainsbury's or a Morrisons? You may have noticed, at least at a subliminal level, how one chain's sandwich is pretty much like another's, how supermarket chicken tikkas all share that haunting industrial gloopiness. Large supermarkets typically stock some 32,000 lines, but a bit like a subscription to endless American or Italian TV channels, it's a quantitative, not qualitative choice. And this supermarket monotony becomes all the more oppressive as the supermarkets recolonise with smaller-format stores the high streets they killed off in the first place.

But as more centres turn into anonymous, identikit trolley towns dominated by the suffocating presence of big supermarket chains, we consumers do have a choice. We can lie down and let the supermarkets take total control of what ends up on our plates. We can stand by, dismayed but passive, as they drive all but the largest farmers and food suppliers out of business by sourcing products from parts of the globe where they can buy for even less. Or we can change our food shopping habits and use them to vote for a different sort of food economy, one that supports small, local and diverse, not large, global and monotonous. I hope that when you read this book, you'll ask yourself which sort of food world you want to live in. We can't have both.

SUPERMARKET SPACE

1

Forgotten people

In June 2003, when a new Sainsbury's Local, complete with cash machine, sliding doors and eight gleaming tills, opened opposite them, the owners of Belmont Mini Market in Chalk Farm were worried. A new shiny supermarket right across the street is every small shopkeeper's nightmare. History shows that when a super-market opens, local shopkeepers can moan and complain all they like, but it's just a matter of time until all but the most exceptional amongst them lose just enough business to the newcomer to make their own enterprises unviable. But the Belmont Mini Market refused to lie down and be ignored. It had been open seven days a week, from seven in the morning until eleven at night, for the last eighteen years. Locals valued the service it provided, and in particular the pleasantness of the hard-working Sri Lankan owners. Belmont Mini Market joined forces with an especially appreciative customer, a creative communication agency, to make local people think twice before bypassing them for Sains-bury's. With the agency's help, the owners sent letters to local residents and printed fly-posters and stickers with photos of the Mini Market's staff that read, 'Sainsbury has got electric sliding door but please do not be forgetting us.' They even posted a man with a placard outside Sainsbury's to emphasise the point. Three months after the opening of Sainsbury's, one of the owners,

Mariathas Suthakaran, told me that although sales of some lines such as bread and milk were slightly down, customers were still coming into his store.

Chalk Farm's residents and workers may not easily forget the endearing staff at the Belmont Mini Market, but statistics show that the UK collectively has forgotten thousands of other shopkeepers. The figures vary depending on the source and its classification of shops, but the overall picture is remarkably consistent, showing a steady decline in small shops as the supermarkets have progressively taken control of the nation's shopping basket. The nation of shopkeepers has become a nation of supermarkets.

In 1950, supermarkets had only 20 per cent of the grocery market while small shops and traditional Co-ops had 80 per cent between them. By 1990, this situation had been more or less reversed, with supermarkets eating up almost 80 per cent of the grocery market. In 1998, when the Department of the Environment, Transport and the Regions (DETR) undertook what is considered to be the most comprehensive governmental assessment of the implications of food store developments, it confirmed a phenomenon that most consumers had already observed first hand. 'Our research has shown that large foodstores can and have had an adverse impact on market towns and district centres ... The level and consequences of impact will vary depending on the particular local circumstances ... Smaller centres which are dependent to a large extent on convenience retailing to underpin their function are most vulnerable to the effects of larger foodstore development in edge-of-centre and out-of-centre locations,' it concluded.

This study underlined just how dramatic the supermarket effect could be. When Tesco had opened a store on the edge of Cirencester in Wiltshire, the market share of town-centre food shops declined by 38 per cent. For convenience shops the study found that the damage was even more acute. In Fakenham in Norfolk, for example, it found that the opening of an out-of-town supermarket had caused a 64 per cent decline in market share for the convenience shops in the town centre. At Warminster in Hampshire, the decline was even more marked – 75 per cent. The trend has continued since the study. When Tesco opened a new 37,000-square-foot store in Hove in 2003, for instance, the effect on neighbouring retailers was almost instant. Within a week, small shopkeepers' sales had tumbled. The local green-grocer said that he had hoped that Tesco would bring extra footfall into the area, but sales were down 25–30 per cent. It was the same story at the post office. 'They [sales] are about 25 per cent down. Hopefully it's only the effect of the opening week. If it is not, we will be stuffed,' said postmaster Nayan Shah.

When the New Economics Foundation examined the phenomenon know as 'Ghost Town Britain' – the slow death of community life in small towns and villages – it probed the mechanism by which supermarkets suck life from local shops and reported:

> Suppose a supermarket opens on the outskirts of a town and half the residents start to do one third of their shopping there. These people still do two thirds of their shopping in the town centre, while the other half of the population continues to do all its shopping in the centre. Although all the residents still patronise the town centre, its retail revenue drops about 16.7% – enough to start killing off shops. This is a perverse market dynamic; a loss to the entire community that not a single person would have wanted. It is also self-reinforcing: once the downtown starts to shut down, people who preferred to shop there have no choice but to switch to the supermarket. What begins as a seemingly harmless ripple becomes a powerful and destructive wave.

Statistics on small shops read like casualties of a curiously uneven war. In 2000, when the DETR Select Committee considered the impact of supermarkets, it noted that the number of independent grocers in the UK had fallen from 116,000 in 1961 to only

20,900 in 1997. Statistics compiled by the Meat and Livestock Commission using figures from the Institute of Grocery Distribution, Taylor Nelson Sofres and the Office of National Statistics show that there were only 23,960 independent grocers in the UK in 2001 compared to 62,000 in 1977.

The same pattern is mirrored in figures for specialist shops. Independent butcher's shops, for example, declined from 25,300 to 8,344 in the same period. Roughly two out of every three butchers have gone out of business in the last twenty-five years. Between 1990 and 2000, supermarkets' share of the fresh fish market increased from 21.4 per cent to over 66 per cent, while fishmongers' market share fell to 20.3 per cent. Between 1997 and 2002, specialist stores like butchers, bakers and fishmongers closed at the rate of fifty a week. Figures logged by the Office of National Statistics show that the number of businesses selling food, tobacco and beverages fell by 37 per cent between 1994 and 2001; if decline persists at the same rate, another 10,000 businesses will have vanished by 2005 and the total number of local shops selling these goods will have been halved in just over a decade. Researchers at Manchester School of Management have predicted that if current trends continue there might not be a single independent food store left in the whole of the UK by 2050.

This projected disappearance of independent food shops is a disturbing possibility, not only because it erodes choice, but also because these shops produce more economic benefits for their immediate community than supermarket chains. It has been calculated that every £10 spent in a local food initiative (shop, farmer's market, farm shop or box scheme) is worth £25 to the local economy because small local food businesses – by using local farmers, the nearest locksmith or printer and so on – support other local businesses. That same £10 spent in a supermarket produces just £14 worth of benefits for the local community.

Obviously the closure of small shops means job losses – and these losses are not compensated for with new supermarket jobs.

The National Retail Planning Forum has calculated that new food superstores have, on average, a negative effect on retail employment. Its 1998 report said that every superstore opening resulted in a net loss in employment of 276 full-time equivalents. A majority of supermarket jobs are part-time, so the arrival of supermarkets means that many full-time jobs in the local community are replaced by part-time ones.

As the DETR Select Committee noted, supermarket blight has been most pronounced in smaller towns, villages and rural areas. By 2000, the Countryside Agency was saying that seven out of ten English villages had been left without a shop. In 2001 the Rural Shops Alliance found that there were fewer than 12,000 rural shops left in the UK; and, according to *The Grocer* magazine, these were closing at the rate of 300 a year.

The haemorrhage of small independent shops that started in the 1980s and accelerated throughout the 1990s has settled down to a steady drip in the last couple of years. In 2001, net closures amongst smaller newsagents, for example, were running at the rate of almost one a day. The Institute of Grocery Distribution has reported that there were 953 fewer convenience stores in the UK in 2001 than there were in 2000: a 1.7 per cent drop. It predicts that this trend will continue, with another 3,700 shops disappearing by 2006.

As far as our large supermarkets are concerned, such effects are just the natural law of the retail jungle. If local shops, even smaller supermarkets, close, so what? Small-scale retailing RIP. As one supermarket expert put it: 'The supermarket groups are running businesses. The success of superstores shows that they are meeting the needs of shoppers, at least the majority of them. The retailers have discovered the right business model, recognized the opportunity; government policy let them rip. People want to use their cars and will do so whenever possible.'

Mention the words 'parking' or 'pedestrianisation' to independent shopkeepers and be prepared to stand and listen for some time. They feel a huge sense of injustice at the large supermarket chains' free-parking advantage over town-based shops. They see themselves as victims of pseudo-environmental town planning, selectively applied. Consumers can drive to out-of-town super-stores and park for free. But if they would prefer to spread a significant amount of their household shopping around local shops, either they will need strong arms to transport heavy shopping by foot – in 2000 the average family food shopping weighed around 36 kilos – or they will have to cruise round patiently in their cars to find one of a diminishing number of parking spaces. When the DETR's Select Committee looked at this issue, it confirmed the disadvantage that small shopkeepers feel so intensely. 'The large amounts of free car parking offered by existing out of town supermarkets gives them an enormous competitive advantage over city-centre stores. In addition, super-markets at these sites generate more car use, making the situation on already congested roads worse. The situation needs to be addressed urgently,' it concluded. To redress this obvious injus-tice, Deputy Prime Minister John Prescott mooted the idea of a tax on supermarket parking. Supermarkets would have had to pay something back to the country for their acres of free car parks. But the supermarkets lobbied successfully to have this proposal dropped. Hence the current status quo in which super-markets dangle a free-parking carrot to consumers while local shops and their potential customers dodge vigilant traffic war-dens keenly enforcing their council's green-sounding, leave-your-car-at-home policy.

For the small, local shops that remain, survival gets ever more complicated too. Small shops have to try to survive a campaign of attrition. Throughout the 1980s and 1990s they had to see off not just the first wave of supermarket openings but also the second and third as rival chains competed for market share in their area. The drastically reduced number of small shops that have survived that period now have to watch these supermarket chains replicating like mutants in a sci-fi film as they extend and refurbish existing stores out of town and set up new ones in smaller sizes and formats in the high street. Life isn't getting any easier for independent shopkeepers.

2

Trolley towns

The term 'company town' was coined by historians to describe centres of population made distinctive by the one-dimensional nature of their employment opportunities and the predominance of the large companies that controlled them. Nowadays it may be more apt to distinguish places not according to how locals earn their money, but by how they spend it. Few British towns have a distinctive sense of place any longer. Most have become trolley towns, shaped by the grocery chains that dominate them.

What does a trolley town look like? Approach any significant centre of population in the UK and you must pass through the supermarket ring. The first thing that greets you is not some distinctive civic monument or landmark but the now familiar supermarket sprawl, complete with its new roundabouts, altered road layout, traffic signals with changed priorities, petrol station and sea of parking. Welcome to Asdatown, or Tescotown, or Sainsburytown. Make it into the centre of one of these places and you're in Anytown, Anywhere. Or even Clonetown. You'll search to find anything approximating to a small greengrocer, fishmonger or butcher. These have been replaced by charity shops, video shops and, in more affluent centres, branches of large retail chains. This is the new urban landscape our large supermarket chains have bequeathed us.

Dundee is a typical trolley town, or city. Once an important port at the mouth of the River Tay, its heyday was during the industrial revolution. Dundee's reputation was built on the three Js: jam, jute and journalism. By dint of its seafaring history, Dundee claims the credit for introducing Britain to the delights of jam made from imported exotic fruits, otherwise known as marmalade. In the nineteenth century, its jute mills swelled its population. In the twentieth century, it was better known as the home of the *Beano* and the *Dandy* comics created by local publisher D.C. Thomson. Now Dundee has a population of around 165,000. On paper, it is an interesting place to live in and visit, and not short of visual attractions. It has the silvery Tay itself and the Tay Rail Bridge, a dark mass of sturdy Victorian metal. You can still see the stump of its notorious predecessor, the one that collapsed into the river. You can visit the historic sailing ship the *Discovery*, famed for its early exploration of the Arctic. But the first thing that hits you when you approach Dundee from any direction these days is not this unique and impressive heritage but supermarkets.

In the 1990s Dundee was home to William Low, a Scottish supermarket chain with relatively small stores throughout the country. It was acquired by Tesco as a quick way for it to build its base in Scotland and compete with the then dominant chain, Safeway. Soon the whole look of Dundee started to change. Locals were amazed when, after the council had spent lots of money improving the approaches to the city, planting floral displays, landscaping and so on, Tesco got planning permission for a superstore on the city's most desirable and scenic location, Riverside Drive, with its long, open views over the Tay. Then Asda started flexing its muscles and Sainsbury's entered the fray. Now most key routes through and past Dundee seem to lead to vast supermarkets. They loom so large that they dwarf the city's outstanding historic and civic heritage. The city struggles to put itself on the tourist map, and no wonder: to the visitor, it might look as though the main occupation of its residents is super-market shopping.

Dundee city centre consists of an area of about half a square mile, large parts of which are pedestrianised. At either end, like sentinels, stand two shopping malls, tenanted with a familiar litany of chain shops – Carphone Warehouse, Claire's Access-ories, Clinton Cards and so on. Fast-food chains are also well represented. Most of the small shop units that remain in the centre have been turned into pubs or amusement centres, or charity or video rental shops.

In the 1960s, before the large UK-wide supermarket chains managed to persuade Dundee's impoverished city council, des-perate for cash, to let them have their way, this area was a thriving centre for food shopping. There were ten bakers; now there are two left. There were eight or nine butchers; now there is one. Of the five fishmongers, one has survived. Where there were half a dozen grocers, one remains. Food shoppers – as opposed to food grazers – will find little to sustain them in Dundee city centre these days.

When I visited Dundee in 2003, the city had four Tescos, two Safeways, two Asdas, one Sainsbury's, one Marks & Spencer and a clutch of discount and low-price outlets. Asda had submitted a planning application to build a third store on a greenfield site. It had commissioned a traffic-impact study to support its applica-tion and was reported to be 'ready and waiting' to state its case to councillors when it came before the planning committee. Residents, meanwhile, had formed an action group to oppose the application. Not to be left out of Dundee's supermarket mêlée, Morrisons was also in talks with the city council over its applica-tion to build a further 90,000-square-foot superstore in the city, close in scale to a Tesco Extra or an Asda superstore. Since both the Asda and Morrisons proposed sites were on council land, Dundee City Council stood to receive a substantial windfall from the sales. 'Some estimates have put the amount the local authority stands to make at anywhere between £15 and £20 million,' reported the *Evening Telegraph*. Dundee clearly did not need any more supermarkets. Yet with this sort of money to play for, you could see why councillors might be sorely tempted to say yes to a couple more.

As it stands, any Dundonian who wants to shop in independent outlets must travel to Broughty Ferry, now effectively a prosperous suburb of the city and home to a thriving rump of small shops that have so far been sheltered from the city's supermarket revolution. Here independent shopkeepers are endlessly resourceful in thinking up new ways of seeing off the supermarket threat. 'We [independent traders] are relying on the overall viability of the area by creating a food shopping cluster,' baker Martin Goodfellow told me. A few doors along, David Craig has reinvented his butcher's shop, Robertson's, as a mini Harrods food hall on the Tay, and it is renowned for its exceptional range and personal service. Both men are optimistic that they can hold the line against the supermarkets, but with new superstores opening and existing ones being extended, they remain far from complacent.

Wherever you go now in the UK, you will find cities and towns whose vitality has been drained by supermarkets. Terence Blacker wrote in the *Independent*:

> I live in East Anglia where the progress of convenience shopping has had a visible effect on the quality of life. My nearest town, Diss, has two supermarkets, squatting each side of the thoroughfare that passes near the town centre. One is adequate, the other cheap but hilariously awful. As a result of their presence, the main shopping street of a market town of 6,000 people consists almost entirely of charity shops, estate agents and, mysteriously, a number of greetings card emporia. As they go out of business, small retailers complain that the life of the town is draining away, but the planning authorities remain unimpressed. It has just been

announced that Tesco has been given permission to build another vast superstore beside the main road.

Writing in *The Grocer*, James Millar drew attention to the irony of the situation where he lived in Gloucestershire. 'A recent survey has just pronounced my local town, Tetbury, the third most desirable place to live in the UK. Tetbury, undeniably, is a nice place to live. Yet the only places you can buy apples, cauliflowers or a bag of potatoes are the local Somerfield and the almighty new Tesco. The fruit and vegetable shop has gone – shut down. We have two local butcher's shops but I wouldn't count their chickens.'

A reader wrote to tell me of the similar effect of a new Sainsbury's on the market town of Bourne in Lincolnshire. Both of the independent greengrocers had closed. One of them had become a doll's house and miniatures shop. The other had turned into a bargain outlet that sold anything, providing it was extremely cheap.

It is not only small shops that close as supermarket leviathans move in. Small or medium-sized supermarkets – the kind that can coexist with independent retailers rather than close them down – are vulnerable. In November 2003, for example, the Midlands Co-op had to close a store in Thurmaston which had been open since the 1970s after it lost the bulk of its business to a new 45,000-square-foot Asda which had opened directly opposite.

It is a familiar story, one that can be recounted time and time again by people living in every part of the UK. When the big supermarkets move in, towns and cities are pushed to what the New Economics Foundation calls 'the tipping point'. When the number of local retail outlets falls below a critical mass, the quantity of money circulating in the local economy suddenly plummets as people find there is no point in trying to do a full shop where the range of local outlets is impoverished. 'This means a sudden, dramatic loss of services – leading to food and finance deserts,' says the Foundation. In the case of big centres of population, this desertification expresses itself in a carbon-copy townscape dominated by omnipresent chains and fast-food outlets. In small places, it manifests itself in one of two forms: either pretty, but useless, main streets with a dearth of everyday services, or wholesale depression and deadness.

3

Small basket

Supermarkets already gobble up a greedy 80 per cent of the nation's grocery spend. Now they want the remaining 20 per cent. The long-term vision of the largest amongst them is that by 2020 or thereabouts, only two or three major players will possess more or less total control of the grocery market. This would make the supermarket sweep to power complete. These players would then have buyer power that allowed them to dictate terms to farmers, food producers and suppliers all over the world. Even the biggest brands, international household names, would be at their beck and call.

If supermarkets get their way, everything we buy, whether it is from a superstore, a smaller city store, a corner shop or a petrol-station forecourt, will be sold by a supermarket chain. There will be small shops, but not as we know them now. They will be run not by independents but by the supermarket chains. To realise this goal, supermarkets have embarked on a new mission. They're after what's known as 'the small basket', those more frequent shopping trips we make for just a few items. This market is what one industry commentator has called 'the new competitive challenge'.

Think of it this way. In the process of sewing up the bulk of our shopping spend, supermarkets have managed to alter our perception of food shopping totally. Where people once shopped for food fairly frequently – if not daily, probably every other day – supermarkets have institutionalised the one-stop shopping trip, a weekly expedition to stock up for the next seven days under one roof. For busy working people this system has its attractions. In theory, the one-stop shop allows us to clear the decks, to get ourselves organised in one fell swoop, saving us from having to think about grocery shopping for the rest of a pressurised week. There are, of course, problems with the concept. Fresh items such as fruit and vegetables don't all naturally last for a week. This doesn't stop supermarkets selling them to us: they simply instruct suppliers to harvest them 'green and backward' so that they don't rot and look OK on the shelves, even if they taste of zilch when we get them back home. And do you know any fishmongers who reckon that fish can be stored in domestic fridges for several days at a time, as supermarkets would have us believe, and still taste fresh when it's cooked?

Apart from making it harder to eat really fresh food, though, the one-stop shop in a big superstore is convenient. If you need to do a marathon shop for Christmas, say, or you have run out of a number of boring basics like toilet rolls, it is indisputably useful. But even the most organised consumers forget things – we run out of milk, salt perhaps; we need a lemon instantly, or dishwasher tablets – and we're getting increasingly disenchanted with having to jump in a car and drive to the nearest superstore to buy them. Five years ago, the average shopping visit or time taken to go round a supermarket was forty-five minutes. Now it only takes thirty-five minutes. Consumers are shopping more frequently for smaller amounts and becoming increasingly reluctant to trail around a vast retail shed to do so. They are deserting superstores for smaller outlets, traditional small shops (butchers, bakers, fishmongers) and convenience stores or 'C' stores which are growing in popularity. Though their ranks have severely contracted as the number of supermarkets has grown, those that are left turn a decent penny or two because we have come to rely on them more than ever before. Why leave that residual business to independents, the supermarkets ask. Their conclusion? Time to mop up the whole lot.

Smaller outlets are attractive to supermarkets because they represent a whole new opportunity to get into a market they simply could not tap with larger stores. Added to that fact is supermarkets' continuing difficulties in getting planning permission for out-of-town stores. At the end of the day, they may well get it, but what chain wants to spend years, and vast reserves of money, arguing with councils and planners when it can simply take over existing stores or sites in well-placed, central locations, with only a fraction of the hassle? What's more, the one-stop superstore market is becoming saturated. Competition is stiff and the scope for making profit or gaining market share is slimmer.

By contrast the potential for growth in town and city centres is huge because, killed off by – guess what? – those out-of-town supermarket developments with free parking, they have become food deserts. As well as buying up small outlets, they are stealing business from them. As the *Guardian*'s Brian Logan put it, 'Not content with all those out of town developments perverting the social geography of Britain, the latest supermarket wheeze is to pop up "locally", right next door to the few remaining independents and, like bogeymen, scare 'em away.' Now, ironically, supermarket chains are colonising the vacant sites that they emptied with new medium-format stores with different fascia: Tesco Metro, Safeway's Citystore, Sainsbury's Central and smaller, convenience-sized outlets such as Sainsbury's Local and Tesco Express. The latter is reported to have caused drops in business of 30–40 per cent for other local shops.

Typically these stores stock a relatively low proportion of fresh, unprocessed food and a high proportion of fast-turnaround prepared foods. When Safeway's pioneer Citystore opened in Glasgow in 2003, its shelves were filled with sandwiches, crisps and fizzy drinks, although its windows were filled with nostalgic black-and-white images of a Victorian high street, complete with trams and thriving small shops, the message being, apparently, that small supermarket convenience stores were the twenty-first-century equivalent. These smaller-format stores leach business not only from remaining independents who have stayed in business – often only by the skin of their teeth, because they offered a good service, most notably long hours – but also from other outlets such as snack bars, bakers, even chain restaurants. Increasingly, supermarkets are widening their ambitions to embrace more of what Sainsbury's calls 'the Food Continuum' – a concept based on the observation that supermarkets have brought about a 'blurring of boundaries' between cooking from scratch from primary raw ingredients and eating out. They have been instrumental in developing 'component cooking' (meals assembled using some prepared items), ready meals and take-aways such as Happy Bags, Hot Chicken and Indian or Chinese Banquets. Having strayed profitably into the 'snacking on the hoof' market and developed 'hand-held' snacks like sandwiches and sushi, the supermarkets' commercial logic leads them to more potential sales, currently made in takeaway or restaurant outlets: hot pizzas 'to go' or hot sandwiches. The further supermarkets move away from stocking raw materials for traditional scratch cooking, and the more they move towards more restaurant-like instant meals, which present various opportunities to 'add value' to the basic raw ingredients by means of food processing and packaging, the better their bottom line will be.

Corner-store formats also allow supermarket chains to charge different prices for groceries. Consumers tend to assume that chains charge the same for any given line in all their stores. Asda, Morrisons, Marks & Spencer, Waitrose, Iceland, Booths, Aldi and Lidl say they operate a strict national pricing policy. But other chains don't. This practice is called 'price flexing', which means that a chain sets a different retail price for a product in different geographical areas to compete with the local opposition. Price flexing cuts two ways. You can end up paying more for tea bags on the high street than you do in that edge-of-town superstore run by the same chain because there is no strong competition from rivals. Or you might be able to pick up tea bags for less on the high street because the market is particularly price sensitive there and so a supermarket chain is offering lower prices on certain lines. Somerfield, for example, told *The Grocer* that it runs extra promotions 'where there is strong local competition'. The Co-op said that although it runs national pricing on key lines, 'other prices vary by format or store size'.

When the *Observer* investigated the prices being charged in seven London stores in 2003, it concluded that customers were paying between 4 per cent and 7 per cent more for the privilege of shopping in supermarket 'convenience' stores compared with what they would pay for exactly the same products in larger-format stores in the same area. A report by the government's Competition Commission in 2000 concluded that when carried out by big chains such as Safeway, Sainsbury's and Tesco, this practice 'operates against the public interest'. Both Tesco and Sainsbury's challenged the methodology of the Commission's analysis, and all chains operating price flexing said that the practice reflected the higher operating costs of more centrally located stores.

You might think that the regulatory authorities would be concerned about supermarkets' tightening noose on the grocery market, but you'd be wrong. When the Competition Commission investigated them, our supermarket chains got lucky. It decided that supermarkets did not have a worrying monopoly on our grocery shopping. It divided the grocery market in two: 'one-stop' at supermarkets and 'top-up' at convenience stores. Our supermarkets had successfully fed the government and the Commission the line that these were two distinct markets without any particular bearing on one another. Any citizen with common sense could see that there is a fairly direct relationship between the decline in independent stores in the town centre and the ascendancy of out-of-centre superstores. But the Commission employed a rather narrow definition of the term 'competition'. In its book, competition in the grocery sector meant competition between rival supermarket chains. Choice for consumer did not mean a choice of both small shops and a supermarket to shop in but a choice of supermarkets run by different chains. The logic was absurd. It implied that if you lived in a small town with a reasonable collection of small shops level pegging with one relatively small supermarket run by chain A, you were positively deprived of choice. The Commission seemed to believe that new competitor supermarkets run by chains B, C and D would give you greater choice. It ignored the fact that another supermarket would accelerate the rate of closures amongst independent shops that were just holding their own.

Given this regulatory climate, it is not surprising that the big multiples' efforts to build their portfolio in the 'small basket' sector are escalating. As Richard Hyman of the market research company Verdict told *The Times*, 'this was always a market that the big boys were going to get into big time'. In October 2002, the Co-op started off the big buying with its acquisition of the grocery chain Alldays. Three days later, it was no surprise to discover that Tesco had got the go-ahead from the Office of Fair Trading (OFT) to buy up the T&S chain of convenience stores, using this two-market yardstick. Tesco gained out of the deal the 450 new Express stores it created from the T&S stores, adding a cool 1 per cent to its market share, without raising a regulatory whimper. The OFT decided that the T&S acquisition gave Tesco only 5 per cent of the convenience market so that was OK. But as one industry analyst told the *Daily Telegraph*, with the T&S deal, 'Tesco had done a land grab which would probably have taken them eight years to do piecemeal and probably 15 years in terms of all the planning wrangles there would have been.' By

4

Working the system

How on earth did Britain get into a situation where independent shops are an endangered species and a handful of powerful retailers are heading for total control of the nation's food shopping – all in three decades? If consumers had been asked to vote on whether this was a desirable set of affairs, the resounding response would have been no; yet this is precisely what has happened. How did our regulatory system let us down?

When supermarkets started appearing in Britain during the 1960s, it was not instantly obvious that they were the forerunners of retail monsters. They were sufficiently few and far between not to cause undue concern. By today's standards they were relatively small. Small shopkeepers were fearful about losing business to the new retail giants, but most people welcomed them. For most shoppers, they were something of a novelty, a new retail experience, a welcome addition to traditional shopping outlets – butchers, fishmongers, grocers and so on – adding to the all-round grocery shopping choice. Consumers saw the new supermarkets as an 'as well as' not an 'instead of' feature of the shopping scene. Local councils often viewed them positively as a whole new pot of rateable revenue.

By the late 1980s, however, supermarkets were multiplying at a steady rate. They were becoming bigger too. The nightmare scenarios articulated by independent shopkeepers were beginning to be played out on the high street. Belatedly, the penny dropped that a supermarket land grab was under way. It became obvious that some restrictions to curb the spread of supermarkets would be needed. In 1988, the Department of the Environment issued a planning policy note (PPG6) for England containing general guidance for local authorities. This said that although the planning system should not inhibit competition between retailers – perish the thought! – it should take into account whether a new supermarket would affect the vitality and viability of a nearby town centre. But this guidance proved totally inadequate to slow down the supermarkets' inexorable push for retail space. A proliferation of large superstores followed.

The supermarket retail revolution no longer meant the odd useful store on the edge of urban areas, but a ring of similar developments creating a supermarket bracelet around towns and cities, a bracelet elastic enough to allow the insertion of ever more links. Chain B would build a new store, bigger and better than chain A's existing store in the area. So chain A would respond with another bigger store to claw back the business the newcomer had taken away. Chain C, meanwhile, not to be outdone, would open its store to make sure it got its slice of the retail action.

People were surprised, and even shocked, to find that these superstores were sometimes constructed on greenfield land, even playing fields, which they had always supposed would never be put under hard landscaping of any sort, naively assuming that they would be protected by local development plans. Such plans proved to be weaker and more open to interpretation than many had supposed. Local planners felt their hands were tied. Even if they had the will to say no, they lacked the regulatory ammunition.

By 1993, the decline of small traders as a critical proportion of their customers began to drift off to the shiny new superstores with limitless free parking had become sufficiently acute for the government to issue a revised version of PPG6. This stressed the need for a suitable balance between developments in town centres and out of centre. It said that the scale, type and location of the supermarket should not undermine the vitality and viability of town centres. A year later this guidance was strengthened by PPG13. This stressed the need to promote more sustainable transport choices and to reduce the need to travel, especially by car. No one disputed that supermarkets were major generators of car travel. Their existence was encouraging shoppers to get in their cars and drive, even for just a carton of milk, when there was a local shop within walking distance.

But even though local authorities now had new grounds on which to cramp the supermarkets' style, the supermarkets' takeover of grocery retailing continued. By 1996, PPG6 had to be strengthened again. But by this point the horse had bolted. A further flurry of supermarket developments on the edge of towns and cities was of particular concern. This time PPG6 required local authorities to give preference to applications for supermarket developments on town- or district-centre sites. Out-of-centre sites were ranked below them and would not be approved if town-centre sites were available. New out-of-centre supermarkets should only be in locations that were well served by public transport.

The situation was and still is different in other parts of the British Isles. In Wales, the regulatory framework is less supermarket-friendly: if a new out-of-centre supermarket is 'likely to lead to the loss of general food retailing in the centre of small towns', this is grounds for refusal. In Scotland, the notion of whether or not a supermarket is needed is not addressed in law. Northern Ireland's planning regulations allow supermarkets on sites outside town centres, providing certain criteria are met. In Ireland, there is a cap on the amount of floor space that supermarkets can have: 3,000 square metres outside Dublin and 3,500 in the greater Dublin area. In addition, there is a presumption against supermarket developments on out-of-town sites and local authorities must safeguard local shops in their development plans.

In the twenty-first century, supermarket chains face tighter planning controls than they did in the previous one. In theory, it is currently quite hard for them to get planning permission for new stores out of town. That is why they have largely turned their attention to the inner cities where they are looking to expand into 'brownfield' sites. Such sites have previously been built on and are usually in an advanced state of dilapidation, and so proposed developments do not attract the same objections as a new superstore on a greenfield site would. On the other hand, because a new supermarket on a brownfield site must fit into an already developed urban area, it is subject to a number of detailed and more specific planning considerations that do not always apply to out-of-town sites: the impact on local views, congestion of small streets, noise and light pollution and so on.

On paper anyway, there are grounds for local authorities to refuse permission for a new supermarket. But more often than not, our supermarket chains succeed. Of 170 supermarket planning applications submitted in the UK in the three years to 31 March 2003, 83 (49 per cent) were approved, 33 (19 per cent) were rejected or withdrawn and 54 (32 per cent) were still pending at the time of writing. John Sweeney, leader of North Norfolk District Council, summed up the dilemma faced by local authorities. 'They are too big and powerful for us. If we try and deny them they will appeal, and we cannot afford to fight a planning appeal and lose. If they got costs it could bankrupt us.' Supermarkets simply don't like to take no for an answer, and come back with one revised plan after another, until they get their way.

5

Sugar daddies

Stopping or even seeking to downsize a new supermarket development is a daunting task. No wonder really organised community opposition is rare. As one pro-supermarket commentator sanguinely put it:

> At the end of the day, most planning authorities have bowed to a combination of consumer apathy – or even tacit support for the new supermarket sites – and the ability of retailers to 'sweeten the pill' on their arrival in a new locality . . . Key local aspirations that had seemed too expensive to fulfil – cleaning up derelict areas, building sports fields and social centres were favourites – gained crucial new support. Hundreds of new jobs were immediately created. The only losers were the collections of locally owned high street stores which had been fighting a losing battle for custom with prices that were perceived as too high, parking that was inadequate and service that appeared and indeed often was both slow and old-fashioned. Furthermore, it was usually months or even years after the new superstore's arrival that the downside consequences became apparent.

Nowadays supermarket chains know that they have a better chance of securing planning consent for a new store if they parcel it up in a mixed development. The Town and Country Planning Act recognises the concept of 'planning gain' or elements included in a planning application to make an application more attractive to local authorities. It allows for what are known as Section 106 agreements. A council and supermarket chain can agree that certain work must be carried out before permission can be granted. For example, the supermarket might have to pay for trees to be replanted, traffic lights moved and roads relaid, or sports facilities provided. Often these take the form of sizeable cash payments from the would-be supermarket developer to the council. Using Section 106 agreements, supermarkets have the perfect sweetener to dangle before local authorities. Developers talk excitedly of 'synergies' with supermarkets that might make possible what previously seemed like unprofitable developments. Supermarkets, arm in arm with property developers, can act as sugar daddies to the community, even to the extent of getting permission for out-of-centre developments that would otherwise be out of the question.

In Coventry in 2000, Tesco won planning consent for one of its biggest stores in the country by agreeing to part-fund a new stadium. 'Sometimes the value of the land is enough to push the deal,' said a Tesco spokesperson; 'sometimes you have to build the stadium.'

In 2003, a property consortium submitted a planning application for a stadium for Wimbledon Football Club near Bletchley and Milton Keynes. This new 30,000-seat stadium and 6,500-seat arena would be part-financed or enabled by a 100,000-square-foot Asda Wal-Mart Supercentre, the largest Asda format. The consortium's website aimed at encouraging locals to write letters to council planners in support of the plan was headed, 'Dreams can become a reality for Milton Keynes and Bletchley.' The consortium's chairman, Pete Winkleman, argued the case as follows: 'Milton Keynes needs an international stadium. Wimbledon FC needs a home. Asda needs a store in the largest city in the UK where it doesn't already have one. Bletchley needs a major investment scheme to kickstart its regeneration . . . Without the stadium, without a revitalised Bletchley, without Wimbledon FC, Milton Keynes remains incomplete. Without Asda none of it happens.'

The more desirable elements that go into the development mix the better, and housing, as well as sport, is usually a winner. In 2003, Tesco announced its plans to build 3–4,000 affordable homes nationwide. Among these were an application for a development in Streatham, South London, where it wanted to build a complex which would include a leisure centre, Tesco store and 250 homes, 40 per cent of which would be for key workers. In Romford, Essex, Sainsbury's new superstore was part of a mixed-use development that included housing, a health club, restaurants, a bowling alley and cinemas.

Just as they were being accused of taking away business from town centres and encouraging traffic by means of such projects, supermarkets have reinvented themselves as urban regenerators with pockets deep enough to make long-cherished community goals possible. As *The Grocer* noted archly: 'Regeneration projects can gain speedy approval from councils and local communities. A whole regeneration package, promising mixed use development . . . is likely to prove far more attractive to planners than just a plain old superstore.' Our large supermarket chains' enormous retail power certainly provides them with the money to make things happen. But the downside of these carrot-and-stick regeneration packages is that they are another way in which supermarkets are insinuating themselves into all aspects of our lives, embedding themselves deeper and deeper in our man-made landscape and hence our consciousness. In Kilmarnock in Scotland, for example, certain areas of the town are listed in local bus timetables according to the supermarket chain that dominates them: Wester Netherton has become Kwik Save and Scott Ellis has become Asda.

The supermarkets are happy to bask in their role as the new

civic developers as long as they get their pound of retail flesh. But the price for planners and their communities is that they may have to say yes to a new store when they would otherwise prefer to say no. Where once people strolled in the park, or walked around the local duck pond, a day out in our supermarket-saturated country is beginning to mean a visit to a shopping and leisure centre of which a supermarket is an integral part. Naturally, supermarket chains are keen to promote their stores as places in which to while away leisure time. Under the headline 'Everyone Asda have a hobby', the freesheet *Metro* told the story of septuagenarian Richard Bunn who, after enjoying a bargain all-day breakfast at his local store in Weston-Super-Mare, had made his hobby visiting Asda stores. When he had travelled some 100,000 miles to visit all its stores in Britain, Asda grasped the public relations opportunity and asked Mr Bunn to open a new store in Oldbury in the West Midlands. 'I know people think I'm batty but I love Asda and once I decided to visit every store, I became a man with a mission,' Mr Bunn told assembled press.

If an obdurate local authority says no to a supermarket development, even if it is cloaked in a halo of urban revitalisation, supermarkets have further avenues to pursue. The original foot-in-the-door tactic was to construct smaller stores – which are more likely to get planning permission – that just happened to have ridiculously large numbers of parking places. This built in a generous margin of surplus land for future extensions. A few years later, the chain could apply to extend the original store into the car park. Little by little, the chain could realise its greater plan. Nowadays the buzz words are 'space sweating'. Chains 'sweat assets' by building mezzanine floors in existing stores where they would not be allowed to extend externally. UK planning law excludes internal building work from the definition of development requiring planning permission. In 2003, Asda Wal-Mart announced its intention to build mezzanine floors in up to forty stores in what *Dow Jones International News* reported as 'a way of increasing space amid strict planning laws'. After a successful mezzanine was slotted into its York store, Asda Wal-Mart set about building floors in stores in Sheffield, and Cumbernauld and Govan in Glasgow. In the Sheffield Asda, the mezzanine added 33,000 square feet to the store – almost the same sales area as the largest supermarket now permitted in Ireland. Friends of the Earth blew the whistle. 'Asda Wal-Mart is making a mockery of planning guidance. By installing mezzanines in existing stores, the company does not even have to submit a planning application to the local authority. This leaves the local authority powerless to assess the impact on local shops or traffic levels and local communities have no say in the development,' it pointed out. Sheffield MP Clive Betts told the House of Commons that the mezzanine expansion in his constituency had made existing traffic problems worse. 'Traffic is considerably heavier, yet there has been no analysis or plan to deal with it, because there has been no requirement for the store to sit down with the highways authority and the planning authority to work out these problems, because there is no need for planning permission.'

Yet another approach is to include housing in proposals for extensions to existing stores. Sainsbury's, for example, got the go-ahead to extend its Richmond store from an already substantial 55,000 square feet to 63,500 square feet largely because it would build 179 flats on top of the existing store and the extension.

Our supermarket chains are determined to get planning permission for new stores and extensions to existing ones. And despite the fact that theoretically they now operate in a tricky planning climate, it is amazing how often they get what they want. As Tesco's finance director told the *Daily Telegraph*, 'Planning approvals have not stopped. It's just more difficult than it used to be. Out of town is very difficult to get but you are seeing brownfield sites redeveloped. Planning changes have not killed development. They have acted to redirect it.'

6

Pimlico v. Sainsbury's

The battle against the building of a Sainsbury's in Pimlico, on
the site of the former Wilton Road bus garage behind Victoria
Station, is one of the most high profile ever fought between a
local community and a supermarket chain. Behind-the-scenes
wheelings and dealings in this controversial case, exposed by the
Sunday Times investigative Insight team, made the front page.
Simon Jenkins wrote a rousing column in the *Evening Standard*
opposing the development as an unwelcome precedent. 'The store
is big, intrusive and will offer parking, thus contriving to offend
every maxim of modern planning ... A superstore is a neutron
bomb. It wipes out commercial life for streets around, while its
parking spaces jam the traffic ... Quite apart from encouraging
more traffic, most of the new stores are large and ugly. That they
may replace ugly gas works or goods yards is no excuse,' he
wrote. The debate continued on BBC2's *Newsnight*. It was rare
for a local community to make such a stand. But Sainsbury's got
its way in the end.

Local residents first got wind of the proposal in 1995. Sainsbury's had been smart. It had got together with a housing association to put forward a mixed development for a superstore with
flats built above it. Half these flats would be private, but the
other half would be low-cost, affordable housing, of which there

was a serious shortage in the area. This type of housing had been given the highest priority in the local council's (Westminster) development plan.

Opposing a supermarket pure and simple was one thing; opposing one linked with such a desirable sweetener to the local council was another. The proposed site was in an area zoned for retail development, so residents' organisations, sensing that all-out opposition was fruitless, set themselves the more reasonable task of trying to get the Sainsbury's plan cut down to the right scale for the site.

They seemed to be on strong ground. Despite its proximity to Victoria, Pimlico is a low-rise, densely populated district, part of which is a formal conservation area. The taller buildings are no more than five or six storeys high. It conforms very well to the notion of the 'urban village' that today's planners are keen to support as an antidote to the 'Anytown, Anywhere' big-box development that strips life and character from urban centres. The planning brief for the area was that buildings should be a maximum of six storeys. In this respect, the scale and height of the proposed development – which was to rise to eleven storeys – seemed totally out of keeping. When one sees the finished development, one local architect's prophecy that it would be 'like having a cross channel ferry in a yacht marina' appears totally justified. As Moy Scott, secretary of Pimlico FREDA, the umbrella group for sixteen active residents' associations, put it, 'it seemed as though Sainsbury's was bringing Victoria to Pimlico'.

The new store would mean more lorries and new car traffic too. It would receive twenty-five deliveries a day, necessitating fifty trips in and out through narrow streets more suited to small cars and bicycles. Already a badly parked delivery van was enough to cause a jam. Sainsbury's had also admitted that it expected 90 per cent of the store's customers to be drawn in from outside Pimlico – Victoria, Mayfair, St James, the City and Chelsea. Inevitably such shoppers would be attracted by the spacious underground car park that was to be built.

Residents were upset not only by the height and bulk of the development and the traffic implications for surrounding streets but also by the impact it would surely have on local shops. Pimlico is relatively unusual in that it has a network of small shops, only a handful of which belong to chains. These independent shops are concentrated in and around Tachbrook Street, the traditional heart of the area, home to a daily market selling fish, fruit and vegetables since 1877. Pre-Sainsbury's, the selection of some 165 shops was one that any urban area would envy. Whether you wanted to buy a newspaper, have keys cut, find freshly ground Parmesan, pick up a bouquet of flowers, get a prescription or source the ingredients for a special meal, you could do it in a small, convenient radius.

But what would become of these shops once Sainsbury's had opened its titan store? With a gross trading floorspace of 30,000 square feet, and eight franchise shops below, it would have more than double the sales space of all the existing shops in Pimlico. It would also be five times larger than the existing Tesco round the corner. Local residents suggested to Sainsbury's that it cut back the size of its proposed store while retaining the same proposed number of product lines. Sainsbury's was already well represented in the area, they pointed out. There was, and still is, a vast, fully comprehensive Sainsbury's at Nine Elms only 1½ miles south and a smaller Sainsbury's in Victoria Street, ten minutes' walk away. Why, local residents wondered, did Sainsbury's need another huge store?

Supported by local objections, Westminster Council refused Sainsbury's planning permission in 1996 and then again in 1997, when it submitted a second proposal with the number of flats reduced from 178 to 160. Sainsbury's appealed against these decisions and the matter went to a local inquiry. There then ensued a David and Goliath struggle.

Not content simply to rely on Westminster Council to oppose the proposal, the local community got itself organised with an experienced planning consultant to put its case. It tempered well-reasoned, carefully assembled, knowledgeable planning arguments with the genuine, heartfelt concerns of local people. Through Pimlico FREDA, the local traders of Pimlico appealed to the inspector in charge of hearing the appeal. They represented all the little shops who worked hard and stayed up late to service the community: Buckles and Brogues, Gastronomia Italia, Park Lane Cleaners, Stanwells Homecare Centre, Sea Harvest Fisheries, Market News – the list went on. Their case had a common-sense logic to it. 'We believe that our area is unique in central London with its local market and small businesses. Many of these facilities would be unable to survive the opening of another supermarket and therefore given the government's policy of city centre rejuvenation, we feel we should be afforded the protection of such a policy. Unless of course we are to have lifeless local communities that are cultural and environmental deserts,' they wrote. 'The survival of our community is at stake. We canvass your support in our endeavours against this appeal by Sainsbury's.'

But prospects didn't look good for the objectors. Sainsbury's clearly had a war chest of money to pay for the costs of the appeal and could afford the best planning and legal team that money could buy. The whole affair had become political too. The outcome of such planning appeals is usually determined by the planning inspector. Pimlico objectors had been informed in writing in 1996 that this would be the case. After the general election in 1997, Deputy Prime Minister John Prescott, Secretary of State for Environment and Transport, had rescinded this decision and decided to 'call in' the appeal and personally determine its outcome. Questions were asked in the House of Commons by Tim Yeo, the shadow Environment spokesman. He pressed Mr Prescott to explain why he had intervened in this particular appeal, and asserted that four months after doing so Mr Prescott had met Lord Sainsbury, a well-known donor to the Labour Party. Mr Prescott confirmed to him that the subject of 'mixed-use housing and retail development' was amongst the topics discussed with the Sainsbury's chairman. He also confirmed that he had held no similar meetings with objectors to Sainsbury's Pimlico proposal. Mr Prescott seemed to be rather keen on listening to supermarkets. His department had just approved a scheme to build a huge and controversial out-of-town superstore near Richmond in Surrey. This had been hailed by planners and developers as Labour signalling that it was relaxing the tougher planning regulations imposed by the former Conservative Environment Secretary, John Gummer. In the event, the inquiry inspector found in favour of Sainsbury's and Mr Prescott agreed. Sainsbury's got the planning permission it was after.

Within ten days of Sainsbury's opening, leaflets were dropping through Pimlico residents' letterboxes. 'Support your local shopkeepers and stalls,' they read. Evidently, Pimlico's independent shopkeepers were already feeling the pinch. Three months after Sainsbury's opening, one local shopkeeper told me that his retail sales had dropped by 18 per cent and that he was increasingly dependent on restaurant wholesale orders for the viability of his business. The ultimate irony, effectively a two-fingered gesture to community objectors, was that this was no ordinary Sainsbury's, rather a 'marketplace' store, in the mould of Sainsbury's Market at Bluebird in the King's Road. It was to be called the 'Market at Pimlico'. It had ten of what Sainsbury's calls 'specialist counters', including a master butcher, a fishmonger, a charcuterie and a hot carvery with 'tailor-made' sandwiches. The message seemed to be crystal clear. Why bother with Tachbrook market or any of the existing 165 local shops when you could drive past the lot of them and shop in Sainsbury's marketplace? Who needs a thriving independent shopping centre when you can settle for Sainsbury's counterfeit lookalike?

SUPERMARKET FOOD

7

Giving us what we want

In the world of British supermarketing, there is a curious gender imbalance. The bulk of shoppers in supermarkets are women. Stores typically operate with a predominantly female workforce under a male manager. As you go up the supermarket tree to the people who make the decisions about what we will eat, the personnel become overwhelmingly male. When you get to chief executive level, you find a handful of fabulously well-remunerated men who are confident that they know more about what the average customer wants than she knows herself. In a sense they do. They can tell us what we want. They know they have a captive audience.

British supermarket chains say that they must be keeping consumers happy or else we would simply push away our trolleys and take our business elsewhere. As one industry commentator put it, 'They [consumers] have voted with their feet – or rather their car keys – patronising the supermarkets and superstores at the expense of other outlets ... The vast gleaming superstores ... St Tesco on the roundabout, St Sainsbury at the interchange, open seven days a week, 24 hours a day – are the clearest possible evidence that consumers are getting what they want.' It is true that in the UK, unlike every other country in Europe, food shopping, for a majority of people, has become synonymous with supermarket shopping. For many people, however, that state of affairs is not a matter of positive choice but the line of least resistance. In a 2001 Radio 4 poll, 71 per cent of listeners who phoned in agreed with the motion that 'We would all be better off without supermarkets'. In 1999, research carried out by the retail consultancy Verdict revealed that six million shoppers – that's one in four of all shoppers – were dissatisfied with the supermarket where they bought their groceries. Two million of these shoppers wanted to abandon shopping in superstores entirely. In 2003, a NOP poll conducted on behalf of the New Economics Foundation found that 70 per cent of respondents would prefer to shop locally rather than in an out-of-town supermarket, while 50 per cent thought supermarkets' size and strength should be controlled to stop them putting local independent retailers out of business.

Even Jamie Oliver, the celebrity face of Sainsbury's, seems to prefer shopping in any place other than a supermarket. Mr Oliver has said that working with Sainsbury's has given him the opportunity to 'influence the food choices of millions of people'. But opening up his personal food shopping address book for *Observer Food Monthly*, he enthusiastically reeled off a list of his favourite independent fishmongers, butchers, specialist food shops, farmgate suppliers and markets.

Supermarket shopping may not be top of many people's favourite occupations, but it seems to be the way of the world. Most people don't see any feasible alternative and the more we shop in supermarkets, the more we forget that such an alternative still might or ever could exist. And when we rely on one supermarket chain for almost all the food we buy, we can easily be manipulated to accept what they want to give us. As a consequence, supermarkets' power to shape our shopping and eating habits is phenomenal, and they know it. The trick is to get us to think that they are responding to our needs and desires when actually we are responding to theirs. 'Giving customers what they want' is supermarket-speak for 'selling what we want to sell'. Super-markets use a number of strategies to pull off this brainwashing.

The number one supermarket ruse is, having created a problem, to present themselves as the solution to it. In countries with a healthy food culture where the population is generally thinner and healthier, people see food shopping as an indispensable, worthwhile and not necessarily disagreeable part of the process of feeding yourself well. In countries where there are still independent food shops and markets, shopping can still be a pleasurable, stimulating, diverse experience which involves interesting, even friendly interaction with other human beings. Food shopping in UK supermarkets, on the other hand, has become a dreary treadmill where increasingly overweight yet undernourished consumers are invited to stock up with food in the same anonymous, automatic way they fill up their tanks with petrol. It is no coincidence that supermarket shoppers regularly complain about spending large sums of money in their store yet being unable to think of anything to cook that night. Just thinking about supermarket shopping is enough to make most of us feel tired and uninspired. Supermarket shopping trips, for many people, are an exercise in extreme alienation. Nor is it just chance that we seem to be getting fatter yet getting less and less pleasure from feeding ourselves. Supermarket shopping makes us into robots, stopping off at pre-programmed points as we always do. Picking the same old stuff. Buying what supermarkets want us to buy. Terence Blacker, writing in the *Independent*, described the experience as follows:

Most people, in order to stay sane, close down their aesthetic sense and human curiosity while being fed through the production line of supermarket shopping. They ignore the other dead-eyed zombies shuffling their way down the aisles as if being led by the trolleys in front of them ... moving in a tranquillised daze to the checkout queue. Here, confronted by an exhausted, hollow-eyed

41

employee behind the till, a brief moment of human contact is experienced but anything more than a hurried 'Hi' or 'Busy today?' will mark you out as an eccentric timewaster.

Columnist Mimi Spencer summed up the supermarket shopping experience perfectly when she said that it had all the allure of going to the chiropodist:

> I just got back from Tesco. Hellish. Personally, I'd rather eat my own liver than have to trolley off to the supermarket . . . I try to enter a state of suspended animation when I visit my local super-store, a bit like I did when I gave birth. My eyes glaze over. My shoulders slump over the wayward trolley, as it fills up with cos lettuces and cartons of soup – which, I know, I will ritualistically throw in the bin ten days later when the lettuce has turned into soup and the soup has turned into something like the stuff that shot from that girl's mouth in *The Exorcist*.

Having made the whole experience of food shopping dehumanising, functional and boring, supermarkets portray themselves as white knights 'lightening the load', riding to the rescue of stressed working women to relieve them of the enormously oppressive burden of food shopping. They promise short checkout queues, a parking space and ways to help you whizz round getting this unpleasant business over and done with as fast as possible. Supermarket language reinforces the idea of supermarkets as the housewife's helper and harassed working woman's guardian angel over and over again in their language. 'Every little helps.' Every meal is a potential problem for which supermarkets have a 'meal solution'. Supermarkets have fostered the stereotype of the 'time-poor, cash-rich' shopper because this gives them another business opportunity to sell lucrative value-added processed food to us. Supermarkets have made not having the time to either shop or cook – and hence living on a diet of processed food – into a sign of social status to which everyone aspires, whether or not they have the means.

Despite these 'solutions', having deprogrammed us as creative shoppers and convinced us that food shopping is necessarily a drag by making it a drag, supermarkets face the potential problem of having to motivate a passive, apathetic customer base. The knack then is to keep us just interested enough to take up their strategically placed special offers and lucrative value-added lines, but not so clued up on food that we realise that the store is devoid of real quality choices and so start looking elsewhere. They want to turn us into trusting customers who can be propelled round the store, following their secret retail map, picking up our masters' ball and dropping it obediently at the checkout. In the overwhelmingly male realm of supermarketing, customers (women) are seen as rather dim subjects who can be programmed, through a series of gimmicks, to want almost anything, seeing a fake diversity and choice in every category shelf.

Safeway, for example, has helpfully colour-coded its bagged salads into 'orange' (sweet tasting), 'green' (mild) and 'purple' (more distinct flavour). Several chains grade their cheese numerically according to strength. Sainsbury's Continental cheeses now come colour-coded: soft cheese is blue, hard is red, goat's is green and blue cheese is aqua. These kindergarten classification schemes make no attempt to educate or really inform consumers about the tastes or properties of food. If supermarkets did genuinely educate consumers, we would soon see the dreary homogeneity of what's on offer. Instead such schemes give chains the opportunity to sell very similar lines in multiple forms, so increasing the likelihood of a sale.

When apathy with a food category or product mounts, supermarkets get together with manufacturers to dream up new ways of selling the same thing to us. In 2003, for example, Safeway joined forces with Unilever and Birds Eye Walls to try out new ways of marketing frozen foods, an ailing part of the supermarket repertoire. 'The aim of the trial,' explained Safeway's frozen category buyer, 'is to create a warmer shopping environment with clearer sub-category segmentation in order to make shopping the category easier for our customers.' He added that one of the main barriers to buying frozen was customers' preference for fresh. 'We have tackled this through food images displayed behind light boxes to convey strong food values along with the use of our new frozen strapline "Frozen For Freshness",' he said. A cynical translation might read: 'Frozen sales are dropping because people prefer fresh so we'll make the frozen stuff look more appealing by selling it beside attractively lit pictures of mouthwatering fresh food and the strapline will make it sound as though the frozen is as good, or even better than fresh.'

Deskilling shoppers by undermining our confidence is another supermarket ploy to make us more easily manipulated. Supermarket press offices regularly spew out carefully designed 'Did you know that the customer doesn't know?' or 'stupid shopper' type of research that characterises the typical shopper as ignorant and desperately in need of the tutoring that only supermarkets can supply. (That supermarkets might be main contributors to this state of ignorance is never mentioned – they want to be seen as benevolent educators.) In 2003, for example, Tesco's press relations office phoned food journalists asking them if they knew that many people use the wrong methods of cooking for joints of meat. Its research showed that only 17 per cent of consumers aged between 21 and 35 had heard of common cuts of meat such as brisket, fore rib, chump and loin. Those aged between 36 and 50 did better – 68 per cent knew what they were talking about – but they were eclipsed by 51–70-year-olds, who knew not only which was which but how to cook them. These results are not surprising when you consider that most younger people's shopping experience is confined to supermarkets, where meat shelves are lined with a narrow selection of mainly prime cuts, and meat counters are often staffed by people who lack the training or experience that the traditional butcher had to explain various meat cuts and their uses.

Safeway carried out a similar exercise in July 2002. It surveyed 1,000 people across the UK to find out how much the nation knew about when foods are in season. A yawning knowledge deficit was revealed: 88 per cent of respondents did not know when certain British favourites were in season. Safeway concluded that 'the vast majority demonstrated a serious lack of knowledge about British food seasonality'. There was no mention that our supermarkets' policy of stocking the same lines 365 days of the year might have been a contributory factor. Predictably, Safeway's research found that 81 per cent of respondents 'look to supermarkets for more education about seasonality'. However, this survey did not nudge Safeway into rethinking its own, self-styled 'uni-seasonal' stocking policy by cancelling standing orders for out-of-season exotica such as Kenyan green beans, Thai baby corn and Peruvian asparagus and then filling its shelves with seasonal British produce. Instead it used the survey to promote sales of its premium The Best range. This, it was at pains to point out, featured not only seasonal fruits and vegetables but also 'prepared products such as recipe dishes'. 'Hero products' in this range included chocolate chip cookies, butter pains au chocolat, prawn selection with Thai dip and ready meals such as potato gratin with roasted garlic and chilli caramelised pork hock whose seasonality was less than apparent.

When supermarkets aren't implying that shoppers are ignorant, they are keen to make them out as stubbornly conservative, almost stupidly inflexible. On a 2002 Radio 4 *Food Programme* about grapes, Tesco's lead technical manager for fruit was at pains to point out that Tesco and its suppliers had a very clear idea of what its shoppers expected in a grape which meant that Tesco stocked no more than six to eight varieties in a year, selected from some twenty commercial varieties available out of a total of 8,000 varieties. Asked why Tesco insisted on selling such a small number of varieties of grapes, which had been picked green and hence had less flavour and sweetness, its expert acknowledged that in grape-growing countries people knew that the yellower the grape, the sweeter. 'But if we put yellow grapes on our shelves, our consumers would think those grapes were over-mature and leave them behind,' he explained. You could almost hear listeners up and down the land murmuring, 'How do you know that? Did you ever ask us?' Might Tesco's choice of grape variety and colour not have more to do with its own need for bulk supply, ease of sourcing and extended shelf life?

A highly experienced fruit wholesaler gave me examples of how supermarkets do not give consumers a qualitative choice but just what they want to stock. 'A prime example is French Golden Delicious apples. Because UK supermarket policy is to sell green Goldens, they mainly source their supplies from the Loire Valley, which is the worst area for full flavour, but they stay green in stores. These apples are virtually unsaleable elsewhere in Europe as the best Goldens are golden and come from higher altitudes, such as Quercy. Another example is salads. Now nearly all the salad produce sold in supermarkets for the greater part of the year is sourced in Holland even though it has no flavour. But it looks perfect and that's what the supermarkets want.'

In 2003, there was another instance of the supermarket assertion that consumers are besotted with appearance to the exclusion of all other considerations. When the House of Commons International Development Committee grilled supermarket representatives about filling their produce shelves with only cosmetically perfect produce, one MP challenged the supermarket contention that consumers would only buy mangetouts, Cox's Orange Pippins or other produce if it were all a uniform size and shade. Senior supermarket figures assured the committee that this was indeed the case. Sainsbury's senior manager for sustainability and product safety refuted any suggestion of blame, identifying the consumer as the problem. 'The UK customer is known to be the foremost in Europe for being fussy about appearance. You can't deny that.' Substitute the words 'UK supermarket chains are' for 'The UK customer is', and you have a sentence that more accurately reflects who calls the shots.

One farmer told me how he goes to Women's Institutes and other community groups talking about supporting local agriculture. He argues that supermarkets are trying to brainwash the public into doing what the supermarkets want. 'I hold up examples of naturally misshapen but perfectly wholesome vegetables and say, "Look, the supermarkets say you don't want these." In every case, they tell me otherwise.' I asked an experienced fruit and vegetable wholesaler if it was true that British shoppers are interested only in looks. He said, 'Mrs Average shopper is now a younger person who only shops in supermarkets and has never known the joys of full-flavoured fruit and vegetables. If her attitude is "If it looks good, it will do," it's not her fault. Supermarkets sell us what they want to sell us.'

8

Feeding bad food culture

It's embarrassing, isn't it, to come from a country with a bad food culture? But that's how other countries see us: as a nation hooked on junk food. It's part of our national stereotype. Au pairs return home to regale their astounded families with tales of what British households eat. Visitors remark on the absence of food shops; their jaws drop at the sight of legions of office workers bolting down their lunchtime sandwiches or school-children breakfasting on packets of crisps and cans of coke.

Theories about the roots of Britain's gastronomic cluelessness stretch back to the enclosures and the Industrial Revolution – the dislocation of food-producing peasants from the country-side to make an industrial workforce and so on. But increasingly, historical explanations seem inadequate to explain fully our current predicament. One contemporary factor is staring us in the face. No country in Europe is so reliant on supermarkets for its food shopping. These days, many British consumers simply see no alternative to shopping in supermarkets. In countries where people eat better, they still do.

The food writer Matthew Fort illustrated this point amply when he described the shopping possibilities in the kilometre-long Via Tribunali in Naples:

In it were nine bars or cafés, one rosticceria, three wine shops, three fruit and veg shops (plus several more round various corners), sixteen grocers/delis, four fishmongers, five butchers, a cheese shop . . . three pizza shops, one tavola calda restaurant, one trattoria and two bakers. And that was besides the hairdressers, electrical shops, tobacconists, shoe shops and clothes shops.

Each was quite small and differed in character from the next . . . an independent entity, a source of occupation and income for the family that ran it. It was as far removed from the homogeneity of the average British shopping experience as it was possible to imagine. In terms of life, social exchange, sense of community, competitiveness, service abundance, variety and sheer energy, it made me realise what we have lost, what our spineless acquiescence to the culture of supermarkets and retail chains has cost us.

Our supermarkets – and the bodies that lobby on their behalf – like to argue that they are the most comprehensive and sophisticated in the world. They can put every food experience to be had on the planet into the British consumer's trolley, setting a standard for safety and quality that no foreign chain can match. 'Food democracy is consumers having access to an unprecedented range of safe food, all year round and at all price points, regardless of where they live. Through economies of scale, innovation and investment, food retailing has helped to deliver a level of food democracy in the UK unimagined before the Second World War,' said Richard Ali, food policy director of the British Retail Consortium. Using this liberation rhetoric, he presented supermarket domination of the UK's grocery spend as a symptom of our healthy open-mindedness, evidence of an improvement in how we feed ourselves. 'Unfortunately there are those who would wish to introduce the modern day equivalent of the Soviet Decree on Food Dictatorship by encouraging collusion and restricting choice. Any such backwards step holds huge dangers to our economy and people's quality of life,' warned Mr Ali. A Britain in which supermarket hegemony is challenged is invariably portrayed by our large retailers as a grim, inconvenient, post-rationing nightmare where no one has ever heard of kiwi fruit and we are all condemned to a monotonous diet of dull, labour-intensive raw ingredients. 'Queuing at one store then trudging down Watford High Street in the rain to another shop ... Is this what people actually want to go back to?' asked Tesco's chief executive, Sir Terry Leahy.

Using this device, supermarkets habitually present themselves as a progressive solution to Britain's food difficulties when in fact their enormous power to determine what ends up on our plates is a major part of the problem of our food culture. It is no coincidence that the country most attached to supermarket shopping has the worst eating habits in Europe because we have effectively surrendered control over what we eat to a few powerful chains. In the guise of giving us choice, they simply sell us what suits them.

A classic example of this is the chilled sandwich. The prototype of the chilled sandwich was pioneered by Marks & Spencer. This non-supermarket food retailer has always been a de facto research and development laboratory and trendsetter for other supermarket chains, which habitually follow its lead. In UK supermarket terms, it is a huge success story, a food-retailing breakthrough. 'The Marks & Spencer sandwich is now an icon, representing freshness, quality and flavour (a welcome replacement for the previous cliché of the tired old British Rail sandwich),' observed one approving industry commentator.

But is it such a great leap forward? Prepacked in its plastic carton, the modern chilled sandwich encapsulates much that is bad about British food. The fundamental concept is flawed because, as any baker can tell you, bread should never be refrigerated. Refrigeration kills any possibility of a proper contrast between crust and crumb because of the prevailing cold and dampness it causes. The best sandwich is the sort that any small shop can whizz up: fresh bread and rolls, straight from a local baker that morning, filled on the spot and sold hours later for more or less instant consumption – a straightforward, simple, sustainable process capable of delivering an end product worth eating. Large food retailers' centralised systems, however, like sandwiches to be made by a few dedicated sandwich factories, the sort that also sell to petrol station forecourts and mass catering outfits. In 2000, one pre-packed sandwich company supplied almost a quarter of all the sandwiches sold by UK multiple retailers. You may have noticed how many sandwiches seem somewhat similar even when you buy them in different supermarket chains. This concentration of production in a few prolific companies is part of the explanation.

From these dedicated factories, sandwiches are delivered to a regional distribution centre and from there to stores. To satisfy the inevitable hygiene implications generated by this extended process and to survive distribution, they have to be chilled to a glacial temperature. Only certain types of technobread are suitable for this treatment: bread that won't fall apart when the moisture in the filling leaks into it as it sits on the arctic takeaway shelves. This bread is sandwiched over fillings made up in the supermarket's prepared food factories: soggy, chopped-up salad leaves, meats you recognise from the ready meals aisles (tikka chicken, barbecue duck, etc.), industrial block cheese, salty tuna and egg mayonnaise without any taste of eggs. It's no wonder that the sandwiches make such unrewarding eating as well as attacking sensitive teeth with their extreme coldness. But we buy them, even though they aren't cheap, because we have got used to them since that's the sort of sandwich supermarkets want to sell us.

The particularly audacious thing about the supermarket prepared-food revolution is the way that supermarkets have taken the culinary limitations of industrial food processing and put a positive spin on them. They claim – erroneously – that their innovation has broadened the British palate, introducing new tastes and flavours, when in fact they are mainly selling us the same standard components, continuously re-assembled and re-marketed in a multiplicity of forms. But since their clientele shop routinely in their stores and so lack any alternative point of reference, this fact usually goes unchallenged. Supermarkets know that because they increasingly control where we shop, the public can be conditioned, by repetition and force of habit, to believe that supermarket TV dinners of the twenty-first century are better than anything they might cook, and possibly even just as good as what they might encounter abroad.

To sustain this tall tale, supermarkets appear to have set themselves a mission of subverting home cooking – the bedrock of any true food culture. Every supermarket chain churns out a stream of recipe cards that purport to encourage home cooking. But home cooking does not make enough money for them. They want the extra margins that can be slipped in with processing. The profits that can be made from convincing people that they don't need to mash a potato or wash a salad are substantial. So increasingly supermarket shelves are filled with foods that obviate, or at least minimise, the need for any home cooking, and make them a tidy profit at the same time. When chef Rowley Leigh was asked to sample Marks & Spencer ready meals, he estimated that a St Michael pasta and vegetable bake, price £1.99, would cost only 40 pence to make at home while a beef casserole, price £5.58, would cost £1.50 if home made. As food writer Matthew Fort put it: 'Hand in hand with the microwave and the deep freeze – and ably supported by manufacturers and retailers who can gouge higher profit margins on these "value-added" products – convenience foods have all but eliminated the tradition of domestic cookery from British homes.' Supermarkets have played the major role in this, providing the means by which the UK has become a 'can't cook won't cook' nation whose idea of a gourmet night is eating a supermarket ready meal on a tray while watching a procession of celebrity chefs cook fantasy food on TV.

Subtly, supermarkets imply that if you've still got the time or inclination to cook on a routine basis, you must be a semi-retired loser, puttering away on the sleepy backwaters of modern life, an endangered species as rare as those who make their own clothes. 'Alongside work, gym, children, partner, friends and chores, who on earth has a spare second to be a domestic star and spend hours preparing a traditional meal?' asked Safeway. 'I certainly wouldn't bother making my own lasagne from scratch now,' its buying manager for prepared foods told *The Grocer*. 'It's [our lasagne al forno] the classic lifestyle option for the time poor, cash rich consumer.' Sainsbury's usually wins the prize for being the most foodie, therefore pro-cooking, amongst the UK-wide supermarket multiples. But even its initiatives to stimulate home cooking are often thinly disguised marketing opportunities to promote sales of ready-made, processed foods. In 2003, for example, when Sainsbury's launched cooking classes for children (for which parents pay £5) during the school holidays in selected stores, it pegged them to its Blue Parrot Café children's brand which features self-styled healthier versions of children's junk food such as chicken nuggets and pizza. Participating children went away with a Blue Parrot 'goodie bag' and a Blue Parrot apron, reminders that if they didn't feel like cooking, they could always get Mum to pick up something ready-made at Sainsbury's.

The Great British Cookery Paradox is evidence that supermarkets have made substantial inroads in undermining the nation's inclination to cook. In spite of the plethora of TV cooking programmes, cookery articles in magazines and newspapers, and cookery books, which should notionally encourage us all to cook, less and less cooking is being done in homes up and down the land. In 2002, UK TV screened 4,000 hours of food programmes; 900 food books and 25 million words about food and cookery were published. But we seem to spend more time watching chefs cook than cooking ourselves. In 1980, the average meal took one hour to prepare; now it takes twenty minutes. It is predicted that this figure will shrink to eight minutes by 2010. The UK has become a nation of food voyeurs rather than cooks, and supermarkets have supplied both the means and the motive. For every person who, after watching Jamie, Gary or Nigella, goes out to buy the raw materials to cook their recipes at home, it seems there are many more who emerge from supermarkets with up-market, ready-meal lookalikes. 'People who are proficient in cooking . . . are now beginning to represent a declining proportion within the population . . . they are arguably also more likely to recognise the difference in cost between purchasing ingredients for home cooking and buying prepared meals,' market analyst Keynote has concluded – an acknowledgement that the more you cook and know about food, the less you are likely to see supermarket prepared food as either desirable or good value.

A central plank in undermining home cooking and boosting sales of more expensive ready-made foods is blurring the qualitative difference between the real thing and the mass-produced supermarket equivalent. Safeway, for example, describes its The Best range as being 'as tasty, near to authentic and home-made as possible'. The slight qualification in this claim was absent when it launched a new winter range of 'traditional British food' ready meals such as pork, cider and apple casserole and toad in the hole – dishes with all the homey, comforting, feel-good virtues of domestic cooking. Safeway cheekily presented it as the 'cheat's guide to making it taste as good as Mum's'. With a little help from Safeway, in the form of ready meals, everyone, it claimed, could be 'a brilliant cook, a domestic legend'. Somerfield's magazine highlighted a reader who was 'planning a "Cheat's Dinner Party", passing off Somerfield ready meals as her own creations!' Sainsbury's used the same strategy big time when it targeted Christmas dinner, the one meal in the year most households would expect to cook more or less from scratch, as a processed food opportunity. 'Who's to know that you've not been slaving away to create a feast? You can take the credit by removing the packaging, safe in the knowledge that Sainsbury's food experts have taken care of all your festive food needs.'

For years supermarkets have fostered the idea that all over the UK, people are passing off ready meals as home-cooked food without anyone being any the wiser. If that is indeed true, it is a sad indictment of our food awareness. But the proposition strains credulity somewhat. Though it might be possible to pass off a supermarket ready meal as home made to those whose only point of reference is pot noodles, most people can easily spot the difference, if only because supermarket ready meals look and taste depressingly familiar. Most recently, supermarkets have developed ranges of 'better-than-the-rest' labels, more upmarket-looking and -sounding 'gourmet' brands such as, Safeway, The Best, Tesco's Finest and Asda's Extra Special, to cater for 'well off young couples who have been known to pass off the pre-packaged food at their dinner parties'. These ranges are an attempt by supermarkets to head off criticism that their food all tastes over-processed and industrial while inserting a more aspirational top range into their portfolio to keep people interested. They look good in the box, and sell for a considerable premium, but on some products the ingredients list is illuminating evidence of the gastronomic gulf between these aspiring home-entertaining specials and the home-cooked article. The ingredients list for a classic French boeuf bourguignon, for example, is relatively short and sweet, containing no unfamiliar ingredients. The equivalent list on one supermarket's 'better-than-the-rest' boeuf bourguignon casserole ran to a substantial paragraph and one needed a degree in chemistry to decode it.

Ingredients in Elizabeth David's boeuf bourguignon (from *French Provincial Cooking*):
Beef, salt pork or unsalted streaky bacon, onion, thyme, parsley

and bay leaves, red wine, olive oil, meat stock, garlic, flour, mushrooms and meat dripping.

Ingredients in a supermarket's 'better-than-the-rest' boeuf bourguignon casserole:
Beef, water, red wine, baby onion, bacon lardons (pork belly; water; salt; dried glucose syrup; stabilisers; sodium polyphosphate, sodium triphosphate, disodium diphosphate; preservative; sodium nitrite; antioxidant; sodium ascorbate; smoke flavouring), onion, modified maize starch, beef stock (concentrated beef broth; yeast extract; glucose; salt; vegetable fat; water, emulsifier; mono- and di-glycerides of fatty acids; rosemary extract), celery, carrot, vegetable stock (with emulsifier: mono- and di-glycerides of fatty acids), vegetable oil, white wine vinegar, salt, pork gelatine, thyme, dried glucose syrup, garlic purée, acidity regulators (sodium acetate; sodium citrate), ground bay, antioxidant (sodium ascorbate).

Even allowing for the additional information for manufactured food required under labelling regulations, such a comparison underlined how a supermarket ready meal in a box was a very different animal from its home-cooked equivalent. An advert for Tesco's Finest range said, 'It's like a top chef preparing dinner for you at a moment's notice.' Tesco had put together a team of '250 of the best of them [chefs]' to create, amongst other Finest lines, convenience meals using 'specially sourced ingredients'. But how many top chefs use ingredients such as dried glucose syrup, mono- and di-glycerides of fatty acids or acidity regulator?

Having successfully planted the idea that there is no need to cook because factory food is at least as good, if not better, than the home-made equivalent, supermarkets have sought to extend their gastronomic empire by fostering the idea that there is no need to eat out in restaurants either.

Here the most daring stunt has been performed by Sainsbury's with its Bombay Brasserie meal kits, named after the celebrated

London restaurant. Launching an extended range, Sir Gulam Noon of Noon Products, who makes the range for Sainsbury's, hailed it as a way for Sainsbury's shoppers who live outside London to 'create their own Bombay Brasserie at home'. He said that his company had worked very closely with the restaurant's chefs 'to ensure all the dishes were produced to restaurant standards', encouraging us to believe the implausible proposition that when we reheat a factory curry meal at home it will look and taste the same as one freshly prepared on the spot by top Indian chefs in one of the UK's foremost restaurants. Only the most gullible would believe that, of course, but such counter-intuitive claims have the effect of making the product being hyped sound better than those that preceded it, so rekindling our interest when it might otherwise wane. Which is exactly what they are intended to do.

9

Why it all tastes the same

If you habitually shop in one supermarket chain for ready meals, you might occasionally wonder if you are missing out on variety by not trying out rival chains' offerings. Don't. There's a very, very strong chance that despite being sold by different chains, the contents of those boxes will resemble one another closely.

Carry out a 'tried and tasted' comparison – a popular consumer journalism exercise which attempts to compare the relative contents of various supermarket chains' boxed offerings – and the resemblance between the appealingly packaged ready meals that line our supermarket shelves is striking. In 2003, Asian food expert Ken Hom carried out precisely such a test on supermarket Thai green curry, sampling those sold by Tesco, Sainsbury's, Waitrose, Somerfield and Marks & Spencer. The parameters of tried-and-tested features are often skewed towards supermarkets – a reflection of their grip on the nation's psyche: usually only supermarket samples are tested, and no restaurant or home-made samples are included in the comparison. Such features demand that there must be winners and losers. An internal hierarchy must be established, even if the entire category is lacking in merit. But the results in this particular taste test were more candid than usual. They spoke volumes about the homogeneity of supermarket food. The same taste criticisms came up with monotony: dry chicken, not spicy, overly sweet, not at all authentic. Though the inevitable ratings implied that one chain's offering had some slight merit over another's, Mr Hom sounded distinctly underwhelmed. One tasted 'more like an airline meal'; another was 'not green curry as I know it'. The highest score went to 'the best of the bunch'. One sensed that given a free hand, he might have been happier offering a Eurovision Song Contest *'nul points'* to the whole lot.

The fact that one chain's Thai green curry tastes pretty much like all the others – and not at all like any green curry you'd ever encounter in Thailand – is scarcely surprising. There's a good chance that it was made by the same company that is supplying its rivals. Between 1995 and 2000, for example, Hazlewood Foods was a major chilled meals supplier to Sainsbury's, Tesco, Waitrose and Morrisons; S&A to Tesco, Safeway and Asda; Northern Foods to Marks & Spencer, Sainsbury's and Tesco; Geest to Sainsbury's and Tesco; and Noon to Sainsbury's and Waitrose. Another company, Uniq, has worked with various chains developing their low-fat, healthy-eating product ranges such as Marks & Spencer's Count On Us, Sainsbury's Be Good To Yourself, Safeway's Eat Smart and Asda's Good For You ranges.

Of course one cannot automatically assume, because of this clubby overlap, that supermarkets can't instruct their faithful suppliers to introduce a genuine 'point of difference' to distinguish their chain's offering from all the others. Recipes may differ, ingredients may come from distinct sources and so on. But taste your way around a few supermarket chilled meals and you will begin to notice how the white sauce in one chain's cod and parsley pie is surprisingly like another chain's moussaka topping, how the tomato goo on top of your pizza tastes oddly reminiscent of the Mediterranean-style pasta in tomato and basil sauce, how the Mexican salsa tastes like the Spanish gazpacho and how, if you sampled the sauce on those Malaysian sweet chilli prawns blind, you might easily confuse it with the gravy on the lamb steak with redcurrants.

Think about it a little longer and you'll pick up the same defining characteristics in almost all savoury supermarket-prepared meals. Any meat will probably be overcooked and dry – a consequence of bulk factory cooking followed by domestic reheating. A salty savouriness without any particular flavour profile prevails. Where a sauce or a liquid element is present, a gloopy consistency is de rigueur. Last but not least, don't be surprised it looks little like the picture on the box. That enticing image, after all, is the product of long hours of toil put in by a team of food stylists, lighting managers and photographers.

Clearly, when so much food is made for our supermarkets by the same companies, the results are likely to resemble one another. The same state-of-the-art factory line technologies and automated short cuts are used to turn out any mass-produced food object. Any slight personality to be found in the ingredients used is beaten out of them by the time they have been subjected to the various interventions of large-scale food processing. Hence the institutionalised sameness of supermarket ready meals.

Lest consumers begin to tire of this uniformity, supermarkets go in for what is known as 'sub-branding' or 'segmentation'. When their shoppers begin to feel like children at Christmas, rather jaded with that new toy, supermarkets like to feed us a stream of novelties that appear to refresh the category even though they are essentially variations of the same thing. It's just like Barbie, the doll with the abundant hair, pert breasts, long legs and impossibly narrow hips. There is Beach Barbie, Air Hostess Barbie, Aerobic Barbie and so on but she always has the same essential hair, breasts, legs and hips. Supermarket ready meals are the food equivalent: they might as well be Thai Barbie, Bistro Barbie, Café Society Barbie, Vegetarian Barbie or Indian Take-away Barbie. They look superficially different but the underlying prototype remains the same. The resemblance stops there though because most supermarket ready meals don't, like Barbie, still look good when they come out of their packaging. They look like what they are, a disappointingly slight, unappetising-looking pile of overcooked food in a plastic tray.

Any positive selling point or new-sounding concept can, in supermarket-speak, be 'rolled out' into stores to create a new range. Better-than-the-rest ranges (such as Tesco Finest or Asda's Extra Special, Somerfield's So Good, Co-op's Truly Irresistible), Ready-To-Cook, Meals in Minutes, lines that promote healthy eating or cater for special dietary needs like Sainsbury's Wellbeing or Safeway's Eat Smart, a celebrity chef collection perhaps, a 'value' range are all concepts that allow the creation of whole new family groups or tiers of products, as desirable and collectable to trusting consumers as Pokemon cards and football stickers. These ranges boost the own-brand power of the chain by increasing the number of 'facings' with which shelves can be filled, preventing ennui from setting in and customers from drifting elsewhere.

Just as we are beginning to notice that our supermarket's chicken korma, for example, is expensive for what it is, not to mention pretty dull, the chain will relaunch it in a new, exciting Regional Indian format, only tweaking the product itself but radically altering its appearance and the marketing pitch on the box. These supermarket strategies encourage us to see diversity and qualitative difference where in fact there is pitifully little. With only minor adjustments, factory spaghetti bolognese can be reinvented as spicy Manhattan meatballs with spaghetti. A change of packaging and hey presto, chilli con carne becomes a chilli beef bowl. A few standard dishes, minimally altered then packed in a brown craft paper takeaway bag, can become a restaurant 'Chinese banquet'. Unable or unwilling to give us the true variety that comes from using a large number of suppliers with geographically distinctive, often seasonal foods, produced with specialist expertise, supermarkets offer instead the phoney choice of the merchandised factory meal in its seemingly infinite chameleon-like forms.

Sainsbury's summed up UK supermarket chains' claims to broaden the British palate when it said that it could supply 'everything you need to launch you on a round-the-world voyage of culinary discovery'. This thinking produces some very bizarre products: Sainsbury's 'American style mini battered chicken fillets with a honey and mustard sauce', for example. These look and taste indistinguishable from any number of other battered chicken products on supermarket shelves. It is not at all clear what is American about them. Their label, though, says 'Produced in Thailand . . . This product has been previously frozen and defrosted under controlled conditions making it suitable for refreezing.' So there you have it, an unremarkable bit of battered chicken reared and manufactured in Asia (where chicken is produced for less than the UK) to a nominally American recipe, which is then sent frozen from the other side of the world to be defrosted in the UK so you can refreeze it at home. Is this a globetrotting foodie adventure worth having?

With such creations, far from broadening the UK's palate, supermarkets have conditioned it to accept traducements of the real thing. Italian chef and food expert Antonio Carluccio has been outspoken about their contribution to Britain's food education. 'Supermarkets have committed huge crimes when it comes to Italian food. It's everyone's dream to supply Tesco or Sainsbury, but I would say to many small suppliers, don't bother. The supermarkets here have such a large share of the market that you have to be able to supply large volumes and quality is compromised. I was once invited by a major food supplier to multiples to improve the own-label lasagne. But when they went back to the supermarkets they weren't interested because it was 10 pence dearer.'

Supermarket convenience foods flirt with foreignness, exoticism and authenticity, but their taste remains essentially conservative, upholding the salty-sweet, gloopy status quo of industrial food production. As Safeway's buying manager for prepared foods put it, 'Authenticity is not necessarily what people want, so we try to marry authenticity with the British palate.' The truth is that supermarket prepared food can't be made to taste like a good example of the real thing, and so supermarkets must feed a dumbed-down version to the consumers with a positive spin put on it. They have done so with notable success. British consumers, for example, spend £7,000 a minute on ready meals, three times more than any other country in Europe. Spending on these is set to soar to £5 billion per year by 2007. Cultural commentator Jonathan Meades once said that supermarkets have thrived on what he calls 'the British indifference to flavour, freshness and quality, the British preoccupation with the appearance of foodstuffs, the British insistence on choice'. How right he was.

10

Fresh is worst

Hardly a week goes by without another reminder that British eating habits are in decline: a survey, or new research, providing more evidence to confirm that we seem to have become a culinarily clueless country, simultaneously overfed yet undernourished, intent on fattening ourselves up on junk in preparation for an early grave. The 2001–2002 government Expenditure and Food Survey was one such reminder. In a nutshell, this snapshot of national eating habits showed that consumption of fresh, raw, unprocessed food had declined within a year, for example fish (–4 per cent) and green vegetables (–7 per cent), while that of processed food was up, chips for instance +6 per cent and processed meats +3.5 per cent.

When consumers are making a beeline for reheatable baked potato instead of baking a fresh one themselves, or selecting a plastic carton filled with mass-produced cauliflower cheese for two instead of a fresh cauliflower, milk and cheese, is this just more confirmation that the UK is, as cultural commentator Jonathan Meades has suggested, 'a country with a collectively defective palate', or does it have something to do with the way we shop?

It could simply be coincidence that the UK's vegetable consumption, for example, has declined by almost a third since the

1960s, just as the supermarkets' retail dominance has grown. Supermarkets would doubtless tell us that this dramatic decline has nothing to do with them. When such worrying trends in UK food consumption surface, our large retailers, even though they supply the bulk of the nation's shopping basket, are always prominent in the rush to distance themselves from any culpability, presenting themselves instead as the purveyors of solutions. After all, supermarkets regularly take credit for giving consumers a wider, more enticing range of vegetables than ever before. Who, they boast, had ever heard of mangetouts or baby corn before the supermarkets came on the scene?

In fact supermarkets positively fall over each other in the stampede to tell us how they are doing their bit to improve the nation's diet. If we are turning into a nation of hypertensive fatties, it is nothing whatsoever to do with what they sell. Their public relations departments issue upbeat and paternalistic press releases telling us how they are filling their shelves with prominently labelled healthy-eating options, helpfully marketing small fruits in child-friendly packaging and so on. They like to be seen as crusaders for top-quality, fresh, healthy food for everyone. In January 2003, for example, Asda claimed that it had taken 1,000 tonnes of salt out of its own-label food products in the preceding four years and pledged to take a further 10 per cent out by the end of 2004. Somewhat embarrassingly, six months later, Asda was indirectly criticised by the Food Standards Agency for loading some of its healthy eating lines with salt. An Asda Good For You lasagne contained 60 per cent of the recommended daily salt intake for an adult. Asda's 'Good For You' korma with rice contained 55 per cent. Popular Asda own-label children's meals – spaghetti with meatballs, shepherd's pie and macaroni cheese – contained 48 per cent, 46 per cent and 42 per cent respectively of a child's recommended intake. If this was an improvement, how much salt had they contained in previous years?

Usually there are strings attached to supermarkets' championing of public health. Often their healthy-eating initiatives are little more than unsubtly disguised self-promotion exercises with a commercial pay-off. In 2003, for example, Sainsbury's launched a scheme in conjunction with the NHS, where GPs would refer overweight patients to the nearest Sainsbury's for a guided healthy-eating tour. Staff would 'point out low fat versions of popular foods, such as ready meals, as well as focusing on cheaper products such as tinned fruit and frozen vegetables'. In a similar initiative, groups of schoolchildren were invited to visit their local Sainsbury's, where a team of trained food advisers and registered dieticians would 'talk to them about the various food groups and how they can choose the best foods to keep them healthy'. Sainsbury's free fruit in schools also sounded like a commendable initiative until you learnt that this was teamed with 'fruitastic store tours' run by Sainsbury's advisers. The message might be 'Eat more fruit', but the missing strapline was 'and make sure you buy it in Sainsbury's'.

In one such initiative by Waitrose, this message was made explicit. It sponsors the Kid's Cookery School (KCS), a charity that encourages children to cook. KCS offers paying cookery workshops with some free places for children from 'disadvantaged backgrounds', which have included workshops run by Waitrose staff, focused around visits to Waitrose stores. In the summer of 2002, KCS ran a two-day sponsored extravaganza during which children toured Waitrose and KCS's principal and chief executive held free workshops for children 'to promote the fantastic range of fruits and vegetables that Waitrose stock'. Likewise every sheet sent out free to schools as part of Waitrose's Food Explorers 'education packs' carries the prominent flag/logo – some would say advert – Waitrose@school.

Children figure prominently in supermarket healthy-eating drives. The food industry has fostered the concept of separate children's food as a distinct category from adult food and this has created a whole new gravy train for retailers. As well as

Waitrose several other supermarkets have come up with special ranges. Somerfield has the Funky Food Factory, Sainsbury's offers the Blue Parrot Café, Safeway has its KIDS 'I'd like . . .' range and Waitrose has Food Explorers. Viewed charitably, these healthy-eating drives are sincere, if misguided, attempts to offer healthier food that appeals to children. Viewed cynically, they are efforts to exploit parents who worry about what their offspring eat by developing highly profitable added-value lines. The ranges comprise a selection of items with distinctly different merits. All include small fruits in special packaging. When I checked Waitrose's offerings in November 2003, Food Explorers bananas cost 19.8 pence each while ordinary small bananas cost 17.9 pence each. This premium charged for Food Explorers was repeated with 'easy peel' clementines. Mini-clementines in the Food Explorers range cost 96 pence per pound while ordinary clementines, larger in size, cost 90 pence per pound. That same month, a Friends of the Earth survey found that in Tesco 'Kids Snack Pack Carrots' were on sale at thirteen times the price of Value carrots, a trend repeated at Asda where 'Snack Pack Carrot Crunchies' cost ten times more than loose carrots.

When it comes to processed food in children's ranges, the chains are very careful about what claims they make, the operative word being health*ier* as opposed to health*y*. The Funky Food Factory components contain 'a minimum of additives' and levels of salt and sugar are 'carefully controlled'. The Blue Parrot Café guarantees 'controlled fat, restricted colours, no preservatives and no added flavour enhancers'. Likewise Food Explorers 'contains no artificial sweeteners, flavourings and colours' and contains 'controlled levels of fat, added sugar and salt'. Safeway says its KIDS 'I'd like . . .' range 'has been developed within nutritional guidelines to contain controlled levels of fat, salt and sugar so you can rest assured they [children] are eating healthier, nutritionally balanced foods'. Favourites in this range include Chicken Ketchup Kievs, mini jam tarts and Cheese & Onion Sky Mix, described as 'cheese and onion flavour 3D moon, star and planet-shaped potato, wheat and rice snacks'.

What supermarkets are aiming for in children's ranges is to provide a tick list of apparently healthy components which encourages parents to put two and two together and make five. They may look good, but in essence they are generally only slightly improved versions of familiar processed foods, often embracing lines which, in any other context, would look like junk. The labelling often seeks to make a major virtue out of every slight improvement. What they should really say on the label is 'Better than the standard food industry equivalent in some respect', which is not saying a lot.

The Food Explorers range, for example, claims to be 'good for children'. Adverts say 'what may sound like kid's junk food is, in fact, healthy food'. This reassuring guarantee, however, is applied to some surprising foods. Parents who thought they understood the basics of healthy eating might be at a loss to understand what was especially healthy about raspberry-ripple-flavoured water, toffee caramel balls breakfast cereal, chocolate chip cookies or toffee sauce. This last item – a Food Explorers 'treat' – is 65 per cent sugars, but it bears the reassuring label '25 per cent less fat than typical toffee sauce'. Many savoury Food Explorers lines are slightly adapted versions of ubiquitous supermarket ready meals such as chicken tikka, sweet and sour chicken, lasagne and shepherd's pie which do little or nothing to extend the boundaries of children's eating as their 'Explorers' title might imply. As food writer Lynda Brown put it:

> The Food Explorers range is not a genuine effort to seriously tackle children's nutrition, but primarily to wean kids and their mothers on processed food in jazzy packaging that has a bit less of the very ingredients causing problems in the first place. Either that, or they have the audacity to reinvent basic items like dried fruit as something specially designed for kids and charge hand-

somely for it. As a Waitrose shopper, I am personally very disappointed. There might be the odd okay item, but how on earth a supermarket chain which prides itself on a passion for food quality can think that their gloopy, sickly sweet toffee sauce has anything to do with good food or nutrition beats me. To call such foods a 'treat' is insulting their customer's intelligence.

Sainsbury's Blue Parrot Café range is promoted as 'healthier food for kids ... specially developed to deliver great taste with improved nutritional quality'. But nutritionists at the Food Commission, the independent food watchdog, were left scratching their heads over several items in the range, not least the blackcurrant-flavoured sparkling water drink.

> You might expect that this product with its luscious pictures of blackcurrant fruit would contain enough blackcurrant juice to warrant Sainsbury's on-pack advice: 'A glass of fruit juice (150ml) counts towards your 5 portions of fruit and vegetables a day'. No such luck. There is so little blackcurrant juice in this product, that a percentage is not even given, which according to food labelling law, indicates that there is so little blackcurrant juice in this bottle that it is simply there as a flavouring. And whilst the product contains some apple juice, sugar is the top ingredient after water.

was the Food Commission's withering assessment.

Sainsbury's interpretation of healthy eating advice has already ruffled feathers at the Department of Health. Along with Tesco and Somerfield, it has spurned the government's five-a-day logo. Sainsbury's says that the government logo is 'too restrictive because it can only be applied to fresh fruit and vegetable products that have no added salt, fat or sugar'. All three chains have their own five-a-day logos, which allow a broader interpretation that can embrace processed food.

There is more than an element of poacher-turned-gamekeeper in supermarkets' attitude to healthy eating, because the truth is that our large food retailers all make considerable profit out of selling over-processed, nutritionally debased, industrial food and have no intention of surrendering that in a benevolent mission to rescue the nation's health. Their apparently high-minded aspirations are given the lie by the relative loading of what they actually sell.

Take a few minutes to walk the aisles of a typical supermarket and roughly measure for yourself how much aisle space is given to each broad category of food. You don't need a tape measure for this exercise; paces will do. Then divide everything edible you see into two categories: first fresh, unprocessed raw ingredients, and then processed food. What will be instantly apparent is how the latter dwarfs the former. You will see that the space given to ready meals frequently outstrips that given to fresh meat and fish combined. Fruit and vegetables, despite being tactically located by the entrance to create the impression of a store bursting with healthy fresh produce, increasingly occupy less gondola (shelf) space than ready meals, crisps, snacks or fizzy drinks. In other words, the selection you see pushes you towards processed food and makes you feel less inclined to cook. In this respect, UK supermarkets are strikingly different from European ones. Phil Daoust, a writer who moved from London to Alsace, summed up the difference in the *Guardian*. 'The other morning I went to the supermarket without any clear idea of what I was going to buy. In Britain I would have come away with some sort of pasta bake, a pork pie, perhaps a Thai-style stir fry. I left the Intermarché with potatoes, lamb's lettuce, steaks and wine. That night my daughter and I ate steak au poivre, garlic mash and salad with a light vinaigrette.' In Britain, fewer and fewer people cook, microwaves are being installed rather than ovens and some homes don't have a table on which to eat any more. More people are going for the easy option, which contributes to them getting fatter and less healthy, and they are strongly encouraged to do that by the supermarket system.

One fresh chilled food supplier observed wryly that UK super-markets would stop selling fresh unprocessed food entirely if they thought they could get away with it. 'Whether it's melons, milk or mince, fresh unprocessed food is just full of hassle. It's a pain in the butt. It doesn't look nice, it's inconsistent, it takes a lot of management by the store. If it stays an extra day or two in depot, they've lost it because it's past its best. The less fresh food they can do the better as far as they are concerned. They stock it because they have to, because people expect it.'

Supermarkets feed this expectation with specialist counters – fresh meat and fish, delicatessen, 'food to go', hot pies, 'curry pots', hot carvery, salad bar, etc. These support the illusion that supermarkets offer all the fresh food virtues of the traditional, more personalised marketplace or vibrant high street, more con-veniently organised under one roof. Morrisons prominently names the aisle with these sections as 'Market Street'. In some newer stores, Sainsbury's tries to create a market feel with an area dedicated to specialist counters at the front of the store. In supermarket language, such counters are 'hero departments' because they have 'pulling power'. They bring people into the store and create an excitement that aisle after aisle of standard grocery products can't. They add 'theatre' or excitement to the supermarket shopping experience.

Some of these specialist counters are more convincing than others. Morrisons, for example, has staff in each store who make up salads daily for self-service salad bars. Asda, on the other hand, has counters which promise that pizza is 'Freshly Made For You', but in the Asda store I visited, 'freshly made' consisted of putting prepared toppings (chopped ham, grated cheese, pepperoni) on top of ready-made pizza bases, then shrink wrap-ping them. At one Safeway pizzeria counter I visited, the pizza oven had a log-effect oven which, to the casual passer-by, gave the impression of a traditional wood-fired oven. Staff behind the counter told me that although the dough could be rolled out into one of two sizes on the spot, it was not made on the premises.

Produce sections also provide supermarkets with an opportunity to create a healthy image and create a mini-high street feel. Launching Sainsbury's 2003 'First For Fresh' – a major overhaul of its produce presentation – the chain's project manager explained that it was about 're-emphasising our excellence in fresh food to the consumer'. When customers first came in they would see 'abundant displays, merchandised with a lot of flair, using colours and varieties to best effect', she said, adding that blackboard-type signage would give it a 'traditional greengrocer feel'.

But even on the produce shelves it is obvious that supermarkets want to sell us processed food. Sainsbury's, for example, has a Food To Go line called 'Fully Prepared Apple Bites' which consists of apple slices dipped in a vitamin C solution and then placed in a 'pillow pack' filled with modified air to stop them going brown. They cost twice the price of an apple. Yet as Brian Logan reflected in the *Guardian*, the apple in its intact form is the original convenience food, a natural 'food to go' with its own edible packaging, perfect for those age-old apple dissecting devices with which we are all equipped, teeth.

Farcical though 'Fully Prepared Apple Bites' might seem, the business logic behind this is simple. There is a limit to what you can charge for straightforward unprocessed ingredients. But add value to them through some sort of food processing, then package them appealingly, and the sky is the limit. There's only so much you can ask, after all, for a kilo of potatoes, no matter how esoteric the variety or well scrubbed the spud. Overdo your margin, and you get the reputation for being a rapacious retailer. But sell those potatoes as a 'just reheat' gratin, or a microwavable potato croquette, and you'll be quids in, with the added bonus that the costing behind the price will be less transparent to customers than it would be with unprocessed food. Provided the 'pick-up' price is attractive, most people will not have any idea whether value-added food represents true value for money. One meat supplier told me: 'They [supermarkets] constantly encourage us to come up with processed food convenience lines on which they can make better margins. They only make about 10 per cent on fresh meat but they need at least 20 per cent to cover their costs. That's why so little promotional activity is around fresh meat. But they have to stock it because it's a "must-have". On processed meat products, they can make as much as a 43 per cent margin and that's why they like to sell them.'

Supermarkets' fondness for processing food in some way so as to add value and make more money is bad news for our health. In 2004, *Which?* Magazine found that processed fruit and vegetables in supermarkets – such as prepared Brussels sprouts, broccoli florets and melon slices – had seriously depleted levels of vitamin C, the most striking example being a bag of Asda sliced runner beans which contained 89 per cent less vitamin C than the typical textbook runner bean.

There is also another reason why supermarkets load their offer with processed food. Mass-produced food that can be churned out over and over again in vast, uniform quantities, made by a handful of big manufacturers who jump to the big retailers' tune, processed food lends itself to supermarket retailing: it gives them the ability to put a standard, regular product into every store nationwide, a product that doesn't require any on-the-spot specialist handling. Big Food and Big Retail are two sides of the same coin. Industrial food lends itself to the supermarkets' heavily centralised, highly mechanical distribution systems, but fresh raw ingredients don't. Unlike cat food and rice crispies, they are irritatingly subject to the vagaries of nature. Apples don't all grow on a tree to the same size to conveniently fit into moulded polystyrene packs of four. A herd of cattle won't all obligingly provide steaks of uniform dimension. Some stubborn types of fruits and vegetables simply cannot be made to grow all year round, however much that would suit supermarket systems. All the plaice that might be fished in the waters around the UK is not conveniently landed at one harbour so that supermarkets can instruct a favoured supplier to buy them all up.

In other words, because fresh raw ingredients are a natural, rather than industrial product, they require more specific, less uniform sourcing and more knowledgeable, experienced and flexible handling than is the supermarket norm. Because of their retailing power, we might assume that supermarkets would handle such perishable cargo in an infinitely more sophisticated and more expert manner than the independent fishmongers, butchers, cheesemongers and greengrocers they put out of business. The irony is that despite the apparently intricate technological infrastructure that supports supermarket food retailing – all those refrigerated lorries pounding up and down the motorway, all those jets transporting food from the other side of the world in a matter of hours, those comprehensive logistics imposed on suppliers in the name of consumer demand – supermarkets have not proved to be supreme champions at delivering fresh and varied food in peak condition. Although supermarkets may be efficient enough at shipping commodities like tinned tomatoes and toilet roll around the country, when it comes to that critical fresh department, their goals and systems actually get in the way of doing a good job.

11

Permanent global summertime

A Briton born a hundred years ago, resurrected and propelled around the typical modern supermarket, would be astounded at the staggering choice that's on offer. Entering via the fruit and vegetable aisle, he or she might even conclude that his children's children live in a latter-day Garden of Eden. How else would you explain that eye-catching cornucopia? Modern consumers who actually eat the stuff, however, are less impressed.

In 2002, an article I wrote for the *Guardian* 'Weekend' entitled 'Strange Fruit', attacking the quality of supermarket fruit and vegetables, received an unusually large, impassioned and supportive postbag. One Cambridgeshire reader wrote in referring to the 'gastronomical tyranny' of the supermarket fruit and vegetable shelves. 'The supermarkets' dumbing down of our taste experience isn't just confined to selecting varieties with longest shelf life and least flavour,' he continued and went on to relate a personal taste experiment. 'Last week I compared a Victoria plum from our garden with one bought from Sainsbury's. One was full of flavour and a succulent mouthful, the other tasteless pap. You can guess which was which,' he wrote. A reader from Gloucestershire yearned for produce that 'tasted good as well as looked good'. A London reader was angered by a supermarket spokesman quoted in the article who had insisted that consumers were happy with their offering. 'He needs to know,' she wrote, 'that people are *not* happy with what they are getting and that we don't want "freshly prepared lines to fit modern lifestyles". We want seasonal produce with flavour. It's time to boycott supermarket produce and refamiliarise ourselves with our local greengrocers,' she concluded.

Increasingly, people have become disenchanted with supermarket produce. One reason is that it is predicated on a new nature-defying order where every conceivable fruit and vegetable grown anywhere is available all the time. I named it 'permanent global summertime' (PGST). Supermarkets' pursuit of PGST means that they cannot be open with customers. In January, for example, a knowledgeable greengrocer would know that there are no peaches to be had anywhere in the world that are worth eating by the time they arrive in the UK and would simply stop stocking them. In May, confronted with a customer seeking parsnips, he might gently suggest that they were out of season and suggest a more appropriate alternative. But supermarkets don't have this option because such candour would give the lie to the dream they peddle in which it is both feasible, and indeed reasonable, for the UK shopper to expect virtually every horticultural product on the planet every day.

Supermarkets promote this artificial reality because they know that fruit and vegetables are a 'destination category': in other words, they form an initial impression that can clinch a consumer's choice of store or might even persuade them to switch stores. The produce section is attractive window dressing for everything else from washing powder to custard creams. It gives chains an opportunity to differentiate themselves from one another. If you have a fruit or vegetable 'exclusive', your whole chain seems more interesting to the consumer. The more unusual or rare, the more environmentally right-on, the better. As a Sainsbury's buyer pointed out, 'Adams Pearmain [a traditional English apple variety] offers a genuine point of difference.' Supermarkets would hate us to get the idea that one chain is very much like another. So to enhance the impression of astounding choice throughout their stores, they stock as many different types of fruit and vegetables as possible.

PGST may look good, but in the name of consumer choice and public health the irregularity and diversity that is part of the natural order has been eliminated, not to benefit consumers but to fit the way our big food retailers like to do business. In essence, this way means sourcing vast quantities of easy-to-retail, long shelf-life standard varieties, grown to rigid size and cosmetic specifications, that can be supplied 365 days a year. 'Quality in supermarket terms means a constant supply of produce that matches their stereotype in terms of shape, size and colour,' one packer told me. 'It must have acceptable sugar and pressure levels and mustn't taste actively unpleasant. Hi-tech, low-taste, odour-free produce is the norm.'

That is why supermarkets have made produce shopping a routine, uninspiring experience, effectively turning shoppers into robotic Stepford Wives, loading up their trolleys each week with identikit purchases. No wonder the nation's fruit and vegetable consumption is declining. Eating 'five a day' is indeed a daunting and unrewarding mission if you shop in a supermarket selling *Midwich Cuckoo*-style produce. And in practical terms, by fostering the concept of the one-stop, weekly shop, supermarkets have drastically reduced the opportunities we have to purchase fruit and vegetables of any kind. Many consumers have simply given up buying pricey items such as plums, strawberries, peaches and apricots entirely because they are such a dismal let-down. The frisson of excitement that true seasonality provides, and the appetite-whetting response it should generate, are absent. Inspiration is shrivelled, for example, by the stultifying knowledge that whether it's March, July or November, you will always find grapes in the middle of gondola three, on aisle number two, and they will always be Thomson Seedless. As food writer Hugh

Fearnley-Whittingstall put it, 'The downside of the culture of infinite year round choice is a kind of options paralysis: there's so much on offer you don't know where to start. Understanding the seasons brings a sense of structure, rhythm and rightness to your shopping and cooking. In a world where the methods of food production are rapidly unravelling into madness, seasonality is sanity, offering the best and quickest solution to the never-ending question: what shall I cook today?' Shoppers no longer see one-time supermarket novelty breakthroughs such as iceberg lettuce, fine green beans, baby corn and mangetouts as a welcome relief from the limitations of native seasonal vegetables. Instead their ubiquity has made them perpetual clichés, a larger-than-life reminder of supermarkets' obsession with creating a new agricultural world order where the sun always shines. When Sainsbury's canvassed shoppers in its prestige Cromwell Road store in London as to what they most wanted from a supermarket, they put their fingers very accurately on our supermarkets' shortcomings. They said they wanted 'very fresh produce, in season, that reawakened their interest in food'; in other words, the opposite of what they usually get from supermarkets, which is unripe, low-risk, far-travelled unseasonal produce that deadens any instinct to cook.

Chef Dennis Cotter astutely summed up consumers' alienation with supermarket fruit and vegetables as follows:

Peaches, tomatoes, avocados, asparagus, broad beans, sugar snap peas, parsnips, leeks, aubergines, sweet peppers, apples, pears ... these are extraordinary foods that can give us unique pleasure. Ironically, the more poor imitations we eat, the less pleasure we take. For many of us, the pleasure associated with these wonderful foods has been gradually replaced in our minds by a dull, nagging ordinariness bordering on disappointment, and ultimately we forget they were ever wonderful. When the foods have finally been reduced to ordinariness, we can pass them in the supermarket aisles without even noticing them.

The problem isn't just the never-changing produce that is on the shelves but what ought to be there yet strangely isn't. Our fellow Europeans expect that the lion's share of produce in their shops and markets will be home produce, coming from identifiable native regions, or at least sold under a generic national label. In Italy, you'll see produce marked *'nostrano'* – literally 'local', a point of fact, but also a statement of pride, evidence of a country with a thriving horticulture. The French use the tag *'pays'* in the same way. To visiting European nationals, accustomed to buying overwhelmingly their own country's produce and only a small proportion of imported lines, UK supermarket shelves must seem positively outlandish. Bizarrely, it is actually easier these days to buy a tropical passion fruit in a British supermarket than it is to buy an English apple. Friends of the Earth found that even at the height of the British 2002 apple season, more than half the apples on sale in major supermarkets were imported. When it carried out the same survey for the 2003 harvest, it found that matters were even worse. The average proportion of UK-grown apples sold in Tesco and Asda stores was 38 per cent. I asked fruit growers why UK fruit was so poorly represented. 'Supermarkets can't be hassled with UK fruit, 300 boxes here, 400 boxes there. They can't even be bothered switching on the computer for that,' one grower told me. 'Even companies with turnovers of £2–3 million are seen as too small to bother with. Supermarkets just want to deal with multinational conglomerates,' said another.

Herbs are another striking example of supermarkets' preference for doing business with major players – even if they are thousands of miles away. Almost all the herbs on sale in UK supermarkets come from Israel where big horticultural companies can guarantee a year-round supply. Yet several popular culinary herbs such as thyme, rosemary and bay grow all year round in the UK. Others such as chives, sage, mint, rocket and parsley will grow in the UK for a good six months of the year.

It is really only the most tender, sun-seeking herbs like basil and coriander that are problematic for our climate. If supermarkets were committed to supporting British production, they could sell British herbs when available and supplement them with ones from abroad only as necessary. When the UK supply is limited, there are many European countries that produce fine herbs. Cyprus, for example, produces a steady flow of top-class parsley and coriander, while Italy has fields of pungent basil throughout the milder months. But it is administratively much easier for our big food retailers to strike a deal with an Israeli consortium for a 365-days-a-year supply.

The sorry state of many less robust supermarket vegetables is an obvious consequence of supermarkets' preparedness to defy local, even European, seasons and source globally at the drop of a hat. Once unwrapped at home, and no longer under flattering produce lighting, these items are likely to resemble airport-weary, jet-lagged travellers. Much supermarket produce never tastes of anything much because it has been harvested prematurely to stop it deteriorating during transportation and on the shelf. Although the big chains all like to make great play of their sophisticated cold chains which theoretically permit all kinds of fragile produce to be transported thousands of miles yet taste as good as when it was picked, the fact is that however much our supermarkets might wish it, fresh produce simply doesn't travel well. No surprise then that consumers are encouraged by supermarkets to shop with the eyes only, all other senses suspended. Smells that might inform the foreign shopper about ripeness, in melons or peaches say, are outlawed. They don't fit in with 'aroma management', the aim of which is to have a uniform smell throughout the store, save for the come-on smells of the instore bakery. Indeed aromas raise a dangerous spectre whose existence UK supermarkets deny: of seasonality, living material in a constant state of flux, development and decay.

One strawberry grower explained to me that he routinely

picked strawberries destined for supermarkets one or two days earlier than those that would be sold in his farm shop. They were less red, less ripe and less sweet to start with, he said, and supermarket chilling methods would not improve them any further. But that's how the supermarkets liked them. Another strawberry grower gave me this vivid illustration of how super-market distribution methods actually get in the way of freshness and flavour:

> When we used to sell our strawberries through wholesale markets they were much fresher. We'd pick all day Friday, for example, a lorry would collect them at 7 p.m. and they'd be in Covent Garden by 9.30 p.m. From there they'd be delivered overnight to secondary wholesale markets all over the UK and they'd be on sale in greengrocers the next morning. Now the supermarkets insist on a 10.30 a.m. pick-up which means that berries picked on a Friday have to be put in cold store overnight. They won't usually get to the central receiving depot until later on Saturday afternoon where they need to be re-apportioned to all the stores and sent out again, probably on the Sunday. The supermarkets have actually lengthened the time between picking and con-sumption.

Or, as one Lewisham stallholder put it rather more bluntly to a reporter from Virgin.net: 'The gear on my stall came from Covent Garden at five this morning. It was almost certainly in the ground yesterday morning. We don't need cold rooms like supermarkets do, we sell the stuff the same day or sling it. Do supermarkets get their stuff delivered fresh from the market every morning and replace it after hours? Like fuck they do.'

One ex-supermarket supplier told me that he sincerely believed that many younger people who only shop in supermarkets have never seen true freshness.

The supermarkets say that their spinach is cut, bagged, labelled, sent cooled to a regional distribution centre then to the store, all within twenty-four hours. That's the theory. In practice, you wait for an unpredictable-sized order to arrive at 10 a.m. You can't afford to let the supermarket down so you keep a least a day's supply in cold store just in case the order is bigger than you estimated it would be, so instantly adding twenty-four hours' life. For a Monday order, you harvest on a Friday. The packhouse will probably bag it on the Tuesday. Spinach can be at least five days old by the time it's on the shelf and then it will have a further three days 'use by' date on it.

Premature picking and over-refrigeration are not the only devices supermarkets employ to create the impression of true freshness, while simultaneously stretching shelf life to its limits. Selecting out certain problematic lines is another. Leeks, for example, are now routinely sold 'de-flagged', without their green stalks. The supermarket justification for this is that shoppers don't have the time or inclination for green flags any longer because they might contain some soil and need to be cleaned. The real reason is that if you leave them on, your leeks look older and sadder more quickly. So it is better for our supermarkets just to whack the flags off and present the de-flagging as a helping hand towards convenience and easing the pressure of modern life. Add to that the advantage that the leeks can be made to fill exactly the shelf space allocated to them. Whole celery is becoming harder to buy. Supermarkets would really prefer to have growers dump the outer stalks and just sell packs of heads because they have a longer shelf life. If they were to sell large-leaf British spinach loose, it would need to be sold in one or two days if it was not to look past its best. So supermarkets have simply stopped stocking large leaf spinach, replacing it with infinitely more expensive baby-leaf spinach, often sold in pillow packs so as to artificially extend its shelf life. As any cook can tell you, the typical supermarket 20 gram pack of herbs is pretty useless. What cooks need is decent-sized bunches. But if you sell herbs in a sparkly stiff plastic carton, most of which is covered by a label, even tired and flaccid herbs can be given the illusion of freshness. Minimally wrapped fresh herb bunches, on the other hand, give a more accurate indication of their age.

To sell really fresh leafy vegetables or herbs successfully, you need experienced greengrocers actively working to achieve a good turnaround. But such expertise is scarce in supermarkets. Store managers simply accept consignments of commodities pre-groomed to reduce all possible risk of spoilage. This skills-and-experience deficit extends to part-time shelf-stackers who are not expected to know whether a Jersey Royal is a potato, a breed of cow or a Channel Island monarch. Further up the horticultural buying chain, there is also a vacuum where experience should be. An importer of Italian salads told me of his experience visiting one of the large supermarkets with samples. 'I met their boss man for fresh produce. He said he was looking to source something a bit different and I showed him a head of trevisse [a red chicory, common in Italy, similar to radicchio but naturally pointed in shape]. "Obviously they must grow these in tubes to get them to grow into this shape," he said. He was so ignorant, I couldn't be bothered answering him.' An English fruit grower told me how one supermarket chain rejected a pre-agreed consignment of Worcester Pearmain apples because they were not round enough. 'The quality controller didn't know that this variety of apple is naturally a bit pear-shaped – hence the name. Help, we thought. They don't know this but they are dealing with our produce!'

The only relief from the standardised tedium of supermarket produce comes in the form of speciality ranges of fruit and vegetables that appear to have more going for them. Complaints about pink sludge supermarket tomatoes, aptly named '*Wasser-bomben*' in Germany, prompted the introduction of 'flavour-grown' varieties. These 'better-than-the-rest' ranges are in themselves an admission that the standard supermarket tomato is grown to satisfy other non-taste criteria. Now the concept has been extended to all manner of produce. Tesco's Finest and Sainsbury's Taste the Difference labels feature items such as sun-ripened Jamaican ortaniques, extra-sweet golden kiwis, Delizia tomatoes 'grown in sandy soil to deliver this distinct, sweet flavour' and bananas 'left to ripen longer and grown exclusively on the tropical terraces of the Canaries'. In 2003 Waitrose launched a new fruit range packed in black and gold livery explicitly called 'Perfectly Ripe', consisting of up-market pears, stone fruit and tropical fruits such as mango and papaya that have been left to mature on the tree. These supermarket specialities cost substantially more than the standard equivalent and seek to make a virtue out of giving consumers what we always hoped we'd be getting anyway: ripe, fresh produce that actually tastes of something.

12

Lost at sea

We are told by the government that we ought to be eating two portions of fish a week, but you can bet that very few supermarket shoppers manage that. When you are buying fish there are two important criteria that ought to be fulfilled. The paramount consideration is that the fish must be ultra-fresh. The secondary consideration is that the wider the changing daily selection of different species – 'the catch of the day' – the better. Supermarkets toil to deliver on both fronts. Take processed products like smoked salmon or marinated herring out of the equation – these pad out the supermarket's fish offering – and you'll see just how little fresh, unprocessed fish is actually on offer. Anyone still lucky enough to have the comparative benchmark of a good independent fishmonger in their area cannot fail to be underwhelmed by the unexciting and lacklustre nature of the typical supermarket offering. Yet as fish expert William Black tactfully put it: 'It's to supermarkets that many of us have to turn, not always happily, for our regular supplies of fish.' It is no surprise that the UK's fish consumption is going down. The government's 2001–2002 Expenditure and Food Survey showed that sales of fish had declined by 4 per cent within the year.

In smaller stores, the whole fish category is generally relegated

to a blink-and-you'd-miss-it zone of shelf space. You'll find fish
in pre-packs sealed with 'modified atmosphere' (air that's had its
composition altered to artificially extend the shelf life of the
product within it), under film so tough and so tight that until
you get home and pierce it with a sharp knife you won't have a
clue whether the fish is, to your mind, fresh or not. Don't have
high expectations. Fresh fish goes through a dumb period when
it is not actively 'off' or malodorous but not exactly full of the
joys of the sea either. Fish in that state is what we are likely to
get when we buy supermarket pre-packs. You're likely to have
the further frustration of being locked into the retailer's idea of
the typical 'meal occasion'. Salmon steaks, for example, commonly come in packs of two, designed for the supermarket's idea
of a cosy *dîner à deux*. So what do you do if there are three or
five people for dinner, or you live alone? Feed the surplus one
to the cat?

In bigger supermarkets with a distinct wet fish counter where
fresh fish is laid out on the slab, there ought to be more flexibility.
In supermarket terms this is a specialist department, so it seems
reasonable to expect that the variety might be less predictable,
depending on what's available on the market and what species
are in season. But here again, our supermarkets seem incapable
of delivering those two crucial criteria, freshness and range. As
the UK's leading seafood chef and authority of fish Rick Stein put
it, 'It's a pity some chains are still taking fish from the quayside to
the multiple depot and then into the store. And it's ridiculous
when you read that some produce has travelled 1,000 miles to
the shop ... I believe the quality and range of supermarket fish
counters still needs a lot of work. I find some of them boring,
given the predominance of farmed salmon.'

Take a couple of minutes to appraise the typical supermarket
wet fish counter and you'll see what he means. The first thing
that hits you is a preponderance of farmed (salmon, trout), as
opposed to wild fish. Increasingly, even species we presume are

wild – like cod, halibut, turbot, tuna, bass and bream – are being farmed. Supermarkets say that farmed fish is just a response to shortage of wild stocks, but that is a partial truth. Supermarkets like farmed fish because it can be bought and sold like ball bearings. It is immune to the whims of the sea and so it fits in with supermarkets' centralised, highly automated, nationwide buying systems. It takes only a couple of conversations between a supermarket fish buyer and Scottish farmed salmon supplier, or a Greek sea bass farmer, to arrange a supply of fish of a standard weight in all stores, at a low price that can be guaranteed for a substantial period of time. By contrast, fleeting, ever-changing supplies of wild fish are a pain in the backside for supermarkets. The catch changes each day; prices and availability fluctuate. Supplies of fresh wild fish are inherently local, patchy and highly changeable. Supermarkets' buying requirements, on the other hand, are national and fixed.

Supermarkets have trialled schemes supplying locally caught fish bypassing central distribution. In 2003, Safeway found that such an initiative in the south-west of England raised sales by 27 per cent. But this method of supply is not typical. Usually, fish and shellfish must pass through one of a few regional distribution centres (RDCs) irrespective of where the fish is to be sold. This is the opposite of the old fishmonger's goal of 'From the sea to the pan as fast as we can'. In the classic supermarket system, haddock landed and smoked at Peterhead in the far north-east of Scotland may well be sent to a distribution centre in England before being despatched to Scottish stores. Whereas traditional fishmongers bought from merchants operating out of local ports and sold what they got as soon as possible, supermarkets routinely transport fish up and down the country. In this way, they have lengthened the time that fish takes to arrive on the slab, not shortened it. And for supermarkets to be interested in doing business with a particular supplier of wild fish, that supplier must be able to guarantee a large enough volume to supply all, or at least a large number, of stores. So the supplier may need to buy in fish from other geographically distant sources to meet the supermarket's requirements.

A common characteristic of supermarket wet fish counters is that a large proportion of fish has been defrosted from frozen. Most consumers assume, not unreasonably, that because fish and shellfish are lying on the slab, not in a deep freeze, they are fresh. Read the small text on the label – it may not be obvious unless you look quite carefully – and you'll see the words 'previously frozen'. Though arguments rage about the effect that freezing has on fish, gastronomic experts agree that frozen is a poor second best to fresh. By buying frozen fish, supermarkets get to have their cake and eat it. They have the ease of buying and transporting fish frozen, without any of the hassle or expense necessarily involved in handling a sensitive product like chilled fresh fish which, to be sold at its best, needs as short and direct a supply chain as possible. Meanwhile, the less than vigilant shopper, who fails to notice the 'previously frozen' small print and refreezes the fish at home, is guaranteed a doubly disappointing, and possibly microbiologically dodgy, eating experience.

Padding out of the fish counter comes in the form of the growing number of 'exotic' species such as tilapia, hoki and marlin which sell, somewhat cheekily, under the label 'air freighted for freshness', though anyone with an experienced eye for fish could tell you that they look exceptionally matt and flaccid, having lost their sparkle after their long journey from oceans on the other side of the world. Now 70 per cent of fish consumed in the UK originates in foreign waters, a figure that clearly reflects our supermarkets' sourcing policies.

Check out your supermarket's wet fish counter of an afternoon, and you can bet on finding 'special offer' bargain fish that's been marked down for quick sale. Whether it's cod or skate or swordfish or tuna, after one look at its tired and lustreless state, you'll instantly appreciate why the staff behind the counter might be having problems shifting it. 'When I walk into a supermarket with a fish counter I can just tell by the smell alone that the fish is not fresh by my standards and the look only confirms that,' one experienced fishmonger told me. He explained that when it comes to supplies of wild fish such as haddock, cod, whiting and so on, there are various grades on offer at a fish auction. This is done not by size but by age: the freshest fish commands the highest price. 'The supermarkets buy the poorer quality fish because they consider the best fish is too expensive. The reason why many of their fillets often contain bones is because they like to buy "block" fish, that's cheaper fish that have been filleted at speed. It's hard to see why supermarkets buy fish from all over the world to sell fresh when they can't even sell fish from the UK fresh,' he remarked.

One young, enthusiastic Surrey fishmonger, Rex Goldsmith, gave me an insight into the difference between fish from the independent fish trade and that from supermarkets. 'I drum into my assistant, "If you wouldn't buy it – don't sell it." I always go for quality,' he told me. On a sunny spring day, the selection on his slab was as vibrantly fresh as the weather: Whitstable oysters, Cornish cod, brill, skate, sole, Scottish mussels, south-coast line-caught sea bass and west coast scallops. None of it had been frozen. It was the sort of selection that gives you ideas and inspires you to cook.

Mr Goldsmith started as a Saturday boy in a fishmonger's at the age of twelve. He always wanted his own shop but then a big new supermarket opened locally. He ended up working there for eight years before realising his dream of going into business for himself. Now each day he trades, he gets up at three in the morning to go to Billingsgate market in London. It takes him one hour to get there and up to three to get back. Such dedication – I asked him why he bothered. 'You'll only sell rubbish to some-one once. They never come back. You have to be good to survive,' he explained.

By Mr Goldsmith's standards, supermarket fish slabs are disappointing, even laughable.

I never miss an opportunity to look at a supermarket fish counter – I love seeing a crap counter. It's good for me. The minute supermarkets start doing fish right I'll be out of a job. Supermarket fish is all about price and availability. They are stocking hundreds of fish counters so they need big, regular supplies, such as little Californian squid that come frozen in 1lb blocks. My fish comes either from Billingsgate or from quite local sources. My south-coast sea bass, for example, comes from two guys who go bass fishing with a small boat and I take all they've got. Supermarkets couldn't be bothered with any supply so small.

Fish expert William Black has criticised UK supermarkets for having staff who do not always appear to be specifically trained to deal with fish and therefore 'cannot match the service provided by a high street fishmonger'. Mr Goldsmith explained to me the consequences of the knowledge deficit.

When I worked in the supermarket we used to have an operation manual for fish. It stipulated the species name and a corresponding number of days that it could be kept on the slab. Cod, for example, was the day of delivery plus two more days. But fish is different all the time. Some fish, such as sole or salmon, is better a few days old, others like mackerel you should chuck out at the end of the day if they don't sell. It depends every day – it's not like bacon. You have to use your instinct and knowledge. Several times I spoke to the fish buyer about quality, saying that species X or species Y that was coming from a certain supplier was no good. The fish buyers were quite open to this feedback but just didn't know any better. Usually they came from cold meats or some other department and had no background in fish.

LOST AT SEA

At the supermarket wet fish counter:

Q. 'What's the best way to cook this [smoked haddock]?'

A. 'I don't usually cook fish. My mum does and she microwaves it.'
  (Waitrose, Marlow)

Q. 'Do you sell fresh (unfrozen) whole squid?'

A. 'We don't do fresh but we do have a stock of frozen which we defrost and sell ready to cook.'
  (Safeway, Inverness)

Q. 'Do you sell bones or trimmings to make a fish stock?'

A. 'No, we don't sell any of that. You'd need to go to a fish-monger.'
  (Tesco, Eastville, Bristol)

13

Bright red meat

At the instore butcher's counter – that's if your supermarket has one – you'll find a curious mirror image of what's happening with fish. The bulk of supermarket meat sells in pre-packs. Asda, for example, has done away with all its butcher's counters. But in bigger stores run by other chains, butcher's counters provide another opportunity to market the same standard lines while simultaneously creating the impression that customers have at their disposal specialists with all the skills and flexibility we associate with the traditional butcher. Stripy aprons, pork-pie hats, even straw boaters help them look the part. Personnel may seem strangely familiar from behind the fish counter – supermarket 'go-between' staff – but they appear to offer the possibility of a more knowledgeable service.

Of course, good butchers need different skills from fish-mongers. While a fishmonger looks for quick turnover to ensure freshness, the classic butcher's skill lies in hanging and ageing meat, and judging when it is at its best for eating. Because the traditional butcher stocked whole sides of meat, almost all customer demands could be supplied. He expected to offer a wide, almost comprehensive selection of possible cuts, at least towards the end of the week. Customers could have meat tailored to their needs. Buy a shoulder of lamb or a whole chicken, and someone would bone it out for you. If you wanted thin, even-sized slices of braising steak to make beef olives, a butcher would cut them to your requirements before your eyes. If a recipe called for particularly finely minced meat, the butcher would change the setting on his mincer and put it through especially for you. There was always the possibility of more unusual items, say lamb or veal mince, because you could point to a chunk of lamb or veal and ask him to mince it for you. On more frugal days, you could be sure of finding bones and off-cuts for making stock or soup: marrow bones, flank mutton and boiling beef. Whether you wanted your stew cut in big chunks for a winter carbonnade say, or in small dice, for an authentic chilli con carne perhaps, you could get it. It was just part of the total service – a service still supplied by the best independent butchers that have survived the supermarket onslaught.

One such butcher is David Lidgate, whose shop in Holland Park in London has been in his family for 150 years, or four generations. His meat has won almost every award and accolade possible and, as he explained to me, that is a consequence of his extensive experience over the years and the long-standing, direct relationships he has built up with his suppliers. All of which is in stark contrast to the meat offering in supermarkets. As with fish, meat is ordered and sourced centrally, and not necessarily by anyone with an extensive background in the field. Meat buyers may not know much about meat because they have not been long enough in the job. 'The supermarket philosophy,' said Mr Lidgate, 'is if you can buy one thing, you can buy anything.'

Although some supermarket meat counters do have skilled butchers, but usually more by default as independent butcher's shops have closed and staff have sought work in supermarkets, it is not necessary for the person who serves you to have any butcher's qualification or experience. You can expect the super-market meat counter, just like the fish counter, to be padded out with processed products – sausages, burgers, bacon and so on.

These are typically much the same lines as those you can buy in pre-packs on the meat aisle, just displayed loose. Fresh meat is usually delivered to the store 'case ready', more or less pre-butchered from the processors in popular cuts of similar weights and sizes which can retail at what supermarkets consider to be attractive 'pick-up' prices. All the butcher's counter staff have to do in most stores is lay it out on the counter and watch that it sells before the date specified on the batch. They may have to perform the odd simple operation. A rack of double loin chops may come still in one piece, to evoke an authentic butcher's shop, and a member of staff may have to use a knife to cut off the number the customer requires. But that is virtually the extent of the skills normally required. Bone a chicken? Prepare a crown of lamb? You'll be lucky. As novelist Julian Barnes remarked: 'If you study those serving in the butchery departments of super-markets, they may be dressed like butchers, but they lack the character; they have the polite, unthreatening manner of corpor-ate employees trained to euphemize the fact that meat comes from dead animals.'

Every now and then, supermarkets try to give their meat counters a master butcher feel. In 2003, for example, Sainsbury's signed an agreement with independent Perthshire butcher Simon Howie to operate his own-brand outlets in all major Scottish stores, in place of the standard meat counter. Banners went up outside stores exhorting shoppers to 'rediscover the meat counter today'. It sounded promising, but anyone who thought this might mean an instore injection of skill and experience was to be dis-appointed. 'Sainsbury staff, in Simon Howie uniforms, will serve it [fresh meat] from behind the counter . . . Obviously, we can't have trained butchers in all the stores cutting up lamb chops or dicing the beef. So, from our production point of view, everything will come pre-cut and, for want of a better expression, idiot-proof,' explained Mr Howie.

The consumer who makes a choice from the pre-packs in the

meat aisle must also conform to that retailer's idea of what most people want to eat. Any attempt to offer a broad selection has been abandoned in favour of standard offerings or 'meal solutions', catering for supermarket pre-ordained 'meal occasions': packs of four pork chops, two sirloin steaks, 'mini-joints'. This has led to a bizarre distortion of the whole meat category. Interested foreign visitors would be puzzled by the selective and arbitrary range of meat that British people appear to eat; they might even conclude that there has already been some major genetic modification of the UK's farm animals. British chickens, they might assume, are bred with multiple breasts, while British pigs don't seem to have a belly. They might think that the British extended family size must be shrinking dramatically, because roasting joints seem to feed only three or four people. If British people still make soup, they must do so from cubes, because there is nothing with which to make stock. Everyone must be rich, since the shelves are stocked with top-whack prime cuts – breasts, fillets, loins – while cheaper, and arguably tastier, economy cuts such as beef shin are nowhere to be seen. As Richard Haddock, a Devon meat farmer, told me, 'Supermarkets only offer the shopper primary cuts and won't buy the others.'

Supermarket buyers also appear to have difficulty appreciating that animals come in all sizes and shapes. They would prefer them to be identical. 'They have very tight meat specifications,' one supplier explained. 'They only want lambs between 18 and 21.5 kilos because they need to make sure they get four chops in a pack. Eating quality is never measured. When you start to pre-pack, you have to make sure that everything in a pre-pack is the same. They are very keen on uniformity but the world isn't that uniform. There's lots of very good product that doesn't fall within their specifications,' another farmer said.

David Lidgate gave me his verdict on what the large supermarket chains have done to British meat:

Until the supermarkets came along, there was a very constant interface between butchers and farmers. They knew each other well and understood what each other wanted. It worked well. The supermarkets came on the scene in the mid 1960s looking for bulk. At first they bought from the market, then couldn't get enough from them and found they could get more supply cheaper from slaughterhouses.

There was no national meat grading scheme until then. Farmers just reared traditional breeds indigenous to their local area, like Aberdeen Angus or Devon Red. But the supermarkets were looking for thousands of animals as cheaply as possible and therefore it was important to them to get a uniform product. So they pushed the Meat and Livestock Commission to standardise grades. Animals started to be judged by their shape and fat cover.

Farmers reacted by saying if those are the standards now operating, let's get Continental breeds because they grow fast and lean quicker. So the quality of meat plummeted. Supermarkets always look for short cuts in meat production to lower costs. For example, you can reduce costs by feeding [animals with] potatoes not corn, but the results are inferior. The supermarkets broke up two millennia of cattle breeding because of their need to buy huge quantities of meat at the lowest price and farmers have been forced to dance to their tune. It's a national disaster.

British consumers, slowly conditioned over the years to supermarkets' re-shaping of the food we eat, are becoming less aware of the erosion of real choice in the supermarket meat sector. Younger shoppers, brought up exclusively on supermarket food, may not even notice the contrast with what went before. It is only mature or adventurous shoppers setting out to buy meat to suit the requirements of a specific recipe and being unable to find it on the shelf who appreciate the inherently restricted nature of the supermarket meat offering. Don't expect much, if anything, in the way of offal. Anything remotely unusual, such as game, is considered by most chains recherché. If they stock it at all, more often than not it will be by special order, or only available in flagship stores catering for well-heeled AB1s where it is sold at a premium. In the autumn of 2003, for example, Waitrose in Henley-on-Thames in Oxfordshire was selling pigeon at £2.49 and partridge at £4.89, while the local butcher was selling them at £1.40 and £2.95 respectively.

Ask your store manager why you can't be sure of finding any cut or type of meat outside the familiar narrow repertoire, and you can expect the standard response: 'We don't have control over what comes in. We just get what's sent to us. If we don't have what you're looking for it's because head office says there isn't enough demand for it.' Occasionally this is seasoned with words to the effect that 'health and hygiene regulations prevent us'. Stated bluntly, in supermarket terms, your shopping needs are deviant. Either buy from what's on offer or bugger off and rear your own.

Whether you buy from a butcher's counter or from the meat aisle, one thing is always guaranteed. In the supermarket food-retailing bible, the cosmetic appearance of meat is paramount and colour is the key; taste is way down the list of priorities. While the traditional butcher knew that to eat well a steak, for example, should be well-hung, mahogany in hue, with a fine marbling of fat throughout the flesh and a creamy cover of flavoursome fat, supermarkets clearly think that consumers would faint with fright at such a sight. As David Lidgate explained, 'Supermarkets have decided that all the public want is bright red meat.' In order to achieve that look, beef, for example, cannot be hung for the optimum length of time necessary to develop flavour and natural tenderness – anything from twenty-one to forty-two days. Instead, it has to be butchered while it is still red, then packed, like fresh fish, in 'modified atmosphere' packaging to ensure that it maintains that colour and profitable moisture rather than darkening naturally as it dries out and matures.

The resulting difference in taste and tenderness is not lost on consumers, as this reader's letter published in *Sainsbury's Magazine* illustrates. 'I usually buy my stewing meat at Sainsbury's; however, for cuts of meat such as fillet steak or lamb chops, I still go to my local butcher, where I know the meat has been properly hung. I have been told that, with the exception of one (not Sainsbury's), supermarkets do not hang their meat, the view being that time is money. Is this the case with Sainsbury's?' the reader asked. In his response, Sainsbury's meat buyer did not try to defend the chain's core meat against the customer's implied criticism. Instead he recommended that she should try its Taste the Difference products, which are 'hung on the bone for an improved flavour and more succulent taste'. Not a huge help to the reader, because this range consists of a very small number of cuts.

Supermarkets are sensitive about the limitations of their meat selection, so every now and then they promote new, more expensive 'boutique' lines in selected, high-profile stores to show that they are not deaf to criticism. In 2003, for example, Waitrose was trumpeting its 'dry-aged' Aberdeen Angus beef in its new store at London's Canary Wharf as the reintroduction of a 'centuries-old method of maturing meat' to increase tenderness and flavour. Sainsbury's followed soon after, with a Jamie Oliver line of '21 day Extra Matured Taste the Difference British Beef', packaged in greaseproof paper to evoke images of traditional butchers. The chain's buying manager for meat explained that the aim was to 'replicate good quality matured beef, the kind of thing you can get in specialist butchers or good restaurants'. The voice-over on the television advert for this beef, which said that 'only Sainsbury's sell a range of tender tempting twenty-one day beef', provoked complaints to the Independent Television Commission by consumers and butchers who pointed out that it was perfectly possible to buy such beef from independent butchers. Sainsbury's responded by changing the script to say it was the only supermarket to sell such beef. While acknowledging

Sainsbury's prompt action in correcting the advert, the Independent Television Commission upheld the complaints and ruled that the original was misleading. For independent butchers throughout the UK, it was a minor victory. Why should Sainsbury's be allowed to claim brownie points for doing what any traditional butcher does routinely?

At the supermarket meat counter:

Q. 'Can you mince lamb for me for moussaka?'
A. 'I'm afraid all our meat's pre-packed now. The butchers don't do any butchering.'
(Somerfield, Eccleshall Road, Sheffield)
A. 'I'm afraid not. The mincer can only take certain meats – they come in packages and go straight into the machine.'
(Tesco, Milngavie, Glasgow)

Q. 'How do you cook this [an individual boeuf wellington with beef fillet, puff pastry, chicken liver and brandy pâté]?'
A. Dunno. Roast it?
(Waitrose, Marlow)

Q. 'I have a Nigel Slater recipe that calls for grilled, spatchcocked [split down the backbone and flattened-out] chicken. If I buy a pre-packed chicken in your store, can you bone it out for me?'
A. 'No, we don't do that – that's a small bird that could fit in your hand.'
(Asda, Arnold, Nottingham)
A. 'We cannot do that at all. You'd have to ask your local butcher again unfortunately.'
(Waitrose, Westbourne, Dorset)

Q. 'I need minced ham or bacon to make meatballs. Can you do that for me?'

A. 'That sounds like you need minced beef, because raw ham is basically minced beef and I can't put cooked meat through the mincer because of contamination.'
(Safeway, Inverness)

A. 'No, we don't do that here. To be honest, I've never seen it. You could try Cranston's [the local butcher].'
(Morrisons, Kingstown, Carlisle)

Q. 'If I come in on a Friday morning, can I be sure of getting a large piece of rolled sirloin that would feed eight people?'
A. 'You'd need to order that in advance so that the butcher could prepare it.'
(Tesco, Eastville, Bristol)

Q. 'I have a River Café recipe for flattened chicken. It calls for the chicken to be boned out through the backbone, keeping the breast in one piece. Can you do that for me?'
A. 'All our chicken comes pre-packed, so you have to buy either the whole chicken or the chicken pieces.'

Q. 'But can you bone it out for me?'
A. 'Well it's all pre-packed . . .'
(Sainsbury's, Chester)

A. 'You could just buy chicken fillets because that's all it is. I mean we could bone it for you but you'd just be left with the individual pieces.'
(Asda, Blackpool)

14

Our weekly bread

Who has not heard the story that supermarkets deliberately pump fresh baking smells into their stores to seduce the shopper's senses? Whether the story is apocryphal or otherwise (no one has ever pinned this one down, by the way), it is true that all the larger supermarkets these days have a prominently sited instore bakery which looks and smells like a proper bakery, turning out wave after wave of breads, rolls and assorted cookies and cakes. Supermarkets like them because they inject some 'retail theatre' into a store.

Consumers are understandably seduced by the volatile compounds that make up these baking smells. Our senses are not finely enough tuned to tell us whether what is being baked is any good or not. Bad bread smells as appealing as good bread. We think that supermarket instore bread smells lovely and assume it must be good. In the sterile, odour-free supermarket environment, it creates a warm, comforting effect, and supports the illusion that there are skilled, master bakers making a fresh product on the spot. 'The smell of fresh bread is almost a permanent presence in stores nowadays,' remarked one market review, 'and along with its sensory appeal, the inclusion of the instore bakery lends an artisan feel to the category.' The instore bakery seems to encapsulate all the virtues of a traditional high-street craft baker. Its odoriferous homespun 'halo' shines a light that makes everything else in the store appear more winsome. The higher cost of instore bakery bread creates an impression of genuine difference from the standard wrapped products. It is only when it has cooled down and you can really taste it that the difference becomes apparent.

Instore bakeries first started appearing in supermarkets in the 1970s. By 1999, it was estimated that there were over 1,500 instore bakeries in the UK. They were devised by supermarkets to compete head on with high-street bakers and give the impression of selling craft bread, as opposed to bought-in, ready-wrapped, industrial bread made to the 1960s 'Chorleywood' or 'no-time' breadmaking process, which is notorious for its pappy, crustless results.

Instore bakeries caused such a ripple of excitement amongst shoppers when they first opened that they would even queue for their products. A joke from that period recounted the tale of one canny old lady who joins the queue to see what all the fuss is about. Once at the head of the queue, she asks the price of the bread, only to find that it is more expensive than the wrapped bread she usually buys. She quizzes the young man behind the counter as to why this is the case. 'That's because it's hot, madam,' he replies. 'In which case,' replies the customer, 'I'll wait until it cools down.' This cynical joke satirises all the fluff and marketing spin that surrounds the supermarket instore bakery offer. The bread may be 'fresh from the oven', but the supermarkets have debased the notion of freshness in bread every bit as much as they have with other fresh food such as fruit and vegetables, fish and meat.

What is actually being baked in supermarkets up and down the land? The most labour-intensive bread you can expect to find is push-button 'scratch' bread. Scratch bread is, in theory, as its name implies, made from scratch from raw materials. In its traditional sense, it is a crusty loaf made by craft bakers from a sack of flour, carrying out all the various stages – mixing, fermenting, moulding, proving, baking – in one continuous time frame. Some chains still adhere to a loose definition of scratch baking, but in a vastly altered sense. They have perfected a highly mechanised operation that can be carried out by relatively unskilled, or rapidly trained, staff. You mix a sachet of bread improvers with a fixed amount of pre-weighed flour. You press a button on a water meter and mix to create a 'no-time' dough. You scale the mixture into pre-set weights. You put the dough through a moulder to shape it. Then you bake it. This method is formula baking, a scaled-down version of the Chorleywood process. It is as skilled as instore baking gets.

The rest of the instore offering is 'bake-off' – frozen dough products that are prepared in a factory, bought in and then finished off in the store. Bake-off is a sort of suspended animation for bread. It can be held instore and wheeled out when it is needed. Since it was developed in the late 1970s, it has been enthusiastically taken up by supermarkets as a way of eliminating labour and reducing risk while at the same time making sure that bread never runs out, and it is sold as fresh bread. Waitrose, for example, has a Fresh from the Oven range. A big sign in stores says 'Enjoy the flavour and freshness of these products prepared throughout the day'. If you read the label, you will see that many of these products have been previously frozen. When I visited Waitrose in Henley-on-Thames at the end of 2003, I checked the labels on the instore bakery shelves. Out of twenty-six different lines of Fresh from the Oven breads and rolls, twenty-three had been previously frozen. Waitrose is relatively forthcoming in this respect, but not all supermarkets are. In Tesco stores, for example, unless you ask someone behind the instore bakery counter, there is no way of telling which bread was previously frozen because there is no mention of the fact on the labels.

In supermarket terms, bake-off is a wonderfully successful innovation, not to mention a moneyspinner. That it produces a supply of what one bread authority described as 'the same Euro-pap from Dover to Dalmatia' is beside the point. It guarantees biddable waves of identikit products: baguettes, paninis, pastries and buns, all with wonderfully evocative names. American-style cookies can be supplied as dough or shaped, frozen and ready to bake. US-style muffins and bagels, Danish-style pastries, French-style croissants and artisan-sounding French and Italian breads can all be bought in ready to bake too. Bake-off bread comes in different forms at various stages of the baking process. Chains can buy in frozen and unproved, frozen and proved or frozen and part-baked. In its most speeded-up form, bake-off bread might need only a few minutes in the oven to give it a crust and some colour. One supermarket baker explained to me that the only tricky thing about the process was remembering to take out of the freezer part-bakes that required defrosting. If certain lines – such as scones – weren't thoroughly defrosted before baking, they turned out to be soggy.

Take a look at the label on your supermarket instore bakery bread and you will see that the 'use by' date is usually the day of purchase or the next. As you may have noticed, such bread dries out and stales very quickly. The irony of bake-off bread is that once baked it has poor keeping qualities because of all the interventions, designed to prolong its unbaked life, to which it has been subjected.

By contrast to products from the instore bakery, the wrapped breads on supermarket bread shelves cost less and seem to last for ever, or at least long enough to conform to the supermarket diktat that shopping should be a one-stop weekly event. Wanting us to think that it is fine to shop for fresh food only once a week, supermarkets have sourced fresh products to fit the bill. Left to its own devices, bread stales as the starch in it hardens. But supermarkets have found that even though bread that keeps for a week can never be truly fresh, it can be made to seem fresh by remaining soft. So they have looked to industrial bakers to supply them with the type of bread it suits them to sell. Since 85 per cent of all bread is sold in supermarkets, they have considerable leverage with the industrial bakers. Two giant companies, Allied Bakeries and British Bakeries, dominate industrial plant baking in the UK with a 55 per cent market share, while other large companies account for a further quarter of the market. As one report on the bread market noted, 'the largest food retailers have attained considerable size and dominate the market, controlling access to consumers'.

This concentration both in bread retailing and bread production makes for clear communication between the protagonists. UK plant bakers have given the supermarkets what they want, bread that stays squidgy because it has been made with crumb-softening enzymes. As the Federation of Bakers puts it: 'Advances in enzyme technology allow bread to stay fresher for longer ... In the UK this has resulted in the shelf life of sliced and wrapped bread, which normally stays fresh for only 2–3 days, doubling to one week.' But these enzymes do not need to be declared on the label because they are conveniently classed as processing aids, not ingredients, so the consumer is none the wiser. That's our supermarkets' way of giving us 'fresh' bread that lasts a week. In supermarket terms, freshness means bread that stays miraculously soft and apparently fresh until it suddenly goes green – a timely reminder that it is time for yet another weekly supermarket shop.

15

Gastro-gap

It was four o'clock on a weekday afternoon and Sainsbury's flagship foodie store, Sainsbury's Market at Bluebird on London's King's Road, was strangely empty. This store had represented a new and promising partnership. Sir Terence Conran, one of the nation's most famous food lovers, had slipped into bed with Sainsbury's, the most gastronomically inclined of the large multiples with nationwide coverage. It sounded like a marriage made in heaven. With this pedigree, Bluebird could become a centre of excellence for good food, with all the choice and variety that specialist food shops might collectively offer, under one roof. It would show that anything independents could do, Sainsbury's could do at least as well – and more cheaply.

Previously a dedicated outlet in Conran's Gastrodrome, Bluebird had re-opened as Sainsbury's Market with a fanfare in April 2003. Both parties sounded full of high hopes for their joint venture. 'The partnership with Sainsbury's allows the creation of a high quality foodstore which can deliver everyday and specialist foods at significantly more competitive prices than we could do on our own,' said Conran Holdings' chief executive. Sainsbury's future stores manager enthused about the alliance which would provide 'the very best of Sainsbury's combined with a new fresh food offer . . . designed with the needs of King's Road shoppers in mind'.

Only three months later, though, the question was: where were all those carefully canvassed King's Road shoppers? In supermarkets, customers always outnumber staff. In Bluebird, it was the other way around. Dressed for the part in upmarket cotton aprons that shouted out 'gourmet' rather than 'employee', staff stood to attention looking hopefully for customers as the slow retail minutes ticked by. It was eerily quiet. Had Bluebird's customers all suddenly found pressing alternative engagements? It was classic Wimbledon weather – sunshine and showers – but the showers were not wet enough to dampen custom. A nail-biting match between Tim Henman and David Nalbandian had begun on centre court, but surely Bluebird's shopper base could not be predicated on customers who could follow a match on the TV on a weekday. Looking around the store at the number of products reduced for quick sale or close to 'use-by' date, one wondered if customers were thin on the ground not just today but every day. What had happened to the critical customer mass that would make Bluebird buzz?

Breezy guarantees barked out at customers. One at the entrance read: 'At Sainsbury's Market you'll find everything you need to put great food at the heart of life . . . The freshest of ingredients . . . Authentic seasonal flavours . . . Expert advice whenever you need it . . . Come in, explore, discover and let your senses guide you . . .' An intoxicating prospect. However, the first smell to hit the nostrils was not perfumed English strawberries or Charentais melons but a mingling of cleaning fluid and the unmistakable odour of a fish counter with a sluggish turnover. Far from flagging a mouthwatering sensory experience, customers' antennae might tell them that Sainsbury's was not entirely convincing in its new role as purveyor of high-quality, specialist food. Indeed the retailer seemed to be having difficulty even understanding the mission. In the produce display by the

entrance, under a sign that read 'Best in season fruit and vegetables', sat a pile of South African clementines – a taste of winter
on the other side of the world, stacked in a rustic wicker basket
half filled with straw to lend that peasant-market effect but still
encased in their orange-threaded, one-kilo packs. Six plastic
cartons of cherries from Kent were more in keeping with the
season, if tokenistic. But they were mouldy. So mouldy, in fact,
that fruit flies were flying around inside the cartons.

As one moved around the store, the disparity between promise
and delivery became increasingly evident. Over the delicatessen
counter another sign read: 'The sourcing of charcuterie is important to us, that's why we only source York ham, Spanish chorizo,
Polish sopoka, Milano salami . . .', demonstrating an almost
touching innocence, as if the presence of a geographical adjective
before the name of a generic foodstuff was some reliable indicator
of quality or provenance. But studying the very small print on
the label of the smoked 'York' ham, a vigilant customer might
feel more cynical about these words. This 'farm assured' York
ham contained flavouring, preservatives and colouring. It had
been 'produced in the UK from pork legs sourced from EU countries'. Was this what Bluebird shoppers expected from a York
ham?

Round the gondola from the York ham sat a less-than-
appetising selection of prepared foods, requiring little or nothing
in the way of cooking at home. Moroccan and Middle Eastern
this, Mexican or Indian that – whatever the title, the dishes shared
the homogenous kitchen-sink ethnicity of all supermarket prepared foods. Thai green curry sat in a pool where the solids
seemed to be separating from watery liquid, but otherwise, irrespective of its supposed national identity, the common factor
in these dishes was a certain gloopy thickness of consistency.
Cooked chicken breasts wrapped in raw oak-smoked bacon, for
example, had been inexplicably blanketed with thick masala
sauce. Labels featured the supermarket convenience-food litany

of 'antioxidant, flavouring, preservative'. Some lines looked reminiscent of Sainsbury's standard boxed repertoire – the goat's cheese and spinach tart 'flamme', for instance. Did Sainsbury's mean 'flambée', the traditional, flat, almost pizza-like speciality from Alsace? And if Sainsbury's couldn't spell this dish correctly, what grounds were there for thinking that it could prepare it properly? You couldn't help getting the impression that, let loose in the specialist delicatessen zone, Sainsbury's was out of its depth.

At the meat counter, at last there was something to get excited about: rump steak from Angus cross north Devon cattle, high-welfare English veal and pork from Gloucester Old Spot pigs. On the counter above sat 'Cajun sprinkle' and 'Chinese glaze', the latter's ingredients featuring sugar, salt, glucose, maize starch, tomato powder, yeast extract, spice extract, ascorbic acid, garlic, xanthan gum, capsanthin, betanin, cochineal and ammonia caramel. Its prominence suggested Sainsbury's was proud of this 'speciality' line and actively encouraging customers to coat their rare-breed meat with it. On the fish slab there was the usual strong supermarket presence of far-flown fish: kingklip, black tilapia, snapper and marlin. About a third of the fish was reduced for quick sale, and it was evident why: it had lost any sparkle it ever had. At the salad bar lank leaves of salad were gumming themselves on to the sides of ceramic bowls. Turning in desperation to the pre-packs, one saw that the bags of 'Cosmopolitan' and 'Continental Four Leaf' salad were decomposing with ugly black and pink veins. Their use-by date was two days off.

Bluebird seemed to have flopped as surely as its salads. It was not a ringing testimonial to Sainsbury's ability to handle fresh speciality food. Yet the chain's alliance with the Conran name was surely calculated to further polish the chain's foodie halo, already shiny from its partnership with Jamie Oliver. The effect of that halo would be, the chain hoped, to build up its food credentials and pull customers into all its stores – customers who, once there, would buy lots and lots of other things. A good food halo shines light on everything a chain does. In their constant imperialistic grab for market share, all the big multiples like to lay claim to this speciality territory in order to create such a halo. They love to take credit for introducing British consumers to a wider, more sophisticated range of foods. Without supermarkets, we are led to believe, all food progress would be frozen in time and we'd be back in the gastronomic Dark Ages, slurping tea and masticating biscuits like Steptoe and Son.

In supermarkets up and down the land, the deli counter fulfils this halo function. It aims to keep potentially disgruntled shoppers happy, those who might intuitively feel, quite correctly, that something is missing in the standard supermarket offering: older people, for instance, who still remember the traditional British grocer with home-cooked ham, giant rounds of butter and wheels of Cheddar; or younger generations, who travel more and encounter small, specialist food shops abroad, if not any longer on their local high street, and might yearn for a proper specialist delicatessen with its intoxicating, seductive smells of freshly ground coffee, cured meats and ripe cheese. When faced with an aisle of antiseptic meats and cheeses mummified in plastic, many people still instinctively crave a food offering that looks and smells different, one that promises something better and less mass-produced than the supermarket norm.

From the supermarkets' point of view, the deli counter is an important tool in upping the store's food profile, reinforcing the idea that the store can cope with not just the basics but all your shopping needs. It helps create the impression that you need never shop anywhere else for anything, because everything you might conceivably want can be bought under one roof. Why use specialists when you've got a superstore? Supermarkets don't want consumers nipping into their stores occasionally for washing powder and cat food, cherry-picking the 'Buy One Get One Free' offers then taking their less mundane shopping business to small independents. They want us to shop exclusively in their stores, and, like well-trained, loyal canines, never to stray elsewhere. In fact, they want us to forget that any alternative might exist.

On the face of it, the supermarket deli counter suggests the availability of food with a distinctive pedigree, food that is more special, more exciting, more diverse than the food elsewhere in the store or in some way extending the qualitative choice we have. Though these counters have appropriated some elements of the style of service we associate with the specialist deli – food sold loose, a proliferation of artisan-looking bowls and, last but not least, a human being behind the counter to interact with – that is where the resemblance stops. The impression of difference is a false one. As at the meat counter, the food on sale is basically the standard supermarket offering, just unwrapped. There will be one or two deli counter-only lines, such as ham sliced from the bone, to create an impression of true difference. But peruse the contents of the bowls and tubs and you will easily identify items that sell in the delicatessen pre-pack or ready-meal aisles only feet away – Thai chicken, Indian samosas, hummus, dips and salsas, prawn coleslaw, quiches and so on. Children bored during a supermarket shopping expedition could easily be set the time-passing game of 'spot the matching pairs' in the aisles and the deli counter. Buy them a couple of ready meals and some cold cuts and deli tubs from the pre-pack aisles, and once home, they could play at recreating their own little supermarket deli counter, simply by unwrapping the purchases and turning them out into rustic bowls. Deli counters give supermarkets another chance to sell us the same lines all over again.

When it comes to cheese, the selection on the deli counter may actually be more limited than the pre-packs on the shelves. And the cheese aisles overwhelmingly rely on a number of mass-produced brands, which, though they might look varied, are portfolio cheeses, supplied in what amounts to family groups by a small number of industrial creameries both at home and abroad – companies big enough to woo the supermarkets. As with fresh fruit and vegetables, true maturity is out of the question. Cheese is hand-picked to sit mutely on the shelves for several weeks and never ever smell like cheese; mature cheese might smell and its sell-by date would have to be much reduced. Cheeses which by their very nature require ripening are packed so immature, then over-wrapped and over-chilled, that there is no hope of them ever maturing satisfactorily, even if opened and left at room temperature to breathe. Cheese experts know that for a Camembert to ripen, for example, it should be stored at 10–12°C. Yet supermarkets routinely keep them at 4°C. As would happen to you if you put a plastic bag on your head and went to bed, the cheese stops breathing and dies. In the case of mild cheese, the best that can be said is that it will taste of little or nothing. Stronger cheeses, whose development has been arrested, might taste positively bitter and twisted. But then does that matter to supermarkets when 'speciality' cheeses are really just window dressing for the main business, which is selling tonnes and tonnes of anodyne slabs of factory cheese?

One independent cheesemonger, Iain Mellis, whose shops throughout Scotland have a loyal following of consumers who seek a true artisan alternative to supermarket cheese, told me that supermarkets try to buy cheese without the bacteria that produce flavour.

Some of these bacteria also produce a gas which blows the vacuum packs. Blown vac-packs are considered unsightly. All the cheese in supermarkets is chosen to look good. Taste just doesn't come into it. Graders selecting cheese for supermarkets therefore go for a 'safe' cheese, which means it is full of acidity, low on bacteria and short on flavour. Many firmer cheeses like Lancashire and Cheshire are selected to suit the packing line. They mustn't crumble too much [one of the traditional tests of fine cheese of this kind] because they'll crumble on the packing line, so causing wastage, and they won't look so good inside their plastic packs.

At the deli counter, though, you'd think that because there are staff to keep an eye on the cheese, you might be able to buy it properly ripened and be given a knowledgeable steer towards cheese that was particularly good that day. But squint at the certificates that line the walls behind many counters and you will get a clue to how those staff have been trained: no mention of knowledge of cheese, just food hygiene. Staff are actively discouraged from sampling cheese; it might even be construed as theft and get you into trouble. One insider explained the system to me. Any knowledge of cheese, indeed even a liking for cheese, is not a pre-requisite of the job. At least 50 per cent of supermarket deli training consists of microbiology and hygiene: how to clean a cheese wire and so on. This is essential because deli counter staff are frequently young or part-time and cannot be assumed to have any existing deli skills and experience. The effect of this training is to breed a fear of fresh food. 'It scares the living daylights out of them. When they look at the counter they just see an army of monstrous bacteria rampaging across it.'

The supermarket obsession with hygiene at the expense of food quality manifests itself in blanket rules and regulations imposed not by the European Union but by the chains themselves. One example of this is the rule imposed by certain chains under which a cheese opened at the deli counter must be thrown away within seven days if it has not been sold, even if it is a firm Cheddar with such a high acidity level that it could be sold for several weeks. Far from allowing cheese to ripen and realise its potential, supermarkets see cheese as a flashing red-alert food-poisoning hazard. Once delivered, it must be displayed and sold quickly.

'Supermarkets have a warped idea of food safety,' said Mr Mellis. 'They assume that the bigger the creamery, the safer and more hygienic it must be because it has more to lose.' This preference for using big players as suppliers is one reason why the cheeses at the deli counter are likely to be even less intrinsically

SUPERMARKET WORKERS

16

My big welcome

Only two months to go until Christmas and the recruitment machine at my nearest Asda Wal-Mart had gone into overdrive. This 100,000-square-foot supercentre was one of the eleven biggest Asda Wal-Marts in the UK. It had a breathtaking weekly take of just under £1.5 million and that did not include petrol or VAT. In the week before Christmas, sales for this store had been projected at as much as £2.3 million – if, that is, there were enough staff to handle them. In theory the store had around 700 employees, but it was seriously understaffed. At the checkouts alone, of some 200 positions only 120 were filled. I was surprised. A recent survey had shown Asda's shop-floor vacancy rate running at 5.7 per cent, only slightly above the industry average. I knew, because it was emblazoned on Asda's recruitment leaflets, that in 2002 Asda had even won the *Sunday Times*'s 'Best Company To Work For' award. OK, supermarket jobs generally have a poor image. They are widely seen as the last resort, offering low wages and long hours. Supermarket jobs figure prominently in the ten lowest-paid jobs for men and women, jobs that consistently come at the bottom of the average pay league. In 2001, being a shelf-filler was rated as the tenth worst-paid job for both sexes, while being a checkout operator was seventh worst for women and third worst for men. Even so, this staff shortage was way out of line with the supermarket norm. This store obviously needed people fast. It sounded like a fruitful place to look for a job.

Sure enough, ten days after I had posted my application form, I had become an Asda 'colleague'. There are no members of staff in Asda Wal-Mart, only colleagues. And, I was to discover, there was more to being a colleague than wearing a badge that said 'Joanna – Happy to Help'. I had to learn how to 'Live the Asda Values'. I had to be trained in maintaining the perpetually smiley face and 'can-do' attitude that would make me a valued, respected member of the warm, cuddly Wal-Mart family. With the aid of simple rhymes, mottoes and ample alliteration I would learn all about 'Miles of Smiles', 'Being a Buddy', 'Smiley Squad Stickers' and 'Pockets of Pride'. Asda Wal-Mart would show me how to 'knock the customers' socks off', how to 'Go the Extra Mile' to 'exceed customers' expectations – *always!*' I was to be given the 'Big Welcome'.

The Big Welcome is a three-day induction course for new Asda recruits. We numbered twenty on day one. A further 100 recruits would be going through the same course in the next week, we were told. My new colleagues were a varied and multi-talented bunch, either young or middle-aged. They included a postman, a landscape architect, a business studies and accountancy student, a road builder, a couple of clothes shop workers, college students (one training to be a fitness instructor, the other trying to get the grades to break into marine biology), a computer hardware programmer and a petrol pump attendant. Not one amongst them expressed any interest in a long-term career with Asda. They were candid: they needed the money. The students needed a job to finance their studies. Many of those already in employment needed a second income to supplement the first. About half the group had opted to work nights because they had to fit the job around other commitments. And the money for working nights was better too. Not what you might call good, considering that you were jeopardising your sleeping patterns; just better. Night shifts paid £6.17 an hour for over-eighteens, rising to £6.75 after twelve weeks. My day job starter rate was £4.62 an hour, rising to £5.06. This was at a time when the national minimum wage for someone my age was £4.50 an hour and the Low Pay Unit was recommending a minimum wage of £5.38. Under-eighteens on day shifts could earn £3.82 rising to £4.18. Our tea breaks would be paid, but not lunch breaks.

Walking in through the staff – sorry, *colleagues*' entrance was a little bit like being back at primary school, or at a Scripture Union playgroup. The first wall display was dedicated to Asda's parent company, Wal-Mart, with photos of corporate HQ in Bentonville, Arkansas, and a potted rags-to-riches history of the chain's spectacular half-century rise from nickel 'n' dime store to the world's biggest retailer, complete with stars and stripes and folksy wisdom from founder chairman Sam Walton: 'Treat every customer as if the world revolves around them . . . it does', 'Never get so set in your ways you can't change' and so on.

The other walls were plastered with motivational league tables on pastel-coloured paper with lots of stick-on stars. There were photos of colleagues who had excelled themselves or, in Wal-Mart/Asda-ese, 'gone the Extra Mile', and 'Our Gold Star Challenge! 100% attendance winners' with prizes, even trophies on display. It was as if a very earnest primary-school headmistress cum Guide pack leader had launched one massive Pavlovian collective behaviour modification exercise. Not quite 'Well done, Darren, for eating your lunch today – a silver star for you. And if you keep this up you'll get a gold star and then a badge!', but that sort of thing. One wall was given over to improving colleague relationships – the 'Big Thank You' from one keen colleague to another. 'Carol! I just wanted to thank you for being chatty and helpful! from Beverly in provisions.' 'A hug to Helen for giving me help when I really needed it from Brett in home and leisure.' Colleagues with such star qualities could put themselves forward to be a 'buddy', helping to motivate newer colleagues. Those with bigger ambitions could go on to win the 'Employee of the Month/ Year' award, a 'Golden Greeter' award or even an Asda Oscar.

Round the corner we came upon the name-and-shame 'Miles of Smiles' corridor, liberally covered with multi-coloured forms bordered with smiley faces, organised by department. On these forms one named colleague after another made a handwritten pledge to give customers better service in future – public declarations made in an almost Maoist spirit of self-criticism, reminiscent of Weightwatchers or Alcoholics Anonymous. 'I will treat customers as I would like to be treated myself,' signed and dated by Lucy in checkouts, or 'I aim to give my customers the best service ever' from Mohammed in produce. On the opposite wall were cheery photos of memorable Asda Days. These featured the most recent 'Pocket Tap Day' when customers and colleagues were encouraged over the tannoy to have fun by simultaneously tapping their pockets, as in the Asda TV advert, and the 'Sing Along with Louise Day', when customers and colleagues accompanied Louise as she launched her new single in store, in a bid to get Asda listed as achieving the biggest ever singalong in the *Guinness Book of Records*.

There was no escape from homilies, pledges, challenges and awards in the colleagues' canteen or even in the toilets. Here, along with reminders about the ongoing overtime possibilities at the checkouts, some eager colleague had stuck up Day-Glo handbills with helpful examples of how to go that Extra Mile. 'I was just finishing my shift when a customer took ill in the canteen. I dropped her off at her doctor's on my way home.' 'I saw a customer looking strangely at an aubergine. The customer had never tried aubergine so I explained the taste and different cooking methods and suggested some recipe ideas for her.'

We were ushered into the training room by Glen, the colleague charged with introducing us to Asda culture. Glen played his role with all the finger-clicking fervour of a revivalist preacher. Asda is part of Wal-Mart, he explained, the world's biggest general merchandise retailer. He directed us to a wall emblazoned with 'Amazing Asda Facts'. Did we know, for example, that if we put all the cucumbers the company sold from end to end they would stretch from Asda House in Leeds to Wal-Mart HQ in Bentonville, Arkansas? Despite its colossal size, though, there were no Misters, Misses or Missuses in this company. We were part of an open, honest, challenging culture, a culture that was quite unlike any other retailers. 'Sainsbury's? Who wants to work for Sainsbury's? It's dull and lifeless,' affirmed Glen with un-wavering certainty. How did it feel, he asked us, to be colleagues in a company as big and powerful as Asda Wal-Mart? Were we comfortable with that? Did it feel good? Okay then, let's see smiley faces and let's hear it!' 'That feels brilliant,' we chorused, somewhat half-heartedly. 'Brilliant' was a word that we like to hear in Asda, Glen explained.

He had lots to tell us about the AWW – the 'Asda Way of Working'. Asda's 'Purpose' was the altruistic-sounding 'To make goods and services more affordable to everyone'. It had a 'Mission' too, which was 'to be Britain's best value retailer by exceeding customers needs . . . *Always!*' and Glen was going to 'empower us' to do just that. There were a lot of aids to help the process along. On the wall directly behind Glen were painted the Asda 'Values': respect for the individual, service to our customers, strive for excellence. We could refer to a booklet for examples of how we could live these values every day. Respect for the indi-vidual, for example, meant amongst other things 'wearing name badges at all times'. Service to customers could include 'continually looking for ways to sell'. One of the ways of striving for excellence was to adopt a 'can do' attitude. 'Combine this AWW with our customer service philosophy and selling culture and what we end up with is a real competitive edge that will make us a winning organization,' said our 'Welcome to the World of Asda' guide.

Next up, a Big Welcome video from Asda's chief executive, Tony De Nunzio. Tony – we were on first names terms already –

greeted us new colleagues with an informal 'Ciao!'. If we met Tony in the store, said Glen, we shouldn't be surprised to find him with his sleeves rolled up. As highly respected, indeed vital colleagues, we shouldn't be frightened to go up to him and let him hear our personal plans for further exceeding customer expectations, particularly if we had a suggestion to make for a new volume producing item or VPI. Colleagues were actively encouraged to identify VPIs and increase sales of that product. We could also share with him our ideas about creating more 'Pockets of Pride' by suggesting cost-busting ideas that would make Asda proud of us. Alternatively we could just fill in a 'Tell Tony' form.

Our training room was stuffy, windowless and lit with naked strip lights and by now our new colleagues' attention was beginning to drift. Some people looked at their watches. I began to compose letters to Tony. 'Dear Tony, Have you ever thought that a better basic pay rate might put an even bigger smile on colleagues' faces?' or 'Dear Tony, I find wearing a first name only badge demeaning' or 'Dear Tony, Turn off the instore tannoy, it's driving me up the wall.' After lunch, one new colleague did not return. The rest of the day passed by in a blur of in-depth security training, covering 'shrinkage' – mainly shoplifting – and how to go about making a citizen's arrest.

By day two, our group had shrunk to thirteen. 'Am I right in thinking that they just tell you the same thing over and over again?' asked the would-be marine biologist. It would be more of the same today, we agreed. 'We aren't brainwashed enough yet,' observed the would-be fitness instructor. But boy oh boy, there was still so much to learn about. Not least, the Mystery Shopper, employed by the company to keep colleagues on their toes. Kelly-Anne from customer services explained that every month the store was visited by a mystery shopper, essentially an inspector from an external company, whose job it was to 'assess colleague behaviour'. To score well if the dreaded Mystery Shopper turned up at your department, good service – 'hello' and 'goodbye' and a generally civil, polite response – was not enough. Asda was looking for 'amazing service', which should deliver a respectable score upwards of 80 per cent. And just in case you weren't sure of the difference between 'amazing' service and 'good service' there was a video to show you examples of the former, prominently featuring 'Smiley Squad stickers' – £1 money-off vouchers – to mollify disgruntled shoppers. Our demeanour was all-important, too. We had to cultivate our 'Ten Foot' welcoming attitude and, having made unswerving eye contact with customers, we should think carefully about the way we talked to them. We should 'inject enthusiasm' into our voices and our tone should 'reflect sincerity and confidence'.

Somewhat embarrassingly, this store had come out seventh from the bottom in the Mystery Shopper company league table, with scores between 50 and 74 per cent. Everyone had vowed to do better. If you did well, you could earn a gold, silver or bronze prize, which might win you a box of chocolates or a bottle of champagne. But the Mystery Shopper would not hesitate to award any colleague a 0 per cent score. This would be followed up with a one-to-one 'counselling session', out of which 'outcomes would be put forward for action'. There were no negatives in Asda, only 'opportunities for improvement'. Make a pledge on the Miles of Smiles wall and even the least smiley colleague could be considered rehabilitated.

Monitoring of colleagues didn't stop with the Mystery Shopper. Asda's 'Penny for your Thoughts' phone line encouraged customers to phone in and say what they thought of the store or a particular colleague. In a Christmas training video there were numerous examples of favourable reports on colleagues who had amazed customers with exceptional service, such as driving harassed mums home when they broke down in the car park even though it was their time off or dashing out with brollies and welcoming smiles to greet shoppers in torrential rain. In case you didn't get the idea, there was a 'SMILES' aide-mémoire, which acted as a prompt to live the Asda values. S for Smile at the customer, M for Make Contact (say hello), I for Information (offer correct information), L for Listen (to what the customer has to say), E for End it well (say 'Is there anything else?' or 'Goodbye') and S for Said it now do it (follow through your promise).

As an incentive to live the Asda values, there would be a colleague bonus each year if the store exceeded certain targets. The happier the customers, the better the bonus would be – perhaps as much as £250 for a full-timer. So colleagues had a direct financial interest in improving store performance, our trainer explained. Our efforts might even extend to confidentially drawing to management's attention any other colleague whose behaviour didn't shape up.

By the end of day two, everyone had got the message: be nice to customers. It was hard to imagine any company with a clearer training goal or one that made such a long-winded effort to communicate it. Which made it all the more puzzling why this store was struggling to improve its Mystery Shopper score and to fill vacancies. And if it was such fun to work at Asda, how come the chain had a 21.2 per cent annual staff turnover rate? I was beginning to see why. Even earning the princely sum of £4.62 an hour, I found that the place got on my nerves. It made me feel as if I wasn't quite an adult. Something about the set-up made me itch to go round with a felt-tip pen and turn all those smiley faces into grumpy faces or even positively naughty faces. I felt a growing urge to snarl some very rude words indeed at the Mystery Shopper. Perhaps I just wasn't cut out to live the Asda values. I didn't go back for day three and I suspect I wasn't the only one.

leaver who had just worked a six-hour shift with one fifteen-minute break, for just under £4 an hour. 'What do you do if you need a pee in between times?' I asked her. 'You just don't go,' she told me. I heard all about the backache and strain too. One girl pointed to her mid-back. 'I feel it here,' she said. An older male checkout operator told me: 'For all the years I've worked here, I still haven't got used to it.' Some checkout staff preferred to sit, others to stand. Several said their chairs were worse than useless however you adjusted them, and many of them told me that they felt uncomfortable a lot of the time.

Then I stumbled upon an article about a Tesco scheme called TWIST – short for Tesco Week In Store Together. This was a scheme for head office top brass to get a taste of what it was like to work on the supermarket shop floor. It started me thinking that I should carry out my own version of TWIST. I knew, because of my Asda Big Welcome experience, that supermarkets were always on the lookout for checkout operators. Even so, I was surprised at the speed with which I was hired. I dropped off my application form to Tesco on a Sunday afternoon, and by the following Saturday I was on checkouts being trained. By the following Monday, I had been let loose on an unsuspecting public, albeit with a sign that read 'Newly trained staff – Your patience is appreciated'. Thanks heavens for that protection.

If you think that being a checkout operator is an undemanding job, let me put you right. True, much of it is robotically mechan-ical, slipping purchases past an electronic scanning eye, but there are a lot of complications too. There are coupons, tokens and cash back. The sheer array of cash and credit cards that can legitimately be tendered these days is truly astounding. The legions of last-minute reductions frequently refuse to scan. There are hot keys (quick cuts) and more ponderous slow keys. To sell high-security goods such as DVDs and CDs you have to find a runner to go and unlock one for you. There are gift vouchers and privilege discount cards, not to mention several denominations of mobile phone top-up cards. Products such as flowers might need special packing. The contents of bulging tills have to be emptied at regular intervals in case there is a smash-and-grab raid. There seems to be a world shortage of £5 notes. I floundered instantly.

I was thankful, after my Asda Big Welcome, that my training was short and sweet and infinitely less corny. The principles were the same, though: be nice to customers and impress the Mystery Shopper. To nudge you in the right direction there was the acronym ECHO – Every Customer Help Offered. The Mystery Shopper had a tick list and offering help with packing was on it. But the Mystery Shopper was a bit dense. You could automatically pack a customer's shopping without asking but this didn't count as offering help with packing. Even a 'Would you like a hand with your packing?' was borderline. You had to utter the prompt word 'help' clear as a bell if you were to be sure of getting that tick. 'Hello' and 'goodbye' were also expected and 'Do you have a Clubcard?' was essential script.

The job didn't stop there. You had to be vigilant for under-eighteens who were trying to buy alcohol and ask for proof of age if suspicious. I learned to spot them easily. They always wear low-set baseball caps and usually have spots. It was quite a responsibility. Mess up on this one, and the store could lose its drinks licence. You had to remember too not to sell cigarettes, lighter fuel or magazines or films with explicit adult material to under-agers. You were expected to be on the lookout for potentially disastrous spills that could result in personal injury litigation; you had to clean these up instantly. And you had to be on the lookout for runaway grapes. Until I worked for Tesco, I had not appreciated the clear and ever-present danger represented by grapes. Forget about banana skins: slip on one of these and we could be talking weeks in court. And just imagine what a careering roll cage full of Pepsi multi-packs could do to a toddler!

When not averting risks to life and limb of staff and customers alike, you had to be vigilant for shifty shoplifters trying to steal small, high-value items like razor blades or batteries. At the checkout, you had to be bright and cheerful at all times, even if you were having a bad time at home. We 'new starts' had a video to watch whose learning outcome was 'Don't bring your problems to work', aptly summed up by a fellow workmate as 'If you need to cry, cry at home.' Not that Tesco was heartless, you understand; it was just that we all had problems but they must never affect customer service.

My first proper shift lasted for four and a half hours, during which I was entitled to one fifteen-minute break. When I took my break, by the time I had walked through the store, gone to the toilet, poured a cup of free canteen tea and drunk it, it was time to be back on the job. At first, the concentration required in mastering the checkout made the time whizz by. The shift didn't seem too bad. The next day's shift was six and a quarter hours with two fifteen-minute breaks. Time began to drag. By now I could chirrup 'Have you got a Clubcard?' in my sleep.

To amuse myself I began to build up a profile of customer types. As a general if not infallible rule, the older the customer, the more agreeable they were and the more likely they were to talk to you. I was given adventurous recipe suggestions by one charming old man and talked the virtues of home baking with several elderly ladies. The more middle-aged the customer, the more harassed and therefore curt they were likely to be. But even then you could almost shame them into being more agreeable by being positively bright and breezy. Men on their own loved to flirt. As for children, adolescents and struggling teenage mothers, chat to them and you had a friend for life. They obviously didn't expect anyone in an official position to be nice to them ever.

I began to notice a definite gender divide. Women, even if obviously not enjoying shopping, actively engaged with it. They tended to be fairly dutiful collectors of Clubcard points, though most seemed pretty hazy about the benefits. 'You get points and then you get, well, I'm not quite sure what, you get something,' one woman explained to her uninitiated friend. Men, either or their own or as trailing spouses, were visibly less interested. Many of them were clearly irritated by being asked whether they had a Clubcard. 'I know it's not your fault, you're told to ask, but I don't have a Clubcard and I definitely *don't want one*, thank you very much,' was a not uncommon reaction. Did we sell 'No, I don't want a Tesco Clubcard' stickers, asked one customer wag. He clearly wasn't the Mystery Shopper, so I'll admit, I sniggered. I subsequently discovered that the notion of merchandising goods with an anti-loyalty card message was not entirely original. Peter Looby, a props man from East Sussex, has designed a T-shirt that reads 'No I haven't got a f**king loyalty card!', aimed at refuseniks who 'don't want a bar code stamped on their arse'. Mr Looby told *The Times* that it was initially meant as a bit of fun but that within a six-week period he had sold more than 500 T-shirts – costing £14.99 plus £2 package – to 'an eclectic mix of customers including vicars, accountants and even European Union workers who wrote their order on European Commission headed paper'.

As the week went on, I began to get to know more about the other staff. They were kind, welcoming and supportive – and not because anyone had sent them on a charm course. It was genuine. There was none of that cheesey Asda Wal-Mart family stuff. They seemed to be very much their own people. Some even refused to wear their name badges and none appeared to have a reverential attitude to management. Many were members of the shopworkers' union USDAW. Tesco actively encourages union membership. At Asda, none of my trainers had volunteered the words 'trade union'.

Snatched five-minute chats with fellow workers at break times were treats that lit up the day, as was the banter with the more amiable customers. But this wasn't enough to compensate for the tedious monotony of the checkout, nor the stressful and tiring nature of the work environment. As the week drew on, I became more and more aware of a stabbing ache between the shoulder blades. Helping customers pack is all very well but doing that and scanning goods at the same time involves twisting and stretching your torso in an unnatural way, often putting downwards weight on wrists. I found myself struggling with twelve-packs of beer and bumper boxes of pet food. It was easier to pack standing up than sitting down, but doing that only meant swapping a sore back for tired legs. TWIST began to take on a whole new meaning. I wasn't in the least surprised to discover that the Health and Safety Executive had found that in a busy four-hour shift a check-out operator might lift the equivalent of one ton in weight, nor that back complaints are common in checkout operators, as are reports of aches and pains in the upper limbs.

Simultaneous scanning and packing is an appealing customer service idea that several supermarkets like to promote. However, in 2003 a Sainsbury's TV advert featuring it fell foul of the Independent Television Commission. It showed Jamie Oliver relaxing at a checkout while an assistant packed his shopping. Two other shoppers complain that Oliver is getting star treatment, only to be corrected by a checkout assistant who explains: 'We scan and pack now.' Sainsbury's customers complained to the ITC that the advert was misleading because in their experience it was usually only the first three or four items that were packed, not all the shopping. The ITC upheld their complaint and Sainsbury's dropped the advert.

I began to appreciate why more often than not checkout staff look jaded. There was no daylight or fresh air. I sat under strip lights. The air-conditioning and heating fans clicked on and off all the time, creating a low-level hum of noise, punctuated by a discordant symphony of repeat beeping as a line of operators scanned goods through checkouts. I constantly felt dehydrated. Frequent changes in temperature as the fans regulated the store temperature left me feeling shivery and uncomfortable.

After several hours at a time, any urge to be cheery or pleasant was overtaken by an all-pervasive, mind-numbing blankness. I began to feel spaced out, as though dulled by drugs. Any energy I might feel at the start of a shift soon ebbed away. The necessity to endlessly parrot 'Do you have a Clubcard?' sapped any willingness left to engage, even superficially, with customers. Even if you wanted to try to be pleasant with people, after only so long it was impossible to keep it up.

In quieter moments, I found myself thinking about Tesco's chief executive, Sir Terry Leahy. He could have a cup of coffee or a glass of water at his desk any time he liked. He could amble over and take a look out of the window when he felt like it too. He didn't have to put his hand up to ask to go to the lavatory. It was a sure bet that he wasn't subjected to random locker or airport-style clothing searches. What's more, he was paid an awful lot of money to be professionally charming to people – his total pay package in 2003 was £4,330,000 – while I was being paid just £4.94 an hour to do so. It would rise to £5.22 after six months and £5.49 after a year but that wasn't much over the £5.38 the Low Pay Unit was recommending as a minimum wage. Neither tea breaks nor lunch breaks were paid.

This was no great surprise considering that in 2003, Tesco was one of the ten lowest-paying FTSE companies in the UK, along with Marks & Spencer and Morrisons. Although Tesco top brass were handsomely remunerated, the average annual salary for a Tesco worker was only £12,945. Low pay is endemic in the world of supermarkets. The GMB union has calculated that supermarket staff as a whole have to work 94 hours a week to achieve the average British wage.

Not long after my stint at Tesco, the company began trialling a scheme to stop paying sick pay to its employees for the first three days to discourage absenteeism. 'How refreshing it would be to see supermarkets competing for the affections of their staff instead of putting pig farmers and corner shops out of business.

It's not as if they can't afford it (sick pay), what with Tesco making enough money to buy a decent second-hand Fiat Punto in the time it takes to type this sentence,' remarked Phil Hogan in the *Observer* Magazine. On a more serious note, Naomi Craft, a general practitioner writing in the *Guardian*, asked the obvious question: 'What are the public health implications of this decision? How keen will we be to buy our fish from the man at the fish counter in Tesco if he has a streaming cold or dreadful diarrhoea?'

Of course there are all sorts of benefits open to staff who stick it out. A Save As You Earn share scheme, a 10 per cent staff discount, a decent pension, career breaks, parental leave and more. But by Saturday, at the end of a killer ten-hour shift (eight and a half hours with an hour for lunch and two fifteen-minute tea breaks), I was virtually brain dead and physically exhausted, fit only for eating a meal and collapsing in a chair in front of the TV. The thought of spending every Saturday like this was downright depressing. I could fully appreciate why many people wouldn't stick around to realise those benefits and why Tesco's annual staff turnover rate was running at 29 per cent.

My admiration for the people who do this job day in, day out, while coping with everything else in life, is enormous. Industry surveys show that the vast majority of them are women working part-time with a host of other commitments. Some of them have other part-time jobs too, such as childminding. They can't just slip off home after work and put their feet up. At the checkout, they face an omnipresent threat of violence. A checkout operator in my store had recently left because she had been assaulted – totally out of the blue – by a couple of men, out of their minds on drugs or drink, or both.

Always, but always, be nice to checkout operators. And if they don't beam back at you, please don't judge them harshly.

SUPERMARKET SUPPLIERS

18

Climate of fear

Friday 13 June 2003 turned out to be a memorably difficult day for Tesco. Annual general meetings are usually rather dull, unremarkable affairs. But even before it began there were signs that this one was going to be different. On the pavement outside the Royal Lancaster Hotel in London, attendees filed past demonstrators dressed up as fat-cat businessmen in grotesquely oversized 'nude suits' – a visual pun on naked greed – holding subjugated farmers tethered on a leash. Real farmers held up placards bearing questions that Tesco might prefer its shareholders not to think about. 'Tesco profits – farmers squeezed.' 'Who's creaming it? Farmer paid 9p a pint Shopper pays . . . ?' 'Who snatched the biggest slice? Farmer gets 7p a loaf. Shopper pays . . . ?' Perhaps the most poignant was the placard that read: 'Cheap Food? 11 farmers go bust every day . . . 1 commits suicide every week.' The adjammers had been at work too, hijacking Tesco's familiar corporate logo, colours and favourite 'Every Little Helps' slogan in an eye-catching banner which read 'TESCO Every Little Hurts'. The message was clear: farmers were in shock, suffering the most severe and enduring crisis in modern British farming history, and they seemed convinced that Tesco had something to do with it.

Inside the hotel, shareholders assembled to hear Tesco's

chairman and chief executive purring over double-digit profit growth and the company's 'outstanding results' – a substantial £1.4 billion profit that year. Plasma screens flashed up heart-warming images illustrating Tesco's solicitous care for its staff, its charitable works, its contributions to job creation and urban regeneration. They bragged about Tesco being not only the leading supermarket chain in the UK but also a market leader in six countries. Almost half Tesco's retail space was already outside the UK, shareholders were informed – a taste of things to come. You could be forgiven for getting the impression that the entire global retailing world, both food and non-food, was Tesco's oyster.

It was a warm day and the audience, composed predominantly of silvery-headed senior citizens, seemed less than riveted to start with. Most looked as if they had come for a change of scene, a day out, a guaranteed seat, a cup of tea and biscuits. Anticipating the inevitable slow exodus to the doors, the chairman announced early on a tacit incentive to stay in the form of a free bottle of Tesco wine at the end for everyone. Some left early. Clearly the offer had proved resistible. Many more fell asleep, some slumping over their neighbours, causing them to spread on to the increasing number of empty chairs.

However, the meeting sprang to life when angry shareholders began to express their considerable difficulty in understanding why directors felt it necessary to pay themselves so much. By 12.40 p.m. – the meeting had begun at 11 a.m. – the chairman was struggling to keep control and was threatening to have one persistent shareholder removed. Some questioners couldn't get over the figures for the income of Sir Terry Leahy, the Scouse shelf-stacker who rose through the ranks to the post of chief executive. His 2002 emoluments or pay package, consisting of salary, benefits and profit-sharing, amounted to £2,838,000. Nor could they come to terms with the £1 million-plus pay packets being picked up by some lesser board members. One shareholder pointed out that they were all 'well established on millionaire row'. Another implied that this generous level of remuneration notwithstanding, they were not doing a very good job, complaining that he could not get fresh bread in his local Tesco, that it was full of out-of-date stock and sold mushrooms not fit for consumption. 'Why can't you have a reasonable wage increase? How much money do the directors need and how much is enough to be rich?' he asked, only to hear the stock supermarket cliché: shareholders were getting 'value for money', responded the chairman, somewhat tetchily.

For the farmers in the audience, these hefty pay packets were particularly hard to swallow. One Lincolnshire arable farmer, Peter Lundgren, pointed out that the average farming income had dropped to £11,000 a year and that 30 per cent of farming families were living on family credit. He congratulated Tesco on its impressive profits but said that these were being achieved through environmental degradation and rural degeneration caused by supermarkets not paying a fair price to the people who grow the nation's food.

Sir Terry Leahy replied in a soothing, almost avuncular tone of concerned sympathy. Tesco, he stressed, was 'very concerned about the plight of British farmers' but he steadfastly refused to shoulder any responsibility for it. He attributed the sorry state of British farming to BSE, foot-and-mouth disease, the euro, Common Agricultural Policy subsidies – anything, in fact, but Tesco's manner of doing business. Tesco was, he acknowledged, 'British farming's biggest customer'. Undoubtedly farming was going through hard times, but 'it is not our [Tesco's] behaviour that has changed,' he insisted.

Another Lincolnshire farmer, John Turner, got to his feet to tell Tesco's directors that he was feeding organic potatoes to his cows because they had been rejected by supermarkets. Brandishing the potatoes in question, he said, 'I'm sure that most people in this room who looked at them would be happy to buy them. But they are getting rejected.' Was Tesco doing enough to help British farmers, he wanted to know. Sir Terry Leahy was at pains to stress that Tesco had 'very good relationships with its suppliers' and was always trying to help. Tesco had tried, for example, to develop organic farming, and even though the market price for organic food had reduced it was continuing to pay organic farmers a guaranteed price higher than market value. That seemed to be news to Mr Turner. 'I produce organic food yet I don't get those guaranteed prices,' he insisted. By this point, the platform's patience with farmers and their difficulties appeared to be wearing thin. Tesco was always willing, said its chairman, to look at any individual case or grievance if it was put in writing to head office. Next question please. As *The Times*'s business editor, Patience Wheatcroft, remarked the day after: 'The selection of suppliers and demands made on them is one of the keys to competitive advantage and Tesco is not about to turn into a charity for agricultural workers.'

For a farmer or grower to turn up at a supermarket's AGM and complain about, or even demur over, how that company treats its suppliers takes enormous courage. Supermarkets have embarked on a constant process of weeding out and streamlining their supply base for many years now, spewing out a steady flow of ex-suppliers prepared to speak out about how they have been treated. But farmers and producers who still do business with supermarkets, or hope to do so in the future, dare not be so candid. A permanent threat of delisting (the supermarket ceasing to stock their product) hangs over them. 'Step out of line [with the supermarkets] and you get delisted,' one supplier told me. 'You are regarded as a troublemaker if you don't worship the ground they walk on. Fall out with one and you get blacklisted by the lot of them because they all talk to one another.'

In the past decade, supermarkets have established a near feudal relationship with their suppliers, tightening their control over them, effectively dictating what they produce and screwing down prices, yet offering no security in return. A Surrey grower, Charles Secrett, gave me a graphic example of the gnawing insecurity suppliers feel. 'One winter, it was so frosty we couldn't get the leeks out the ground. But we knew if we didn't get them to the retailer, it would be a black mark against us and probably affect the growing programme they gave us next season. So we literally went out and chiselled the leeks out of the soil rather than tell them that we had a problem.'

Speaking to a wide range of suppliers one builds up a picture of British supermarkets behaving like the most mercurial, impossible-to-please mistress of British agriculture. A mistress who must be kept sweet, who stamps her little feet regularly, expecting everything yet guaranteeing nothing in return. It is a one-way trade, not a dialogue, and no criticism or grumbling is permitted. 'As soon as you put your head above the parapet [complain] that's a nail in your coffin,' is how one supplier summed up the predicament. 'If you blow the gaffe on supermarkets, they can turn nasty and there can be repercussions. All of a sudden they might find a "quality problem" and use that as an excuse to delist you,' confirmed another seasoned supermarket insider.

There is no doubt that reprisals for disloyalty can be swift and painful. Devon beef farmer Richard Haddock told me of his experience. Mr Haddock had been supplying meat direct to processor under a supermarket scheme. 'I went to a supermarket producers' meeting where representatives of the supermarket in question and its abattoir/processors were present. I stood up and talked about my negative experiences with the supermarket and got backing from other farmers. Shortly afterwards I was told by a fieldsman working on behalf of the supermarket and its processors that he was sorry, but he could no longer come to look at my cattle. Because I had spoken out publicly, they couldn't take my meat any more.'

In the same way that many consumers dislike having to shop in supermarkets, many farmers and growers deeply resent having to supply them. The supermarket modus operandi is so different from the dignified, gentleman's-handshake agreements between equals that used to characterise dealings between farmers and growers and their clients. Many suppliers would dearly like to be able to tell their supermarket masters to take a hike, but because the supermarkets have an effective stranglehold on the nation's food spend, they feel they have to do business with them if they want an outlet for their produce. But the resentment smoulders away. 'Supermarkets are irascible bastards who won't countenance anything that's bad for their margins,' one supplier told me, definitely off the record. 'People [suppliers] are petrified of them [supermarkets],' said another. 'Suppliers are scared stiff of supermarkets. They operate a rule of fear,' explained yet another who, predictably, dared not be named.

Fear? An exaggeration perhaps? Not according to the Competition Commission, when in 2000 this independent body reported the conclusions of its enquiry into supermarkets. 'We received many allegations from suppliers about the behaviour of the main parties [supermarket chains] in the course of their trading relationships. Most suppliers were unwilling to be named, or to name the main party that was the subject of the allegation. There appeared to us to be a climate of apprehension among many suppliers in their relationships with the main parties.'

'Apprehension' is putting it rather diplomatically. In fact, such was the fear of supermarkets that when the Competition Commission asked suppliers to tell it about their dealings with supermarkets, it found it extremely difficult to reassure them that they could do so safely without fear of repercussions, noting:

Even very large suppliers were concerned about what action their supermarket customers might take if they found adverse evidence had been given against them. Most suppliers were extremely concerned that their submissions and comments should be kept confidential. Many refused to give evidence or complete questionnaires unless we were prepared to guarantee confidentiality and many more refused to identify the relevant main parties [the supermarket in question ... Even large multinational suppliers expressed concern] ... Some suppliers expressed what appeared to be very real fears that any hint of involvement in our enquiry would threaten the existence of their commercial operations ... We assured suppliers that we would maintain their confidentiality in so far as we were able since it was clear to us that without such an assurance, we would have had the greatest difficulty collecting any evidence whatsoever. Even so, many suppliers refused to submit evidence or complete our questionnaire.

Why were supermarket suppliers so reticent? The answer was not too hard to uncover. Suppliers' organisations were slightly more forthcoming with the Commission than companies and individuals, as their umbrella nature gave them some protection, allowing them to be forthright. 'Many of our individual members are extremely reluctant, or refuse point blank, to comment on specific cases. Many of these organisations have 40, 50, 60 or even 70 per cent of their sales with a multiple. The resultant power that the multiples have is huge,' one commented. A consultant to the packing industry told the Commission that 'the degree and variety of pressure upon the suppliers was extremely alarming – all complied with the retailers' demands because of the dread of delisting'. One lone company, in supporting its case for anonymity, pulled no punches, saying it would be 'commercial suicide for any supplier to give a true and honest account of all aspects of relationships with retailers'.

No wonder suppliers have to watch what they say about supermarkets.

19

Extracting the best deal

Our supermarkets are keen to portray themselves as loyal and supportive customers, nurturing suppliers in their quest for the best deal for consumers. Tesco says that it is 'committed to maintaining strong mutually advantageous relationships with our suppliers', Asda asserts its 'belief in good relationships which we work to improve all the time' and Sainsbury's says 'we are very proud of the good relationships we have with our suppliers'. Bounce that supplier-friendly image off many supermarket suppliers, though, and they'll ask you to pull the other one – it's got bells on.

At the higher echelons of supermarket hierarchy, and especially in public forums, all the supermarket chains are fond of outlining their 'corporate social responsibility' strategy, which, amongst other objectives, lists treating suppliers decently. To the consumer, it all sounds comforting and reassuring. We want to believe that the people who produce our food are finding it profitable and worthwhile to do so, and supermarkets are never shy about grasping any opportunity to foster this positive image. At the start of the UK foot-and-mouth epidemic in 2001, for example, they set up a compassionate fund of several million pounds to help farmers in distress. The public might have been impressed, but most farmers were not. 'Is that not just a bloody joke?' one farmer quipped. 'Who the hell put them in distress in the first place?'

Occasionally, the mask of benevolence slips, as was the case in an interview with the chief executive of Safeway, Argentinian businessman Carlos Criado-Perez. Pushed as to why there was growing unrest amongst suppliers and complaints that Safeway was acting aggressively, Mr Criado-Perez insisted that its relations with its 2,000 suppliers were good. But he offered an unusually forthright insight into Safeway's current business strategy. 'We are very keen negotiators and, increasingly, it becomes a more challenging dialogue. It's our job to prise every penny out of suppliers. Every single penny comes either from them or the customers. We try to do business ethically, but we also want to do what is best business for our shareholders.'

Speak to suppliers directly and they will tell you precisely what they make of that. The fine words supermarket generals reel off about their dealings with suppliers do not seem to filter down the ranks to the foot soldiers who actually carry out their business and generate their profits. 'The supermarket high-flyers are all protected by great screeds of people round about them, so much so that they don't even meet major suppliers, that's people who are supplying them with hundreds of millions of pounds of raw material. They work at the strategic level way up in the clouds. They say they'll give farmers fantastic support. They say that they are going to do X, Y and Z and then the buyers move in and just kick the suppliers to ribbons,' one experienced farming figure told me. Another supplier confirmed this. 'As soon as the chief executive officer walked out the room, it was business as usual. The buying team was just a bunch of thugs.' So common is this view within the grocery world that the term 'buyer bullying' is a well-used industry catchphrase.

The public image of the Dudley Moore-style cuddly supermarket buyer, tirelessly scouring the globe for food finds like a latter-day Indiana Jones, is wide of the mark. The typical supermarket buyer for a large multiple, the person who negotiates the detail of any business with suppliers, is likely to be in his or her mid to late twenties and routinely changed at short notice. One minute he or she could be in charge of pet food, the next Christmas gifts, then ready meals or toiletries and so on. 'When we first started trading in the early 1990s,' one supplier explained, 'the buyers were relatively knowledgeable people with whom you could build a relationship. They might not have known that much about your category but they knew how to deal with people and products. Now some supermarkets have made a lot of them redundant. Increasingly, the buyers are younger and there is no continuity. They're here today and gone six months later.'

Even within the world of supermarketing, this knowledge deficit is recognised. When the small, family-owned, regional supermarket chain Booths trounced every other supermarket chain to win the title of 'Overall Wine Merchant of the Year' in *Wine Magazine*'s 2002 Oscars, it publicly attributed its success to the fact that its knowledgeable wine buyer had been in the job for four years, an uncharacteristically long tenure amongst the ever-changing personnel of supermarket procurement. 'Many supermarkets swap buyers between departments and this often means that the frozen vegetable or lingerie buyer of today may well be the Bordeaux or Riesling buyer of tomorrow. This can easily lead to difficulties in telling a claret from a carrot or a hock from a sock,' remarked Booths.

Several established suppliers told me of their difficulties when trying to present products to inexperienced and uninterested buyers. 'You're in this cubicle deep in the chain's HQ. You're talking away passionately about your product, waxing lyrical to a 26-year-old and you can almost see the cartoon bubble coming out her head saying "yawn" or "bored". All she wants to know about is getting the maximum sales from each square metre and the only way she knows how to do that is by reducing wastage, increasing sales by price cutting and increasing margins,' said one. The wine writer Tim Atkin gave readers an insight into the world of supermarket wine buying, recounting his experience at a wine tasting. 'Tesco buying managers have a reputation for securing the hardest bargains ... One of them was given a new wine to taste ... and was asked for his reaction. He sniffed the contents of his glass, tasted it and replied "Not enough margin". This would be funny if it weren't so alarming.'

Supermarket buying is rapidly turning into a know-nothing, profit-obsessed occupation. To get a job as a supermarket buyer, no substantive knowledge of the product category is required and it is questionable if it is even seen as a benefit. In the words of one recruitment consultant, 'all he [a buyer] needs to know about is profit margins and doing deals'. Buying is just a job requiring the same set of negotiating skills for each product category. One product is just like any other. Of course this could mean that, as inexperienced newcomers, buyers have an open-minded approach to suppliers, waiting to listen and learn about their products before they start trying to cut a deal. But that is not how it works. By constantly moving buyers around, supermarkets can ensure that they do not become too reliant on regular suppliers, which might blunt their desire to get the best deal. As one supplier told the Competition Commission: 'Multiples switch their buyers around every six to twelve months in order that relationships and loyalty to suppliers can be avoided. The new buyer is given carte blanche to delist suppliers, who are frequently treated with complete contempt.' All buyers must realise that any supplier can be replaced and it is up to them to make the supplier fully aware of that too. Some buyers keep a 'supplier storecard' and 'supplier financial performance card', benchmarking suppliers against targets to remind them who calls the shots. With typically only twelve to eighteen months in the job, buyers have to get results within that time and their whole approach is necessarily short-term. 'The attitude is, I've got to make this much savings in less than eighteen months to make my mark. Some of them resort to clumsy threats of delisting and so on. They aren't going to be around long enough to worry about the effects of their decisions on the long-term health of the category,' one supplier told *The Grocer*.

With supermarket head office car parks, I am reliably assured, full of a stream of hopeful suppliers, clasping their cool boxes, waiting for an audience with a buyer, a bit like a queue for a theatrical audition, it is no surprise that some big companies will go to expensive lengths to cultivate a new supermarket buyer. I learnt about 'Spanish trips', for example.

> This big Spanish company wants to sell to a UK supermarket chain. It will invite the buyer out for a weekend, ostensibly to look at produce. He will be taken out on the most expensive golf course and told that there's a villa down the road if he wants to stay on another week. The company will say, 'This won't affect our business of course, but there is a villa there, if you want to stay. Oh and bring your wife and family too.' The company will take him out to a restaurant. It's sickening what goes on. It's a case of what's the most expensive dish on the menu? We'll have that. What's the most expensive wine? We'll have that too. One meal I was at in Spain, the bill came to £1,000 for six people. All just to impress this new young buyer.

One UK supplier not financially equipped to compete with this sort of buyer wooing told me of his altogether more chilling encounter with a new vegetable buyer. This buyer had previously been in charge of paper goods and had been in the vegetable job for only two weeks when he came to visit the supplier. 'He told us how he had worked in the paper department. When he came into the job, he told us, the chain was paying £13 a thousand for this particular product. By the time he'd been in there two months it was paying 75p a thousand, he had kicked out all the main suppliers and moved the chain's margin up from 20 per cent to 50 per cent. He told us that he intended to do the same thing with vegetables.'

Failure to go along with a buyer's requests can be disastrous. In 2002, a story circulated throughout the book trade about a publisher whose key account executive was unceremoniously dismissed from a buyer's office as a result of refusing to give a 65 per cent discount on the publisher's lead spring title. 'If you are not willing to negotiate on that title, you may as well pack up now. I don't want to see the rest of your list,' the buyer was reported to have said. One supplier went so far as to express his feelings to the Competition Commission in a particularly heartfelt way: 'On the whole, supermarket buyers and store managers are blackmailers, they are not fair and always have their own way, hence the reason why our business is no longer trading . . . Thank you for giving people the chance to express themselves and show supermarkets for what they really are.'

But it is not just that suppliers feel bullied by buyers. The buyers themselves are constantly looking over their shoulders at their superiors further up the supermarket sourcing chain. These superiors in turn will be in the firing line of the remorseless profit-driven supermarket machine if they don't get results. 'Senior managers are under almost unbearable pressure to perform,' one supermarket insider said.

Most supermarket buyers, in common with colleagues in other divisions, are paid a basic salary with a performance-related bonus. In most chains the margins obtained by buyers are directly reflected in their pay packets, so they have a personal financial incentive to get the best deal from suppliers. If they don't reach target, both buyers and category directors have to worry about losing their jobs or being downgraded. As David Smith, chief executive of the National Association of Master Bakers, put it: 'They [buyers] are going to get promoted by screwing the suppliers. Saying "I'm going to sustain my suppliers" isn't going to play well with their bosses.' Graphs and maps may be put up on office walls to chart daily progress on targets and indirectly humiliate anyone who is not meeting them. Everyone has to work to an appraisal system and regularly demonstrate their performance against targets, usually assessed on the basis of a simplistic good/bad tick list. The demands put on them are ratcheted up at regular intervals and competition and rivalry for internal empires is encouraged. The worse the company's financial results, the more intense is the pressure heaped on buyers to justify their existence by extracting extra margin or 'financial support' from suppliers.

Head office 'streamlining' is a constant worry. In June 2003, Sainsbury's, for example, axed 200 HQ positions as part of its ongoing 'business review'. In the fallout around 100 buyers – one out of every four – was sacked. These cuts were followed later in the year by another wave of job cuts, this time in the technical division. In May, Tesco – whose profits looked fine and healthy at the time – had slashed 100 executive jobs from the intermediate ranks of managers 'mainly responsible for buyers in different product categories'. I understand that the job cuts made in 2003 in some of our leading supermarket chains typically represent anything from one quarter to one third of key divisions and that no rank is protected.

As supermarket competition gets more intense, and buyers are laid off, those that remain have increasing workloads and are put under even more pressure to get results. One seasoned negotiator remarked:

Being a supermarket buyer for one of the big multiples must be the worst job on earth unless you're someone who loves the power you can exercise over people. These people are youthful and inexperienced, but suddenly it's all up to them. They find themselves handling multi-million transactions. They have to screw the guy that they're dealing with as hard as they can, but not so hard that he goes out of business. On some occasions they do squeeze too hard, and the supplier does go out of business. I've seen a supplier – a grown man – come out in tears after a meeting with a super-market buyer.

By all accounts, to succeed these days in the world of supermarket buying you have to be starving hungry to get on and keen as mustard to submit to life as a company clone, with a corporate message chip inserted in your brain. You are expected to believe that your chain is fantastic, uncritically parroting its virtues at every possible opportunity. You must become thoroughly steeped in its culture and positively belligerent in your assertion of its virtues over other competitors. Suppliers are expected to feel tinged with glory just because they have the privilege of doing business with your chain – and grateful too. Their powerlessness makes you feel ever more important. A supplier told me how its marketing team was insufficiently humble during a meeting with one influential supermarket buyer. They were consequently blacklisted by that retailer as the buyer moved up that chain's management ladder.

In the high stakes atmosphere of supermarket sourcing, buyers have to be psyched up for doing their jobs like soldiers going into battle. Though rewards, in the form of bonuses, can be high, the penalties for failure are too. There are 'cascade' sessions when senior directors make rousing speeches to their staff, weekend re-treats or in-house training courses where team leaders play out war games, practising negotiating with suppliers or out-manoeuvring competitors. 'The appraisal system becomes a machine. You have to conform to it. There's no master architect, just an all-pervasiveness. Individuals either cannot grasp the wide-ranging consequences of decisions being made or have gone into denial, maybe as a way to survive or keep their own positions,' one manager explained. It is an environment where the toughest and most ruthless flourish.

20

Pay to play

You would think that if a product was wholesome, safe and reliably supplied at a price that, as well as sustaining the supplier, offered a decent margin to the retailer, supermarkets might be interested in purchasing it. But these days in the lord-and-vassal world of grocery retailing, that proposition is not necessarily sufficiently enticing. If suppliers want to deal with supermarkets, it is a lot more complicated than that. They may have to approach the supermarket buyer not only armed with something the consumer might like to buy, but also, like the ancient Greeks, bearing gifts.

The concentration of power that has taken place in food retailing in recent years – a horticultural co-op gave me an illustration of what this means in practical terms: 'When we started up 15 years ago we had 45 different customers taking vegetables every day, anything from five tonnes upward. Now we have only four, all major multiples' – has not just given our large supermarket chains a stranglehold on the nation's food shopping. It has effectively assigned them the role of gatekeepers whom farmers, growers and manufacturers must get past if they want to supply that market, with extraordinary negotiating power. If they are to let suppliers through, supermarkets expect to be kept sweet. If you are a supplier you are expected to play by the rules of the supermarket game – rules that are drawn up by the supermarkets themselves, and are effectively non-negotiable. It is not like a game of Monopoly where the ultimate penalty is going to jail. With losers getting delisted, which could mean you go out of business, the stakes are high.

Our supermarkets have developed a number of practices which, in one way or another, have the net effect of improving the supermarkets' margins at the expense of the supplier, pushing what should be the retailers' costs back down the supply chain to the producer or manufacturer.

What sort of practices are we talking about? Perhaps the most striking example ever to be made public is Safeway's now infamous 1999 'Focus' promotion. The chain wrote to suppliers of 1,000 of its most popular lines asking for a £20,000 contribution for each line they supplied to guarantee its availability. A supplier providing four different products to Safeway, for example, was asked to contribute £80,000. Some suppliers faced bills of several hundred thousand pounds. The National Farmers Union felt outraged enough on its members' behalf to break its tradition of never going public with its grievances about supermarkets and reported Safeway to the Competition Commission. It pointed out that keeping shelves well stocked should be a retailer's responsibility and that Safeway was just passing the costs of its instore promotion on to farmers. Safeway defended itself by saying that it was a voluntary scheme and that if any supplier felt he could not support it, Safeway would withdraw his product and no penalty of any kind would be imposed. Some supermarkets charge their suppliers for delisting them.

In July 2003, there was another example of how supermarkets may seek money from their suppliers when it emerged that Tesco was asking for payment from suppliers to cover the costs of compliance with the Ethical Trading Initiative, an alliance of organisations that promotes fair trade. One angry Tesco supplier leaked a letter to *The Grocer* in which Tesco stated it wanted

£69.50 per quarter per supplying site from all primary suppliers to cover these costs.

To do business with some of our largest supermarkets these days, suppliers may have to 'pay to play'. They may be asked for a large sum to put their product on the shelf in the first place, also known as a 'bung', and they may have to come up with a 'promotional package'. That means a large sum of money up front and a preparedness to come up with more at intervals thereafter. A representative from a minor wine-growing region gave me this illustration of what it takes to be a player, recounting his meeting with a buying manager. 'I asked him what we could do together in the way of a wine promotion, suggesting a tasting in all stores (with the wines provided at the expense of the producers). He said we hadn't enough money to do a promotion with them. I asked how much an instore tasting would be. Answer – £100,000.' This 'money talks' supermarket culture acts as a major disincentive to small and medium-sized suppliers and militates against quality. 'The demands placed on suppliers are so huge that only big branded companies can afford to play the game . . . For the retailers, the deal is everything. To provide it, producers are obliged to cut corners and bottle inferior wines,' wrote wine writer Tim Atkin.

Whatever product suppliers want to sell to supermarkets, it seems they have to take the attitude that they really want the business and will put up with a long list of demands in order to win it and then retain it. When the Competition Commission carried out its investigation into supermarkets in 2000, it identified 'a substantial number of serious concerns' about supermarkets' trading relationship with suppliers. It therefore put to the supermarkets a list of practices alleged by suppliers and asked them to tell it which of them they had engaged in during the last five years. 'We found that a majority of these practices was carried out by many of the main parties,' it reported.

The Competition Commission concluded that when 'requests'

came from a supermarket with buyer power (large multiples with more than 8 per cent share of the grocery market), they 'amounted to the same thing as a requirement'. The Commission also said that thirty of these practices, when carried out by the 'major buyers' (once again, large multiples with more than 8 per cent share of the grocery market), 'adversely affect the competitiveness of some of their suppliers and distort competition in the supplier market – and in some cases the retail market – for the supply of groceries'. Furthermore, it said that twenty-seven out of the practices 'operate against the public interest', citing possible consequences such as lower quality, less choice for consumers, higher prices for consumers shopping at smaller retailers and reduced choice of retailers.

Some supermarkets raised objections to the design of the Commission's research questionnaire. Tesco, for example, said that it was 'wholly unsatisfactory' and said that it had not been possible in the time allowed to conduct a survey of all the buyers. It also felt that yes/no tick lists, taken out of context, 'ignored the complexity and heterogeneity' of Tesco's relationships with suppliers. Sainsbury's said that the format of the questionnaire had not been appropriate for some questions. It also said that it had 'not been possible to check that its policies had been consistently and uniformly applied by each of its buyers' in the time given. Safeway said that the Commission had not allowed for the fact that it might no longer be engaging in a practice, nor asked about the frequency of such practices. Waitrose was unhappy, amongst other things, with the equivalence the Commission had given to 'requested' and 'required'.

Here is a detailed list of practices which the Commission concluded some supermarkets engaged in and the chains involved as named by the Commission. In the interests of fairness, a précis of responses by named supermarkets to each supplier allegation is included. Readers who do not want this level of detail can skip to page 166 for examples suppliers gave me of supermarket requests for money.

- Required or requested payments from suppliers as a condition of stocking and displaying their products or as a pre-condition from suppliers for being on the list of suppliers
  Chains named: Budgens, the Co-ops, Iceland, Morrisons, Safeway, Somerfield, Waitrose

  (Safeway said payments were required occasionally but infrequently. Budgens, the Co-ops, Morrisons, Somerfield and Waitrose said they requested but did not require payments. Iceland said suppliers made payments in return for minimum orders.)

- Required or requested payment from suppliers for better positioning of products within stores
  Chains named: Asda, Booths, Budgens, Iceland, Morrisons, Safeway, Waitrose

  (Asda said it might request a contribution in certain circumstances. Safeway said that suppliers occasionally paid for more prominent space. Budgens, Morrisons and Waitrose said they were requested but not required. Iceland said that payments were for positions that generated greater sales. Booths said that payments were for secondary promotional displays only.)

- Required or requested an improvement in terms from suppliers in return for increasing the range or depth of distribution of products
  Chains named: Aldi, Booths, Budgens, the Co-ops, Iceland, Marks & Spencer, Morrisons, Netto, Safeway, Sainsbury's, Somerfield, Tesco, Waitrose

  (Aldi, Marks & Spencer, Safeway, Tesco and Waitrose said they requested better terms where a supplier would increase its volume of sales. Safeway said increased volumes benefited the supplier. Sainsbury's said payments might be negotiated if a product was extended subsequently into further stores. Asda said it was not correct to say that it required or requested better terms in such circumstances. Aldi and Somerfield said suppliers offered improved terms for extended distribution. Morrisons said it requested but did not require payments. Budgens said such payments were not compulsory. Booths said it requested these as part of on-going normal negotiations. The Co-ops said this could be part of a negotiation.)

- Required or requested a financial contribution for a promotion from suppliers – 'pay to play'
  Chains named: Asda, Booths, Budgens, the Co-ops, Iceland, Marks & Spencer, Morrisons, Safeway, Sainsbury's, Tesco

  (Asda said it might ask suppliers to contribute. Safeway said it would generally seek to recoup lost profits and promotional running costs. Tesco said any such payment was not a charge but the chief means by which suppliers competed with each other. Sainsbury's said it was not unusual to discuss sharing of costs in certain limited circumstances. Morrisons said it requested payments but did not require them. Booths said that payments were part of normal promotional negotiations. Marks & Spencer said promotions would always be the subject of negotiations which would cover the sharing of costs. Booths said it requested these as part of on-going normal negotiations.)

- Discriminated between suppliers in the length of credit period
  Chains named: Asda, Booths, Budgens, the Co-ops, Iceland, Marks & Spencer, Morrisons, Safeway, Sainsbury's, Somerfield, Tesco

  (Iceland, Morrisons and Budgens said they negotiated credit terms. Asda, Marks & Spencer, Safeway, Sainsbury's, Somerfield and Tesco said that variation did not amount to discrimination.)

- Delisted a supplier or caused a supplier to reduce prices under threat of delisting

Chains named: Aldi, Asda, Booths, Budgens, the Co-ops, Marks & Spencer, Morrisons, Netto, Safeway, Sainsbury, Somerfield, Tesco

(Aldi, Netto and Tesco said that if a product was not selling they might consider delisting. Asda said delisting was rare and might be used as a threat during negotiations. Morrisons said it delisted only in extreme cases. Somerfield said delisting was related to product performance review. Marks & Spencer said if it could source a product at a more competitive price it would discuss this with its current suppliers and negotiate accordingly. Sainsbury's said delisting was a feature of rationalising sources of supply.)

- Suggested to a supplier that the chain would delist a product and later withdrew suggestion having received a discount on an unrelated product or a general improvement in terms
  No chains named. The Commission noted that 'The responses from major buyers which said they engaged in the practice did not address the question as asked.'

- Required or requested suppliers to make payments for specific promotion (e.g. gondola or aisle ends, advertisement allowances) where the payments exceeded the actual costs for the supermarket
  Suppliers named: Booths, Budgens, the Co-ops, Somerfield

  (Somerfield said there might be times when funding exceeded cost but the overall effect on margins on adversely affected products also had to be considered.)

- Required solus supply of a product (the supplier must not supply that product to any other retailer)
  No chains named. This practice seemed to be limited to own-label products.

- Sought to influence a supplier not to supply a product to another retailer where the retailer was, or was believed to be, offering the product at a lower price

  The Commission noted one isolated incident and said that it had no other clear evidence that the practice was more widely observed.

- Sold a product on which the labelling indicated, or might be taken to indicate, that the product was of UK/British origin when it originated overseas (such as 'packed in the UK')

  Chains named: Asda, Morrisons, Somerfield

  (Asda, Somerfield and Morrisons said they complied with UK labelling laws and regulations.)

- Required or requested 'overriding' or 'in anticipation' discounts from suppliers

  Chains named: Booths, Co-ops, Safeway. The Commission remarked that 'On the evidence of Asda, Sainsbury's and Somerfield we cannot be satisfied that they carry out this practice. But we believe it is probably widely carried out in one form or another.'

  (Booths said they were negotiated with suppliers. Safeway said it required overriders on some goods. Budgens said they were not mandatory.)

- Sought retrospective discounts from suppliers

  Chains named: Asda, Booths, Budgens, the Co-ops, Iceland, Morrisons, Netto, Safeway, Sainsbury's, Somerfield

  (Asda said it negotiated projected volumes and might renegotiate if there was a variance. Safeway said it might renegotiate but could not compel. Morrisons said it might seek such discounts where it seemed apparent that other retailers had been charged lower cost prices. Somerfield said it sought such discounts, sometimes to clear over-stocks. Budgens had ongoing negotiations. Booths said it would only try to negotiate to do so when it was left holding stock where the market price of the products had reduced since the original negotiations. The extra discounts would be reflected in the retail price. Iceland said it sought such discounts if there were changes in the marketplace which it wanted to pass on to customers. Sainsbury's said that it had agreed retrospective bonuses with some suppliers.)

• Required or requested compensation from a supplier when the profits were less than the supermarket expected
Chains named: Asda, Safeway, Somerfield, Marks & Spencer, Netto

(Asda said if a product did not perform and Asda incurred unforeseen costs, it would ask the supplier to share them. Safeway said it would look to share the risk with the supplier. Somerfield said it might seek compensation. Marks & Spencer said it discussed with suppliers the sharing of costs in limited circumstances. Netto said it occasionally requested compensation when a reduction in retail price caused it to become unprofitable.)

• Sought support from a supplier to match a low retail price of a competing retailer
Chains named: Aldi, Asda, Booths, Budgens, the Co-ops, Iceland, Morrisons, Netto, Safeway, Sainsbury's, Somerfield, Waitrose

(Asda said it might negotiate part or full funding with a supplier to reduce the cost price. Safeway said it sought support from suppliers but did not always get it. Somerfield said it sought but did not require margin support to improve terms or prevent loss of profit. Waitrose said it sought to establish the advantage to other retailers and match it. Iceland said it might seek such support. Aldi said it might do so by negotiation and mutual agreement. Iceland said that if another retailer was selling at a lower price it might ask the supplier for support to enable it to sell at a lower price.)

- Required or requested suppliers to make payments to cover product wastage
  Chains named: Asda, Booths, Budgens, the Co-ops, Marks & Spencer, Netto, Safeway, Sainsbury's, Somerfield, Tesco, Waitrose

(Sainsbury said it requested payments from suppliers of short shelf-life products. Sainsbury's, Booths and Marks & Spencer said they asked for payments from fresh produce suppliers when the wastage was caused through substandard products. Asda said it might ask for a contribution when the waste was more than expected. The Co-ops, Safeway and Waitrose said that they asked suppliers to contribute following the introduction of a new product where wastage might be far higher than normal. Somerfield said payments related particularly to products on promotion. Netto said that fruit and vegetable suppliers were required to contribute 1 per cent of sales at cost to cover wastage. Tesco said it did not require or request payments retrospectively; suppliers' agreement would be sought when terms and conditions were agreed and payments were rarely deducted in practice.)

- Required or requested suppliers to buy back unsold items or failed to pay for them outside a written 'sale or return' agreement
  Chains named: Asda, Budgens, Safeway, Somerfield

(Asda said that if it had stock it could not sell, it might ask the supplier to take it back. Safeway and Somerfield said that if they delisted a long-life product, they might ask the supplier to take it back.)

- Failed to compensate suppliers for costs caused through the supermarket's forecasting errors or order changes
  Chains named: Asda, the Co-ops, Safeway, Sainsbury's

(Asda said that it did not deliberately make forecasting errors, but where these occurred it would not compensate a supplier. Safeway

said that forecasts were only best estimates and that it worked closely with suppliers to ensure that these were as accurate as possible. Sainsbury's said it did not compensate suppliers although on certain products where forecasting was more difficult its contractual arrangements made allowances.)

- Levied charges on suppliers for consumer complaints that exceeded actual costs, or were not for a product fault or for which written information was not provided to the supplier
  Chains named for carrying out 'some aspects' of this practice: Budgens and Sainsbury's. The Commission said 'the level of complaints we received from suppliers would seem to indicate that this is widespread. However we cannot be satisfied that any of the main parties [supermarkets] other than Budgens and Sainsbury's carry out any part of the practice as no other multiple admitted doing so.'

(Sainsbury's said that it had not levied charges on suppliers for consumer complaints that exceeded its actual costs or for which written information was not provided. All customer complaints were dealt with under a procedure that had been in force for several years.)

- Delisted any producers/growers who had failed to deliver agreed quantities owing to weather conditions
  No chains named. The Commission thought this only occurred in one or two isolated incidents.

- Sought information from a supplier on the supply and pricing of its products to other retailers
  No chains named. The Commission said that it had received no clear evidence to suggest that any undue pressure had been used.

- Required or requested suppliers to make a financial contribution if any promotional activity carried out by the supermarket failed to meet the expected target
Chains named: Asda, Iceland, Somerfield

(Asda said that when a product did not perform and Asda incurred unforeseen costs, it would seek to renegotiate terms with suppliers. Somerfield said that targets and supplier funding were agreed ahead of promotion; suppliers knew the risks and knowingly accepted them. Iceland said that any contributions were agreed with the supplier.)

- Required suppliers to bear the cost of surplus special packaging ordered by the supermarket for a promotion when the sales did not meet the expected target
Chain named: Somerfield

(Somerfield said that targets and supplier funding were agreed ahead of promotion. Suppliers knew the risks and knowingly accepted them.)

- Debited suppliers' invoices, or otherwise claimed from them, without their agreement
No chains named. The Commission noted: 'We believe it [this practice] is probably widespread.'

- Delayed payments to suppliers outside agreed contractual periods, or by more than thirty days from the date of invoice, where deliveries had been made to the supermarket's specification
Chains named: Asda, Safeway

(Asda said that over 90 per cent of invoices were paid on time but delays could occur usually when there was a mismatch between order and delivery. Safeway said it generally abided by agreed terms but its efforts to even out cash flow sometimes resulted in negotiations and often a two-way deal around the year end.)

- Changed the quantities or specifications of a product previously agreed with a supplier with less than three days' notice without financially compensating the supplier for any losses
Chains named: Asda, the Co-ops, Netto, Somerfield

(Asda said it would not normally compensate a supplier. Whilst it did forecast, or place provisional orders, most were real-time-based sales, typically with a 48-hour lead time. Somerfield said it was rare for it to change an order at short notice; changes in terms and conditions were at the behest of suppliers, or at Somerfield's request if there was a change to products a supplier was to provide, following a range review. Netto said that short-notice changes were made occasionally, by agreement with the supplier.)

- Required suppliers to maintain a lower wholesale price pre-viously renegotiated for an increased order when the volumes purchased were subsequently reduced
Chains named: Asda, Booths, Budgens, the Co-ops

(Asda said that if a product did not perform and it incurred unfore-seen costs it would negotiate with a supplier to share those costs. Budgens said it would negotiate with a supplier.)

- Over-ordered goods at a promotional price from suppliers which the supermarket subsequently sold at a higher retail price without compensating the supplier
Chains named: Asda, Booths, Budgens, the Co-ops, Morrisons, Netto, Safeway

(Asda said that the dates on which the discount on a cost price would be agreed would tend to be the dates between which the promotion was running. Asda and Morrisons said that they incurred losses on goods in stock at the commencement of a promotion. Safeway said that 'investment buys' used to be fairly common but the practice had declined owing to lack of capacity.)

- Debited suppliers' invoices or otherwise claimed money for promotions in amounts which were not for the sum previously agreed with the supplier, or were for promotions that had not yet taken place or were without provision of back-up data to the supplier

  No chains named. The Commission said that it was not persuaded that it was reasonable for a supermarket with buyer power to debit suppliers for promotional activities without their agreement but it was not entirely satisfied that the practice adversely affected the competitiveness of suppliers or that it distorted competition in the supply of groceries.

- Instigated a promotion on a product without the agreement of the supplier and requested the supplier retrospectively to fund the promotion

  Chains named: Asda, Budgens, Safeway

  (Asda said that if it lowered a price, and sales volumes grew as a result, it would usually seek an improvement in terms. Safeway said that its pricing strategy involved mounting localised hard-hitting price promotions at short notice and it had not always been possible to give advance notice to a supplier; it said in respect of its 1999 'Focus' promotion that, assuming the sales growth projections were achieved, its suppliers would get a healthy return on their investment very quickly, adding that there was no question of this scheme being imposed on anyone.)

- Required or requested suppliers permanently to reduce the price of a product previously agreed in support of a multiple's marketing initiative

  Chains named: Asda, Budgens, the Co-ops, Tesco

(Asda said its initial negotiations were on the basis of projected volumes; once the volumes were actually ascertained, there might be renegotiation on price. Tesco said that where a promotional retail price led to a significant improvement in volume, it might request, but not require, that suppliers maintain the cost price in order that Tesco could pass on lower retail prices and continue to drive volume.)

- Delisted any suppliers of branded products in favour of super-markets' nearest own-label equivalent
  No chains named. The Commission believed that this practice could distort the supplier market but on the evidence received could not be satisfied that this had been the case.

- Required or requested suppliers to contribute to the super-markets' costs of buyer visits to new or prospective suppliers, artwork and packaging design, consumer panels or market research, or to provide hospitality to the supermarket or its employees
  Chains named: Aldi, Asda, Booths, Budgens, the Co-ops, Iceland, Marks & Spencer, Morrisons, Netto, Safeway, Sainsbury's, Somerfield, Tesco, Waitrose

(Sainsbury's said it financed the costs of buyer visits but this had not always been the case in the past; suppliers' contributions to artwork and packaging were negotiable; suppliers might be asked to contribute to independent panels and market research. Asda said that suppliers had paid for buyers' visits especially outside the UK, but this was now an exception. Safeway said it recharged costs for artwork to the supplier, which agreed an amortization rate for their recovery that was reflected in the cost of goods purchased by Safeway; it expected suppliers to cover costs of long-distance travel. Aldi, Booths, Iceland, Morrisons, Netto and Somerfield said that they requested payments for artwork and packaging design, Netto adding at cost price only. Waitrose said it requested payments for buyer visits. Marks & Spencer requested payments for artwork, consumer panels and market research. Tesco said that suppliers might occasionally be invited to contribute to joint market research but this was not a requirement.)

- Levied charges on suppliers for discrepancies in supply where the source of the discrepancy was not agreed with the supplier, or where written information on the circumstances was not provided to the supplier
  No chains named. The Commission noted: 'We believe it [this practice] is probably widespread.'

- Required or requested suppliers to contribute to the costs of a store refurbishment or the opening of a new store
  Chains named: Budgens, Morrisons, Safeway

  (Safeway said that some suppliers were asked to contribute on the basis that they would enjoy higher sales.)

- Introduced a change to any aspect of the supply chain procedures which reasonably could be expected to increase a supplier's costs without compensating the supplier or sharing any savings achieved
  Chains named: Asda, Booths, the Co-ops, Iceland, Netto, Safeway

  (Asda said that although it made every effort to consult its suppliers on changes it introduced to improve efficiency and service to the customer, inevitably some changes would be introduced that were not discussed. Safeway said that improvements to its procedures were continually being made to the benefit of its business, customers and suppliers; short-term costs to suppliers should be offset by increased volume of sales. Iceland responded similarly. Netto said it had introduced a charge per pallet to frozen-food suppliers.)

- Unilaterally imposed charges on suppliers for not meeting product specifications without proven investigation that the problem might have originated at the store
  No chains named. The Commission said that it was not persuaded that it was reasonable for a supermarket with buying power to impose charges on suppliers without their agreement but it was not entirely satisfied that the practice adversely affected the competitiveness of suppliers or that it distorted competition in the supply of groceries.

- Required suppliers predominantly to fund the cost of promotions such as 'Buy One Get One Free'
  Chains named: Booths, the Co-ops, Marks & Spencer, Morrisons, Tesco

  (Marks & Spencer said that each promotion was negotiated case by case; in some cases it bore the majority of the costs and in some cases the supplier bore them. Tesco said that where a promotion would largely benefit a supplier, it would expect the supplier largely to fund it.)

- Required or requested suppliers to make a financial contribution to the costs of bar-code changes or reduced-price-marked packs
  Chains named: Booths, Budgens, the Co-ops, Morrisons, Safeway, Sainsbury's, Somerfield, Tesco

  (Tesco said that it incurred additional costs when a supplier of a branded product instigated a promotion which required a bar-code change. Sainsbury's said that payments were negotiable. Somerfield said it did not always require payment. Safeway said it would not expect to pay for bar-code changes on branded products, and on own-label products the packaging was paid for by the supplier so it, too, would fund the changes.)

- Invited suppliers to make contributions to charitable organisations
Chains named: Asda, Booths, Iceland, Marks & Spencer, Morrisons, Safeway, Sainsbury's, Somerfield, Tesco, Waitrose

(Asda and Waitrose said that suppliers were not invited to make such contributions as a condition of doing business. Safeway said there was no requirement. Tesco said it invited suppliers jointly to fund charitable events. Morrisons said that suppliers which voluntarily donated prizes for a charity raffle were publicly thanked. Somerfield said suppliers were advised of the charity they were supporting. Iceland said contributions were jointly agreed. Marks & Spencer said that suppliers contributed at their own discretion. Sainsbury's said it had invited suppliers to participate in events it hosted; participation in such events would not impact on its purchasing decisions.)

- Required suppliers to purchase goods or services from designated companies such as hauliers, packaging companies
Chains named: Asda, Budgens, the Co-ops, Iceland, Marks & Spencer, Morrisons, Netto, Safeway, Sainsbury's, Somerfield, Tesco, Waitrose

(Sainsbury's said that it sometimes required this; where possible it offered a choice of companies. Tesco said its quality control necessitated the designation of preferred haulier and packaging companies; it received commission from them; it believed this was widely known. Asda said it imposed such requirements where commercially sensible but in recent years had not accepted any commission. Safeway said it received overriders from third parties it required its grocery suppliers to use. Somerfield said it received rebates from the third parties. Morrisons said it insisted on designated third parties for own-label products only and received no commission. Waitrose said it received benefits from third-party suppliers. Budgens said it required suppliers to use designated third-party labellers. Iceland said it had nominated suppliers to guarantee standards of quality and service; packaging costs were passed on by suppliers to Iceland. Marks & Spencer said it imposed certain restrictions on the third parties its own-label suppliers used. It would discuss any payments by these third parties with the finished goods suppliers. Netto said it received commission from designating bagging and labelling companies.)

- Instructed intermediaries not to allow goods to be handled that are intended for delivery to other retailers, where the goods originate from producers with which a multiple has ceased trading No chains named. The Commission said that this practice could, in some circumstances, lead to a distortion in the supplier market. But on the evidence it had received concerning two chains, it could not be satisfied that this was the case.

This list of supermarket practices, with its cool, circumspect, quasi-legal tone, does not give the full flavour of the many, varied and highly inventive ways in which supermarkets may look for financial support from their suppliers. But the information supplied to the Commission by suppliers gave a fuller picture. They spoke of 'support packages' for a new product, sums of £2–5,000 for distribution of point-of-sale material (such as recipe cards), 'new line entry fees', 'wastage allowances', 'catalogue contributions', 'year end rebates', 'margin enhancement', 'marketing subsidies', advertising support for a departmental 'kitty', 'stock cleansing allowances', 'magazine contributions' (to the chain's instore magazine), 'supplier's marketing budget', 'listing fees', 'free stock in lieu of fee' (for listing), 'loss of profit claims' and 'gate fees'. They might be expected to fund a 'Buy One Get One Free' promotion or pay for money-off vouchers. Having paid to get their product onto the shelves, which might include an extra payment – say £10,000 to have it put in an advantageous position such as a gondola end – suppliers said they might then be asked to come up with some 'mid life' promotional event (price cut) to 'support' it once it was there. They spoke of the odd donation to the supermarket's charity, 'sponsorship' for the London Marathon, fees for technical audits and product testing or a contribution to new packaging labels and many other types of payments.

I asked suppliers to give me concrete examples of the cash demands made on them by retailers. There was no shortage. Here is a selection. When I put these anonymous complaints to the supermarkets, they largely denied them; their comments are included in Supermarket Responses, pages 313ff.

One day I was phoned up by the stone fruit buyer. 'Oh, by the way,' he said, 'I'm now instigating a half per cent on all your sales as a sampling rebate.' But the chain never did any sampling [product tasting]. We had to pay the rebate but we had no control over what he did with it.

We had a manufacturing problem in our factory, so we had to stop production and put the problem right. We informed the supermarket about that but it meant that for three days they were without product. They reckoned that the product sold £6,000 through their tills each day and they fined us £18,000. Not just the profit margin on the product they were making, which would have been about a third of that. They billed us for the total sales value. This sort of thing happens to lots of suppliers. I learnt that some manufacturers keep a fund for paying supermarkets for precisely this sort of eventuality because it is so common.

Often we get a demand for money in some form around January/February at the end of the supermarket's financial year. You'll get the buyer on the phone saying he needs more margin [profit] and so he wants to discuss rebates [discounts]. He tells you that he needs it agreed by 5 p.m. that day, calculated retrospectively for the last year . . . and he wants to discuss next year's rebate as well.

If a customer complains or brings back an item, then the supermarket will charge you [the supplier]. Say it's a bag of pears. The complaint is logged. The customer gets his or her £2 back. It becomes a 'return to manufacturer' (RTM). We get automatically charged £25 by the supermarket. Quite often they don't come back to us with the bar code or the right information so we don't know what the product was. It might be that the customer just doesn't like it or that the product is bad because of a problem at the store. Perhaps the pears have been left in light in a warm place for too long. But the supermarkets always take the view that any customer complaint or rejection is the supplier's problem.

Customers see 'barker cards' or shelf labels with comments on them like 'As featured in X magazine' or 'Gold medal winner in competition Z'. We [the supplier] pay £500 for those.

The supermarket will announce that it's doing a '50p off every bag of apples' promotion for eight weeks. We tell them there are not enough apples. They simply say we don't care, that's your problem. If you don't go along with it, some other supplier will. They aren't building sales or promoting the product, it's just price-cutting. Occasionally supermarkets will contribute a small proportion to the promotion, but that's rare.

I have been asked to pay a supermarket a delisting fee towards the cost of discounting the line that our product was replacing. I was asked to support the promotion by giving £1 a case for 3,000 discounted cases.

However the demands are presented, supermarket suppliers are accustomed to being asked to put their hands in their pockets for something or other. Most of them are resigned rather than angry about it. 'When we first started supplying them [supermarkets] I was smarting with the injustice of it all,' one supplier told me. 'Now I have become inured to it.'

21

Green beans from Kenya

In October 2004, in the midst of a season when autumnal British vegetables are diverse and abundant, Tesco took out eye-catching green and white adverts in weekend magazines. Beneath a picture of two shiny sugar snap peas, posed to give the impression of pirouetting dancers, the wording ran: 'Sugar snap peas. Flown fresh from Guatemala. By jet. Then delivered to your house by Tesco van. Oh well, you can't have it all.'

While the recipe writers in the same publications were encouraging readers to pulverise new season's Jerusalem artichokes into soup, or roast that fresh new British beetroot, Tesco, defying the greenness of its advert, was promoting 'exotic' out-of-season vegetables – available 365 days a year and flown in from the other side of the world – as the ultimate consumer aspiration.

The irony of the colour choice was not lost on readers, especially as the advert had coincided with articles on rising carbon levels and greenhouse gas emissions and our unsustainable dependency on oil. 'To explain why carbon levels soar, need we do more than turn to Tesco's advert?' asked one contributor to the *Guardian* letters page. 'While many companies now employ senior staff to tell us how impeccably green they are, Britain's biggest supermarket is bragging about its environmentally ruinous practices.' Environmentalists rail at the folly of air freighting fresh produce thousands of miles around the planet. Bear in mind that air freight produces nine times more CO_2 emissions than road freight and fifty times more than shipping. British growers, meanwhile, bemoan their difficulties in selling home produce to supermarket chains whose shelves are stacked high with imports. But our large retailers justify their enthusiasm for imported food as giving customers what they want. A secondary line of defence, often used to deflect environmental objections or when fielding questions about the conditions of Third World growers supplying these goods, is that the supermarket trade brings foreign currency into needy countries from which all manner of social and economic benefits flow.

But as rival chains vie with one another to have the lowest retail price, Third World growers tell a different story, one that echoes those British farmers who are beaten down on price by major supermarket chains. This is the tale of one Kenyan green bean grower, who told me how his experience of supplying UK supermarket chains was rapidly turning sour.

I started growing vegetables and salads in Kenya in the early 1990s. I worked for companies growing for British supermarkets. I enjoyed it and learnt a lot. By 1997, the supermarkets wanted their suppliers to have their own farms, so my wife and I found a farm of our own. We ran it as a mixed farm with dairy and beef cattle as well as goats. On the arable side we grew cabbages for the local market as well as beans and courgettes for my former employer. It was quite a struggle, as the farm was run down and the land poor, but we were able to expand. The basis for our expansion was export crops – first green beans and then baby corn. At first the prices were OK and we were paid regularly. However, as time went on, more and more demands were made of us. We had to abide by a series of increasingly demanding 'protocols' set by the supermarkets. Some were fairly easy to accept, such as the recording of chemical use, but others made little or no sense. We were just informed that they were 'what the customer wanted'. We were told, for example, that we needed a secure store for our stocks of chemicals. We explained that since we try to use as few chemicals as possible, we carry no stock on the farm and just buy from local companies as and when we need any. But the response was that this was not good enough, so £6,000 later we have bought a smart chemical store of no use to us but pretty impressive if any outside inspector wanted to look at it.

The supermarkets gave us no choice other than to conform to assurance schemes such as Nature's Choice (which promises consumers more natural farming methods), all at our own expense. These schemes allow the retailer to tell the consumer that what they sell is good and healthy to eat and produced sustainably because there are two folders full of useless paperwork signed by the grower. For us they mean many additional costs – we have had to employ someone whose job it is to fill in the myriad forms – yet they return to us no benefits other than the ability to continue to supply supermarkets. Our grading shed, for example, is built out of wooden slats, well aerated, cool, open at one end with large entry and exit areas. We put in covered lights and ensure that it is always neat and tidy. Now to keep the supermarkets happy we have to label each individual light and then have a person checking the lights daily. To an already cash-strapped company, this means employing one more person we really don't need and can't afford.

The supermarkets demand worthwhile-sounding standards but don't pay a price that allows us to meet them. All tractors are meant to be fuel efficient and green, for example. But we feel like telling them that our tractors are usually second-hand, because they are squeezing us so much on price that we can't afford to buy newer, cleaner ones.

The bigger we have become, the tighter the grading requirements have become too. One supermarket asked us to grow baby carrots but it rejects close to 50 per cent of what we send in. We never get to see our rejected produce, because it goes into their system as sliced carrots – free to them at our expense. When we said we could not afford to grow baby carrots, we were labelled as difficult. Over the last five years we have found that their packers have increased the proportion of our vegetables that they reject from 10 per cent up to 30 per cent, so eroding any gains we might have made by scaling up our production.

While these conditions have been imposed, prices for our produce in the supermarkets have been going up, but our returns have been slashed. When I first started supplying UK supermarkets in 1997, the price we were paid for beans was around fifty pence a kilo for something retailing at around £4 a kilo. Now in 2004, we are being paid twenty-six pence a kilo, a reduction of nearly half on a product retailing at no less than £5.30 a kilo on supermarket shelves.

We made the mistake of thinking that by expanding into supermarket export crops we would be able to get off the farming treadmill by virtue of economies of scale. Now it seems to us that we have made a rod for our own backs. The supermarkets like the idea of traceability and accountability from large units such as ours but want to pay the same price as they would pay for produce bought at the side of the road from the small African farmers who are in the same boat as us. The downside of all this is that while we have several hundreds of acres of crops, we struggle to pay ourselves and our staff a fair wage. And the most galling thing is that being paid even ten pence more a kilo would make a massive difference to us and all the other growers of so-called exotic produce. The obvious thing to do is stop growing for supermarkets and return to growing cereals for the Kenyan market. However, we have around 600 people working here. It looks attractive to get out of vegetables, but as there is no social security here, what will our workers do? Some have worked on flower farms and seem to us to have been weakened by the chemicals inhaled while in greenhouses. Others are in varying stages of infection by HIV. They cannot get work anywhere else: most farms medically screen prospective employees before employing them. AIDS has left quite a few grandmothers with children to bring up. Our policy is to give them jobs that they can do easily. Most can manage weeding or picking peas. While a fair proportion would be able to find jobs, many wouldn't. We employ two teachers for the local school, where the student-teacher ratio is 100 to 1. We supply the school with basics like paints, colours, Manila sheets. Free medical examinations, also paid for by the company, would come to a halt. But as time goes on, I see no real future in supplying the UK multiples. Somewhere between our farm in Naivasha and the supermarket shelves there is a black hole that swallows up over £5 of cash. Air freight is around £1 or so, but who is taking the rest?

This tale is typical of Third World growers' captive powerlessness in the hands of their supermarket masters. The same plot lines are repeated wherever you look: that familiar mix of enforced low prices, ever-growing cost-producing requirements and a lack of long-term commitment and security. One academic described the situation in Zambia as follows:

For farmers supplying the export market, the product is graded at buying, when the farmer is present, and regraded at the packing house, where the farmer is not present. When rejected, fruit is thrown out and the farmer isn't paid. It is sold informally on the street. Farmers are just told that X per cent of their product was accepted. Large-scale commercial farmers, who are mainly white, get better prices and are paid in dollars, whereas indigenous farmers are paid in kwacha. There is a scheme to help small farmers negotiate with exporters, but it has helped the exporters more than the poor farmers.

Speaking directly to growers in South Africa supplying UK super-markets, Oxfam opened up a Pandora's box of grievances. One apple picker told the charity:

> There is less permanent labour and fewer perks and lower increases for those that remain. This is the result of over-production and the suppression of prices by retailers. [Real export prices for South African apples have fallen 33 per cent since 1994.] Many of the farmers are retrenching their permanent workers because they say they cannot afford it any more ... Where must we go?

A table grape grower gave this example of how supermarkets demand complex packaging and labelling requirements without reflecting the additional cost in the price paid to growers:

> One chain wanted us to change their grape packaging from open to sealed bags. The new bags were three times as expensive – up from 2.8 rand to 8 rand. And the productivity in the packhouse went through the floor because it took workers 20–30 per cent longer to seal those bags. But the price (to the grower) stayed exactly the same– it wasn't even discussed. And the other super-markets all demanded it too. That's the way it goes.

As Oxfam puts it, 'Supermarket shoppers have never had so much low-cost choice and worldwide variety delivered to their shopping baskets. But Oxfam research ... has found that, across different national contexts, supermarkets and food industry buyers are capturing the lion's share of gains from this trade, while passing risks and costs on to farmers.'

22

Get it in writing

The big supermarket chains love to tell their customers about their 'partnerships' with suppliers. The word 'partnership' has a nice warm quality to it. It projects the right image to customers. A caring, responsible retailer arm-in-arm with a supplier. An informal, democratic agreement between equals. A long-term commitment from one partner to the other. A secure relationship between people who know and care about one another. Above all, it implies a certain loyalty. It is a lovely idea, and one that the big supermarkets' public relations and corporate social responsibility departments work hard to promote. But it could not be further from the reality of the supermarket–supplier relationship. A master–servant analogy would be more apt. As one supplier told the Competition Commission, supermarkets 'talk about partnerships, but these do not exist, and they ruthlessly erode suppliers' margins with no consideration of the damage they are doing to the company or its employees'.

Incredible though it may be to business people outside the supermarket world, the agreements between supermarkets and suppliers are worked out on an ad hoc, informal basis. Even though the business concerned might run into hundreds of thousands of pounds a day, written contracts between suppliers and supermarkets are highly unusual. The Competition Commission noted, 'Day-to-day negotiations (particularly on price and quantity) are usually conducted orally. Some of the larger main parties [supermarkets] told us that full written agreements were not generally applicable in the industry.'

Everything, even an important matter such as price, is agreed at meetings, on the phone or by email, with the buyer or indirectly through the supermarket's representative – a packer, processor or category manager. Many companies never have any direct contact with a supermarket, despite the fact that it is a major customer: everything goes through a middleman. Key suppliers might be invited to one of a chain's 'producer club' meetings, which are normally hosted by the relevant buyer and category manager. Tesco, for example, holds such meetings, the aim of which is to 'improve communication and understanding of the whole supply chain'. Suppliers described them to me as 'more like a lecture on why the chain is so great and how lucky you are to be doing business with it'.

This does not mean that suppliers are left unsure as to what supermarkets expect of them. They receive a 'product specification' and are notified of details such as payment schedules, delivery times and invoicing dates. Growers will be given a 'programme' indicating what volumes they are meant to supply. Suppliers will be sent a written copy of the retailer's terms and conditions of trading and asked to sign it. They are at liberty to send the retailer their terms and conditions or attempt to confirm an oral agreement in writing. But they do not have a bit of paper to refer back to if there is a problem. They have no document that states an overall commitment to do business with them for a specified period of time or details possible eventualities and sets out codes of behaviour for both parties. There are no such things as a required period of notice before cancelling an order, agreed credit terms or terms for promotional activity. None of these things is thrashed out in advance; instead they are dictated by the retailers on the hoof. Even companies who have been trading with supermarkets for decades have no formal commitment from or contract with them.

As a consequence, if the supermarket wants to ditch a supplier tomorrow – an increasingly frequent occurrence – there is nothing the supplier can do about it. A trade organisation told me that of all the grievances suppliers raised about their dealings with supermarkets, the lack of contracts, and hence security, was the foremost. 'A phone call from a buyer can destroy a significant part of their business. That worry and constant anxiety keeps them awake at night. They dread getting a call on Friday saying they are going to lose all their business from Monday.' This is precisely what happened to one company that grew beetroot for processing for one major chain. 'We had planted twenty acres of beetroot. We had lifted half of it when suddenly the chain decided to stop selling this beetroot line. Just like that, we got a phone call saying the chain couldn't take any more beetroot. They had given us a programme for twelve months but we had nothing in writing. All because the buyer, a twenty-five-year-old lad, had decided not to stock it. What are you meant to do with ten acres of beetroot all of a sudden?'

Another supplier told me what happened to his company:

We had built up a nice business with this multiple over ten to fifteen years: £10–12 million a year and going upwards. We'd heard that they wanted to bring in other suppliers – that's normal commercial life – and we were concerned. However, we got a letter from the head of buying saying that our business was totally secure. He acknowledged that we had built the business. Then the buyer turned round and said that he didn't want us to supply them with lettuces any more. Bit by bit, they stopped all our business, first cauliflowers, then cherries, sometimes overnight or with two days' warning at the most, then everything stopped. It was all done with great duplicity. There was no commercial reason for it. Dealing with us just didn't suit their system and the system has to win. They had given the business to another supplier. That supplier wasn't interested in these products. He was just told to take them on or the multiple would stop buying all the rest of his stuff.

I heard the story of a vegetable grower who had been supplying several supermarket chains. One chain came to him and asked him to supply it exclusively. The grower was reluctant to say to other retailers that he could no longer supply them in the absence of a guarantee of future business from the chain demanding exclusivity. But the chain in question would not deal with him unless he stopped trading with the other chains and so he went along with it. After a couple of years the chain said that it wanted his product packed in a certain way or else it could not take it. The grower had to buy an expensive piece of packing equipment costing a five-figure sum in order to do this. Six months later, the chain dropped him. By this point, he had no other customers and the only outlet for his product was as cattle food to neighbouring farms.

The supermarkets' ultimate sanction of delisting means that their suppliers have to accept practices that are manifestly unfair and skewed in favour of the retailer. One common grievance amongst supermarket suppliers is the unreliability of the sales forecasts on which supermarkets base their programmes. For example, a supermarket will give a lettuce grower a programme to grow so many heads of iceberg lettuce every week for a year. The number of icebergs required is a guesstimate of what the supermarket expects to sell. The lettuce grower goes off and plants the icebergs. To ensure that he can supply the right volume, like most growers he has to overproduce in order to be absolutely sure of having enough because he dares not let down the supermarket. I asked suppliers why they could not grow less to avoid waste and simply explain their circumstances to the supermarket on the odd occasion that they were unable to supply enough.

'You could only do that if you didn't care about getting the business again. We need to be seen as always coming through with the order,' one supplier explained. Supermarkets in turn often encourage waste by overestimating how much they might sell to be sure that they do not have empty shelves – during a surprise spell of hot weather, say (to continue the iceberg example), when consumption of salads goes up. If it is a particularly wet summer, however, and the forecasts do not materialise, or if the estimated sales on which the programme is based do not materialise for any other reason, the surplus icebergs become the grower's problem, not the supermarket's. Forecasts are not orders and the grower has to find another home for the icebergs or simply plough them in. As far as the big supermarkets are concerned, whether the product is a lettuce, an own-label ready meal or a pork chop, supply is just a tap that can be turned on or off at will with no financial penalties. The ramifications of that decision down the supply chain are irrelevant.

This attitude causes growers major headaches. 'At the start of the season we have a meeting with the packer and the supermarket's rep and they tell us what varieties to grow,' one potato grower explained. 'If it's not on their list of approved varieties, they won't take it. They keep changing the varieties and seem to think you can just suddenly change from one to another. If you want to supply a new variety, you have to start two years beforehand, sending them to the supermarket's HQ for cooking tests, and it's usually about a year until you hear back from them. When they do come back they just think you can produce it there and then, that season. But it can take three years to build up a supply.'

A supplier told me how one chain brought his meat company to its knees and the company was powerless to do anything about it. The company had had several meetings with the relevant buyer, including a visit by the buyer to the supplier's plant. In the course of these meetings, the supermarket clearly undertook to take an agreed volume of meat from a certain date. In order to ensure that it could fulfil this commitment, the company contracted other farmers to rear animals for it. But the supermarket delayed taking the meat as agreed for a period of months, offering one excuse after another. Meanwhile the animals were reaching maturity, and the meat was stacking up and having to be sold off cheaply; the contracted farmers were looking for the money they had been promised and the company had to keep paying them what it had undertaken to pay even though it had no income from the supermarket. Had it discontinued the contracts it might not have been able to supply the volume when the supermarket eventually wanted it. So it had to maintain them and absorb the loss. 'It nearly cost us our business,' they told me. But the company just had to take it.

Among supermarket suppliers, insecurity extends not just to the volume of supply but also to the most basic consideration – price. One potato grower explained to me how the price he was paid by supermarkets was set each week, invariably downwards. 'They will not give us a price for the growing season, not even a minimum–maximum price.'

Suppliers try to hedge their bets, but the more business a supplier has with a supermarket, the more it demands exclusivity, not allowing the supplier to deal with rival chains, forcing the company to put all its eggs in one basket. One packer told me how he supplied four different chains but maintained the impression of giving each chain exclusivity. 'When one retailer comes round we have to hide away all the trays we use for the others.'

The supermarkets' informal, almost casual way of doing business, which creates an imbalance in power between retailer and supplier and gives the former plenty of room to manoeuvre while the latter has none, is not a reflection of an easy-going, relaxed partnership between supermarket and supplier. It is an institutionalised way in which supermarkets keep suppliers in a constant state of insecurity. This creates a pressure to cut corners

– for example, by using poorly paid casual workers in a bid to keep the wages bill down. In its informality you might liken this way of doing business to a gentleman's agreement, except that supermarkets don't always act like gentlemen. Rather they use the looseness of the 'partnership' to unilaterally impose conditions on suppliers who, in turn, have no comeback. As one food processing company explained, 'They offer no stability, no security, no sense of working together. They can make or break a company by switching their business away from it. They are entirely callous and in a position to get out of you just exactly what they want.'

23

You've been category managed

Most supermarket shoppers recognise that different chains tend to stock much the same choice of food. If it is standard super-market commodities you are after, such as bumper multi-packs of crisps, ready meals or sliced bread, one supermarket is as good – or as bad (depending on your point of view) – as the next. We consumers usually settle on a particular store because its location is convenient and familiar, occasionally making a longer trip to a more distant store either because it has a more pleasant shopping environment or a better selection, or because we perceive it to be cheaper.

Nevertheless, for most of us there are a few products that we associate with a particular chain, products that other competitor chains don't stock which make us inclined to favour supermarket A over supermarket B, C or D. More often than not these are what are known as 'secondary' or 'tertiary' brands from small suppliers and manufacturers, which have a bit more personality to them: non-standard lines whose presence on the shelves makes you think that this supermarket is really serious about giving you the depth and range of qualitative choice you might associate with well-stocked independent shops.

Over the last few years, though, vigilant customers may have noticed that such lines are thinner on the shelves, while big, ubiquitous brands seem to sing out. Those distinctive, special items that helped clinch our choice of store are becoming few and far between. Why? They are the victims of retailers' drives to cut costs and maximise profits by cutting down on the number of suppliers, even if that means diminishing customer choice. Most likely your favourite items have been 'category-managed' off the shelf. If they haven't disappeared already, they may do soon.

Category management is the rationalisation of the choice of brands available in each category – and currently the big super-markets' key tool for streamlining their supplier base and increas-ing their margins. Ideally, supermarkets would like it if everything they sold was own-label – those that bear only the name of the retailer not the manufacturer or producer – because this offers the possibility of higher margins, keeps suppliers faceless as far as customers are concerned and allows the multiple to dictate terms to the supplier more readily. Consumers, however, expect branded lines, so supermarkets have to stock them. But rather than supply a profusion, they give customers a simple choice: a majority of own-label lines and a few household-name branded equivalents, regularly refreshed with new ideas designed to steal a march on competitor chains.

Our supermarkets did not always operate this way. In the 1980s, when UK supermarkets were expanding at a rate of knots and had lots of new shelf space to fill, they took on a portfolio of new products. That period was a heyday for suppliers, who were grateful to get their products into stores offering mass distri-bution and the possibility of vast sales. Small and medium-sized producers were particularly enthusiastic about the new opportu-nity that supermarkets presented. For the consumer, it seemed that supermarkets had outstripped the independents in the range they offered.

By the 1990s, however, when supermarkets had taken control of the lion's share of grocery supply in the UK, category management became the new way of doing business. The concept was pioneered in the US by the supermarket behemoth Wal-Mart, who figured that its shelves were cluttered up with a number of different lines, many of which – however cherished by a proportion of their customers – were selling too slowly. They might be proving profitable and enhancing customer choice but stocking them was an inefficient use of sales space. This conclusion prompted a long, hard look at what was on the shelves and a rationalisation of the range in order to squeeze the maximum revenue from every square inch.

Nowadays, all the big retailers who operate nationwide use category management. A category is not a single product line, but a group: not tinned tomatoes, for instance, but all tinned vegetables. The supermarket looks around for a supplier who is a household name in the category – usually a leader in its field, a player with enough manpower and muscle to do the job – and appoints it category 'captain' or 'partner'. The captain is charged with managing the category in partnership with the retailer. The captain's job is to look at the category and design an 'offer' that makes money for the retailer while giving a carefully constructed choice to the consumer.

Designing an offer means analysing sales figures to identify major profit generators and then planning the 'fixture' or physical shelf space accordingly. The category captain comes up with a computer-generated 'planogram', which maps out what should be stocked on the basis of projected sales and where it should go. In baby food, for example, the category captain helps to decide how much space is given to wet and dry food, how much to rusks, how much to drinks and so on, and identifies what products should be put at eye level or in the centre of aisles (both fast-selling hotspots) or at floor level (a dead zone). Pride of place in the planogram goes to own-brand products because these make more profit for the supermarket and those from companies who can guarantee substantial financial support for promotions for their product. The category captain suggests what area to commit to different sizes or formats of products known as stock keeping units (SKUs). He makes sure that the category is competitive, by keeping an eye on competitors and analysing how they stock their shelves. Research and technical development, plus coming up with new ideas and strategies to keep the category fresh and competitive, are also part of the category captain's responsibilities. These mean everything from picking up the tab for trials of new packaging to bearing the costs of new product development.

The creed of category management is the fewer suppliers, the better; the more lines a supermarket can source from one supplier, the merrier. Sainsbury's, for example, already says that half its sales come from 100 suppliers and that half its suppliers have sales through it in excess of £10 million a year. Category management does not just apply to branded goods. Supermarkets increasingly use category captains, often packers or leading producers, to source fresh own-label products such as fruit and vegetables or cheese. Consequently chains that used to have twenty different suppliers for a line – such as strawberries, or citrus, or stone fruit – now have only two or three. By 2004, Asda was sourcing its milk from only one supplier. The chairman of the National Farmers Union's potato committee has predicted that by 2005, 80 per cent of the UK potato crop will be produced by just 250 growers, down from the current 5,000. By 2000, 90 per cent of supermarket herbs that come in pots, such as basil, were grown by only one company.

A former employee of a large supermarket has estimated that in 1987 it had 800 fresh produce suppliers and by 2000 fewer than 80. One researcher has summed up the prevailing situation as follows: 'The major supermarkets now deal with just a handful of suppliers in key product areas and take every opportunity to pass responsibility and associated costs for quality control and procurement, storage and distribution upstream to their key suppliers, in return for which the chosen few are rewarded with volume growth.' Now the large retailers are looking for a system where a category captain might be responsible for even larger categories, like all fruit or all vegetables.

For the supermarkets, the advantages of category management are obvious. You avoid all the hassle of dealing with a pool of suppliers of varying size. In financial terms, the potential savings are enormous. You don't need such a big buying team at head office because your category captain will do all the legwork and present you with a ready-made package. Some supermarket chains even have their category captains second staff to the chain's head office to carry out work previously performed by supermarket employees. Fewer suppliers means less administration and lower costs for the retailer.

Category management is part of an ongoing process whereby supermarkets are shedding knowledge and responsibility and pushing them back out to their supply base. 'Why do it in-house when you can just make the supplier responsible?' is how one senior manager described the system. There is a power and control advantage too. When a chain's category captain has so much business with the supermarket, it will be prepared to come up with whatever it takes to keep it. Among other things, that means offering the retailer a better deal on price than anyone else. Category captains are supermarkets' single-minded and dedicated servants.

For the company appointed as category captain, there are obvious advantages too. Although it is as unlikely as any other supplier to have a written contract with the retailer, it has considerably more security. If nothing else, it is less likely to be ditched peremptorily. It also gains a distinct advantage over its competitors – not least privileged access to sales figures. Theoretically, category captains should behave in an even-handed way and be fair to rivals, ensuring that they get whatever representation on the shelves their product merits: the category captain's job is to build the category not boost its own sales figures. The reality, though, is that inevitably category captains favour their own products at the expense of smaller companies, aided and abetted by the retailer.

Speak to suppliers left out of this 'I'll scratch your back if you scratch mine' system and they will tell you that category management has proved to be a nightmare for them. The first casualties have been the many companies who have been eliminated from the chain's list of suppliers, generally not for any quality issue, such as a poor product or bad service, but because the company was too trifling to deal with or could offer too few lines or lacked the requisite financial muscle to put behind its product, or because the product was not earning its keep. In category management terms, big is always beautiful – not to mention profitable and efficient. The system favours the biggest, often multinational companies with greater resources and negotiating strength who already dominate the category. The effect of this remorseless business logic is to squeeze out all but the largest suppliers under the guise of economies of scale. 'The major retailers' policy has been increasingly to stock, within a given category, the brand leader, possibly a strong second and their own-label. Brands lower than number two in the market, and sometimes number one, have been delisted, unless they have a strong niche appeal,' one supermarket authority noted.

Many suppliers, both large and small, now find it harder under category management to get listed (have their product taken on) by a supermarket. Where once they dealt with the supermarket's buyer direct, now they may have to deal with a category manager, who may be indifferent to their product at best or actively in competition with it at worst. It is a system that has cut a swathe through suppliers. One supplier told the Competition Commission that it had lost £6 million turnover from a major supermarket as a consequence of category management. Another said category management had caused it to be delisted by two major retailers. Yet another said it had lost all its business with one chain after nine years of supply because of a bigger category management deal not related to price or service. I heard how the manufacturer of one Continental food range (a household name) was struggling to get it listed in UK multiples even though it was the number-one brand in its country of origin.

Category management's drive for fewer suppliers means that suppliers who do get listed often find themselves with a gun put to their heads. If they want to retain a supermarket's business in product X, they have to also take on the supply of product Y. A company that was quite happy supplying a retailer with vegetables, for example, will suddenly find itself under pressure to start supplying it with prepared vegetables – julienne carrots, ready-trimmed beans and so on. The Spanish Gallia melon man who was pleased to supply a multiple with his own produce throughout its native growing season will be asked to become the sole supplier of melons, which means sourcing melons – ogen, charentais, canteloupe, honeydew, watermelon – from around the globe all year.

Product 'innovation', in supermarket speak, otherwise known as gimmicks to grab the consumer's attention, is the key to keeping supermarket business because it produces added-value products that the chain can use to make a bigger margin. New varieties of fruit and vegetables that purport to be sweeter, juicier or crisper or have improved visible characteristics; new formats such as pre-prepared meal components, stir-fry packs, mixed salads with sachets of dressing and so on; anything with an extended shelf life or which is deemed to be more efficient, such as easier processing and better storage – all are deemed to be a feather in the supplier's cap.

When invited to become a category captain or partner suppliers face the nagging worry that if they cannot get geared up to supply such additional or innovative new lines, they will lose their existing business. As a result, category captains find themselves struggling to generate cash surpluses in order to extend reluctantly into new areas that require considerable investment in the hope of bigger volume sales, without any long-term undertaking from the retailer that the business will continue to come their way. The supermarket effectively says to the supplier, 'We'll take everything you can handle unless it suits us not to, in which case we won't.' That insecurity means that they have to keep costs as low as possible and think short-term. Category management is a system that looks after the supermarket, not the supplier. Even so, category captaincy is an offer that is hard to refuse.

As for the consumer, with its mission to supply not great quality or true choice but just an increasingly predictable selection of safe-bet products refreshed from time to time with new gimmicks, all calculated to feed the retailer's bank balance, category management just means more boring shelves and a duller range. Category management has become a sort of one-stop shopping system for retailers, who rely on a sole category manager to cover disparate areas of sourcing. Within this streamlined system, it seems perfectly logical for a supermarket chain to have, say, a manufacturer of industrial block Cheddar as cheese category captain, in charge of sourcing all the chain's specialist cheeses, even though the block Cheddar company knows zilch about small-scale or artisan cheese. By downgrading product knowledge and experience category management encourages dumbed-down, uniform, mass-produced food. One supplier summed up the situation to the Competition Commission thus: 'They [supermarkets] stand between manufacturers and the public and dictate what is on offer to the public even though the public might prefer alternative lines. Multiples usually only stock the national brand leader plus own-brand. This limits the choice to the public and even regional brand leaders in the independent sector are not considered by them. This will lead to the demise of small manufacturers with a consequent permanent reduction of choice.'

So if you are the kind of shopper who is looking out for

24

Business as usual

When the Competition Commission shone its torchlight on supermarkets' treatment of suppliers in 2000, it recommended that action should be taken to correct some of the worst abuses of 'buyer power'. It recommended a code of practice. The Commission did not believe that a voluntary code would be adequate. It concluded that larger supermarkets with 'buyer power', chains with more than 8 per cent market share – Asda, Safeway, Sainsbury, Somerfield and Tesco – should be required by law to comply with a code. It felt it was 'highly desirable' that chains with less than 8 per cent should comply with a code also.

The code that was set up as a result sounded promising. At last, some protection for suppliers from supermarket bullying. But by 2003, only a year after it had been in operation, the code and its conspicuous ineffectiveness in achieving its stated aims had already become something of a bad joke. An expensive one at that: vast amounts of public money had gone into the Competition Commission's deliberations and the consultation and the drawing up of the code by the Office of Fair Trading. Not one single complaint had been made against any supermarket in the year that the code had been in operation. Did this mean that the supermarket superpowers had radically altered their behaviour, leaving suppliers blissfully content? It rapidly emerged that the real state of affairs could not be more different. The resounding silence from suppliers was due to fear. They were simply too scared to complain. Six months after the code had been introduced, Clive Beddall summed up what was happening in *The Grocer*:

Anyone who believed that suppliers, large or small, would complain was living in cloud-cuckoo-land, given the understandable fear amongst farmers in particular, of retribution from the high street giants ... In confidential conversations I have had with suppliers recently ... it appears that pressured buyers from the multiples have increased the unreasonable use of their powers since the code was unveiled ... The claims point the finger at two of the Big Four and three so-called second tier retailers which currently are not covered by the code ... Some buyers at least are laughing at the code to the tune of umpteen thousands of pounds in unexpected demands.

In February 2003, a month before the code celebrated its first birthday, complaints arose against Safeway. A number of supermarket suppliers contacted *The Grocer*, accusing Safeway of demanding 'outrageous' cash sums. Here is an edited extract of one of the letters published. The name and address were supplied but withheld by *The Grocer* for obvious reasons.

Having supplied Safeway for many years, we have got used to the delisting threats and extra demands as Safeway's year-ends approach, but this year-end is quite exceptional ... Safeway's management is working hard to extract the last penny from its suppliers by threatening to delist and introduce new suppliers who are prepared to pay handsomely for the privilege ... Demands for six figure payments (in cash and by the end of March, if you please) breach the government's code of practice, but no matter. Safeway's suppliers, who have had to manage numerous other breaches, are not expected to do anything about that, as any report to the Office of Fair Trading could damage their business even more.

Safeway vigorously denied all the allegations. 'We are not making cash demands,' said its director of communications, Kevin Hawkins. 'It is laid out in our terms and conditions, which are in accordance with the OFT code of practice, that we may "request" directly or indirectly, lump sums from suppliers. These could support promotions, new products, or cover the retailer's risk if sales of a new product did not come up to scratch . . . Where it is reasonable, we may request money from suppliers to cover artwork, packaging, refurbishments and so on.'

So who was right? From the detail of the code, it looked as though Safeway might have had a point. The code of practice that had finally emerged from the Office of Fair Trading following consultations, or what Friends of the Earth preferred to refer to as 'close liaison' with the supermarkets, was a very pale shadow of the Competition Commission's recommendations. No sooner had the code of practice been made public than it was criticised as being toothless and woolly. Non-supermarket interests thought their submissions to the Office of Fair Trading had been ignored. The National Farmers Union, for example, said that the code would leave farmers and growers bitter and angry. 'None of the critical points made by the NFU in its submission have been taken into account. The result is that it could still be open to wide interpretation by the retailers.'

So what were the bones of contention? Top of the list came the fact that the code was voluntary, not legally binding as the Competition Commission had recommended. Then there was its limited scope. It applied only to the then Big Four (Tesco, Sainsbury's, Asda and Safeway). It did not apply to suppliers who sell to supermarkets through an intermediary, such as a packer. Neither did it cover suppliers of plants or flowers, described by the NFU as 'a vulnerable group'. And then there was the wording itself. In the code's twelve pages – it was a remarkably slight document given the task it had set itself – every prohibition to supermarkets was hedged with qualifying words. 'Reasonable/reasonably/unreasonably' appeared eighteen times. Any reader seeking elucidation of what was meant by 'reasonable' would not find it in the footnotes because the OFT had not defined it, saying that it 'depends on the circumstances of each case'. As one food manufacturer remarked, 'If you are a small supplier negotiating with a retailer with more than 15 per cent of the market, you can bet it's not you who defines what is "reasonable" ... If you don't like it, you can lump it.' The qualifying term 'unless' also turned up twelve times. The document was peppered with phrases such as 'in good faith', 'with due care' and 'transparent', all of which were so open to different interpretations that they could easily be used to let the supermarket off the hook. Waitrose, not a signatory to the code, subsequently remarked that the code was 'heavily weighted in favour of the buyer and lacked enforcement mechanisms'.

No wonder, then, that the word from both suppliers and supermarket buyers was that, despite the code of practice, it was business as usual. When senior executives of supplier companies were polled in May 2003, 83 per cent said the code had had no effect on the buyer behaviour of the big chains. This was not just supplier whingeing, for a month later the Competition Commission itself confirmed that situation, and went a bit further. 'Evidence received to date suggests that for the vast majority of suppliers, the code of practice has made no difference to their negotiating position with the large supermarkets. For those who thought that it made a difference, more thought that it had made the position worse than thought it made it better.' In September, the House of Commons Environment, Food and Rural Affairs Committee reinforced the Commission's assessment in its 'Gangmaster' report (so called because it criticised the supermarkets for fostering an environment which allows gangmasters to recruit foreign casual workers who are paid a pittance to pick fruit and vegetables). 'The evidence we received in the course of this inquiry suggests that the code of practice has failed ... A more interventionist approach may now be needed,' it concluded.

Later that month, the Competition Commission published its long-awaited report on the sale of Safeway and a possible merger with other supermarket chains, which concluded that '... the code of practice has not been working to protect suppliers. This suggests that, given that buyer power will increase as a result of the acquisition of Safeway, the situation would worsen for suppliers if the code remains substantially in its present form.' *The Grocer* summed up suppliers' verdict on the code as 'a waste of space'. When suppliers were asked 'Is the code of practice workable?', 81 per cent said no and 75 per cent thought there should be an independent ombudsman to regulate the activities of the multiples.

Far from improving matters, it seemed that the code had actually made matters worse.

SUPERMARKET WORLD

25

Pruning horticulture

Secretts pick-your-own, garden centre and farm shop in Milford, Surrey, was formerly one of many large vegetable-growing concerns in what was once a highly productive growing area. The sign you see as you approach proudly reads 'Growers since 1908'. The original Secretts was set up then by Frederick Augustus Secrett, one of the most influential figures in early twentieth-century British horticulture, who had six farms spread throughout Surrey, Kent and Cornwall. Secretts is an impressive place. Behind a huddle of red-tiled, black wooden buildings surrounded by clipped yew hedges sit elegant glasshouses the size of a football pitch. Frederick Augustus's grandchildren still run it, but it is a very different business from that in their grandfather's day. Once Secretts was a grower pure and simple. But as supermarkets have stamped their mark on UK horticulture it has had to diversify in order to survive.

Now Secretts grows a range of salads and other crops such as asparagus, squash, sweetcorn and flowers. These are either snapped up by restaurants or sold direct to the public through the farm shop. The latter has the square footage of a small city-centre supermarket, but the range on offer is refreshingly different from that which you routinely see on supermarket shelves. It is a seductive showcase for Secretts' own ultra-fresh produce and that of other local producers and small-scale suppliers: about 20,000 different lines. Shopping in Secretts would make you optimistic that there still is a future for British agriculture, that it can be productive and bountiful. It shows that there are still many British artisans and small producers who can produce great food.

But as Charles Secrett told me, it is one of the few local growers that have survived the last thirty difficult years for UK horticulture. 'The supermarkets have presided over the virtual decimation of the Thames Valley as a rich, varied horticultural production area,' he said. What happened?

In the 1960s and early 1970s Thames Valley really was one of the foremost areas for horticultural production in the country. We grew butterhead, cos, Webb's Wonderful, Little Gem lettuces, a full range of brassicas – spring greens through to purple sprouting broccoli – spinach, beetroot, all the root crops, globe and Jerusalem artichokes, celery, celeriac, angelica and herbs like parsley and mint, carrots, spring onions . . . there was an enormous diversity of crops. With the backing of the National Farmers Union, Thames Valley Vegetable Growers was set up. It had seventy members, all thriving vegetable growers in the area, and this didn't represent the total number of growers, just those who chose to join.

Initially the supermarkets offered a very good outlet. You were able to meet their specifications and protocols without ridiculous levels of input. They would also pay a reasonable price. Then they started changing the face of the crops we grew. Outdoor butterhead lettuce was one of the very first to go. Supermarkets just didn't want to handle it because it was dirty, it didn't look right for them and they wanted a glasshouse grown lettuce. So we lost one of the nicest types of lettuce that you could ever hope to eat. They didn't want crops like Swiss chard or large-leaf spinach because it was far too bulky. They only wanted leeks with eleven inches of white and one inch of green, and so on.

The supermarkets very quickly increased their share of the market, which meant that the wholesale markets lost a lot of volume. You still had growers using the wholesale market as their outlet but there weren't enough buyers around to take it [the quantity of produce]. So prices were consistently depressed, year after year. Growers either had to align themselves with supermarkets or go into catering, which is very fragmented. If you sold through a packer to a supermarket, you would get a fairly low price. The alternative was to go to the supermarket direct.

In the early 1980s supermarkets would still talk to you if you could offer a crop which they were struggling to source. They would encourage you but slowly the requirements would get tougher and tougher. You had to get bigger to supply them because supermarket X wanted carrots that are six inches long and an inch in diameter and supermarket Y wanted carrots that are five inches long and three-quarters of an inch in diameter. You'd grown this crop with a spectrum of sizes and you needed three or four supermarkets to cover the size spectrum to sell your crop.

By the late 1980s things got really cutthroat. The supermarkets started to knock out the smaller growers who they were not interested in and focus more on the large ones. Growers were partly at fault because they weren't very good at getting together to present a united front. Supermarkets were playing one grower off against another and promising things that wouldn't materialise. You'd go into partnership with a supermarket one year with a major growing programme, only to be told you wouldn't be needed next year. You had made all the investment but they said that if you wanted to supply them, you had to do it through another company. All they were doing was looking for fewer suppliers and bigger volume.

That process hasn't stopped and now supermarkets are focused on sourcing from organisations that have gone beyond being producer-based, conglomerates that can source product from anywhere round the world. Unless you are an enormous player in this country, they really aren't interested. Now there's all this talk about sourcing local food. We've heard it so many times. It's a great appeasement to the public at large but in practice, it doesn't happen. And now there's hardly anyone left to source it from anyway. Of the seventy growers who were originally members of Thames Valley Vegetable Growers, for example, there are no more than five still growing. It would be impossible to start up this type of business now because our skills have been decimated, so it's difficult to find skilled labour.

Before the supermarkets arrived, we were self-sufficient in vegetables here in the UK. The supermarkets have destroyed British horticulture. The chink of light for growers who have hung on is that over the last five years, we've noticed that more shoppers are fed up with clinical supermarket produce that looks good but tastes dreadful when you take it out of its crinkly polypropylene film. They are looking for produce like they used to be able to buy. A sector of the public is clamouring for the real article. You only have to eat English asparagus and compare it with the imported equivalent to realise what a difference there is. But as long as people continue to buy their fruit and vegetables in supermarkets, I really do not think that UK growing has much of a future.

Although like many other once-productive areas of the country Surrey was well appointed with supermarkets, the sad tale of the Thames Valley growers showed that very few local growers were managing to supply them. So where was all the growing for supermarkets happening in the UK? Browsing through Tesco's recipe magazine – strapline: 'passionate about food' – I got a clue about where to look. The magazine featured an article about Tesco's celeriac (one of the crops that Thames Valley Vegetable Growers used to grow) and Tesco's current supplier, Jack Buck Growers, who was based near Spalding in Lincolnshire. 'The company must be doing something right,' it read, 'because Jack

Buck now produces 80% of this country's celeriac crop.' One grower produces four fifths of the entire national supply of celeriac, which is then sold by just a handful of retailers? OK, celeriac isn't quoted in the UK's Favourite Veg Top Ten, but was this happening with more everyday crops too? A quick look through government horticultural statistics confirmed that a lot of vegetables were being grown in Lincolnshire. In 1998 – the most recent year for which figures were available – Lincolnshire and Nottinghamshire combined produced 56.7 per cent of the cauliflower, 53.5 per cent of the winter cabbage and 68.3 per cent of all the calabrese (broccoli) grown in England and Wales. I decided to go and see the area for myself.

Driving along the road from Boston to Spalding, I had no trouble believing that this was the brassica capital of the UK, if not the world. It felt like being on a boat on a dark green ocean. On either side of the road lay vast tracts of land, seemingly stretching to the horizon, undulating with neat, green waves of leafy crops: sprouts, broccoli and cabbage. These were punctuated by the odd taller, blacker crop of trendy cavolo nero, doubtless destined for some supermarket boutique vegetable range, and vivid orange pumpkins. Locals informed me that there used to be signs by the road saying 'Grown for Asda' and so on, but these had been taken down. Perhaps they invited graffiti, or alternatively the knowledge that these crops were being grown for supermarkets was so obvious to locals that it didn't need saying.

Pretty much the only things that broke up this landscape were sprawling clusters of glasshouses, filled with indoor crops like tomatoes or the odd field-scale crop trial. Lincolnshire is prime horticultural research-and-development territory. Some of these are trials of genetically modified crops. In the first round of GM field-scale evaluations begun in 1999, Spalding was host to three. Throughout Lincolnshire as a whole, there were twenty-one.

This fen country, traditionally know as blackland, has rich

peaty soil, known as Grade I agricultural land. It is the ultimate growing medium for intensive crop production, perfect for the anchorage of plant roots and the soaking up of chemical fertilisers and pesticides. It is the sort of soil that seems almost inexhaustible. You can farm it intensively, crop after crop, with little or no fallowing. Areas with poorer soil could not take this level of commercial exploitation: as with oil or coal, the soil's fertility would eventually run out. But here, although cracks in its perfection are now showing in the form of soil erosion and reduced fertility, volume production of uniform, pesticide-manicured vegetables destined for supermarkets is the order of the day. The general flatness of the land helps too. It lends itself to big fields that can be laser levelled, a practice which farmers tell me results in fewer rejections or 'pack-outs' by supermarkets. These nice big fields allow more mechanisation, the use of machines to cut and pick up the vegetables – work previously done by hand.

Everything seemed big here, not just the fields. As I approached Spalding from the north, the oceans of brassicas gave way to a sea of windowless industrial warehouses whose grey shimmery roofs shone out from far off, making Spalding look more like a sprawling industrial estate than a pleasant market town. As it began to rain heavily, I lost my way and pulled in to consult the map in the car park of a local pub called the Packing Shed, an apt name and a clue to the main business of Spalding. Nowadays, these warehouses are home to a number of companies more or less dedicated to supplying our supermarkets. The business has gone way beyond just hi-tech packing: now the companies' facilities include sophisticated chilled distribution, nitrogen generators for 'controlled atmosphere' storage, pre-pack equipment, grading machines, water flotation tanks, ripening rooms, chill-blasting and rack storage. Suppliers can no longer afford to do only one thing well. To be sure of keeping supermarket business and remain on the shrinking list of supermarket suppliers, they have to add value. So if these warehouses are not HQ for the production of those hauntingly familiar garlic baguettes, or herbs in pots, or puffed-up salad bags and stir-fry kits, they are producing that familiar supermarket coleslaw, those dips that look and taste oddly similar from chain to chain, pizzas, ready meals, soups, sauces, deli-style salads or even sushi. If you see a warehouse-factory around Spalding that is not churning out prepared, chilled food or cut flowers, or bottling, freezing or canning food for supermarkets, there is an odds-on chance that it is dedicated to providing packaging for them, or labels, or machinery; or that it is maintaining equipment or servicing the trucks that transport the whole shooting match. Flick through the local business listings for Spalding and you will marvel at how a small fenland town has become a strategic nerve centre for supermarket supply.

These companies sell themselves in mission statements that stress their ability to give large retailers an all-year-round supply of 'innovative' products. These are made possible by their alliances with large, powerful agricultural trading consortia abroad. They pull product in from Spain, Holland, Israel, New Zealand and South Africa to be processed in their state-of-the-art factories. Those articulated lorries that thunder along narrow Lincolnshire roads are not just picking up local cabbage and leaving it at a nearby factory to be made into coleslaw. Effectively, Spalding has become a 365-days-a-year one-stop shop for supermarkets, a huge infrastructure underpinning a supermarket-dictated supply chain that has less and less to do with anything local.

Theoretically, though, it should be good for jobs, all this value-added activity. Certainly as I passed through nearby Tunnel Bank, there was a large sign outside Bourne Stir-Fry, 'Recruiting now ... Come in and find out more'. These days, if you live around Spalding, you are more likely to have a job chopping up Spanish Lollo Rosso or Dutch red peppers in a factory than you are to be working the land. One local farmer told me that because he grew organically he needed to employ more people proportionately than the big, highly mechanised intensive grow-ers. Commonly his workers were the younger members of what had formerly been farming families, who had been forced to give up largely because supermarkets had eradictated the outlets – independent greengrocers and wholesale markets – that had given them an outlet for their produce. Other locals told me how many of the casual, seasonal agricultural jobs that were once performed by local women as second earners were now being carried out by casual workers from abroad, of every nationality from Lithu-anians to Iraqi Kurds, who were often bused in en masse from Peterborough and Rotherham. The House of Commons Environ-ment, Food and Rural Affairs Committee highlighted this situ-ation in its 2003 report on casual labour in the horticultural industry. It said that largely because of supermarkets' 24-hours-a-day, 365-days-a-year demands, 'local communities can no longer supply the volume of labour and flexibility of labour required'.

As I spoke to many people in and around Spalding, I kept picking up a strong undercurrent of resentment at the grip that supermarkets have on the area. In 2002, MP John Hayes expressed these sentiments when he gave this rousing account of the issues raised by his constituents in the area in the House of Commons.

That [observation] brings me to . . . the power of the supermarkets – I would go as far as to say, the pernicious power of the super-markets – over producers . . . I believe that supermarkets are commercially capricious. They know no loyalty to most of their suppliers. Of course the suppliers cannot say so because they would be talking about their customers, but I can say it . . . The truth is that supermarkets have distorted the relationship between producer, retailer and consumer. They have done more than any other agency to damage the business of local supply . . . Unless the government face[s] up to the issue of the unaccountable power of a handful of retailers, we shall not address the problems of the relationship between producers and consumers, or re-establish in the consumer base a degree of market intelligence ... I suggest that supermarkets have produced a situation where people neither know the price nor the value of good food. That needs to be addressed by this government – or by a government – as soon as possible.

Smouldering discontentment with some supermarkets even seems to be affecting some of their largest suppliers. Sir John Banham, chairman of Geest PLC, a company well represented in and around the Spalding area, turning over approximately £800 million, 90 per cent of which is with the major grocery retailers, wrote to the Competition Commission in 2003 to outline some of the company's concerns. Some UK retailers, he told the Commisssion, lacking the scale and ability to pursue the 'Every Day Low Pricing' strategy begun by Asda, were 'suffering competitive and financial pressures in consequence as demonstrated by share price reductions ... The more marginal UK retailers, who had not been able to contrive an effective partnership sourcing approach, had responded by putting pressure on their suppliers.' Tactics included demanding upfront payments to keep existing business, creating phantom bids at e-auctions (internet auctions – see Chapter 28), demanding recompense for 'lost profit' if the supplier failed to meet the entirety of the order, demanding, without consultation, a disproportionate supplier's 'contribution' to the retailer's promotional costs and requiring that a supplier from whom the retailer might receive overriding discounts or payments should be used for items such as packaging and transport. He concluded: 'The practices listed above, taken to extremes, could undermine the financial health of suppliers and compromise their ability to innovate. This would lead, inevitably, to job losses, more imports, lower wages and lower incomes for local growers.'

Curiously, Spalding is the place where supermarket electronic bar codes made their debut back in 1977 – an event that heralded their connection with each other. Supermarkets and Spalding seem to go together. But I can't help getting the impression that the supermarket food revolution has proved to be a mixed blessing for those living and working around Spalding. Wherever you go in the area, you cannot avoid seeing the profound imprint left by supermarkets on both the natural and built environments. But the industry all makes perfect business sense to our large chains. In place of an irritating multiplicity of growers of various types and scale, well distributed throughout the country, they like big 'efficient' clusters, vast tracts of monoculture adjacent to packhouses and other value-added infrastructure, strategically situated close to trunk roads, ports and airports to smooth the passage of produce imported from all over the world. Our supermarkets like a system more tuned to buying trimmed South American asparagus all year round than local spears in season. Spalding could well be a harbinger of things to come. If the supermarkets' grip on the nation's food supply tightens further, all round the country there will be a few intense pockets of supermarket sourcing activity while large areas of the countryside produce nothing. Smaller food producers throughout Britain will face a choice, just like Thames Valley Vegetable Growers: attempt to join the supermarket rat race or be frozen out of production.

26

Market grab

Even when it opens for business at three o'clock in the morning, New Covent Garden Market is a strangely eerie place. Outside its gates, on the Nine Elms Road, stands a confident sign, 'New Covent Garden – The Larder of London'. When you see the set-up inside, this sounds a bit like wishful thinking. Once you pass through a manned security barrier which looks a bit like a rather shabby motorway toll station, you see several parking areas, clearly built to accommodate many more vehicles than now occupy it. Just over the back wall looms the well-lit, security-patrolled bulk of a giant Sainsbury's.

Traditionally, Covent Garden Market was a supremely important wholesale market. It was a funnel for produce destined for wholesale markets throughout Britain. It was also London's greengrocer. In a sense it still is, but only for those citizens who eat in restaurants: the fruit and vegetable pavilion, which hums with nocturnal retail activity, is now focused almost exclusively on supplying the restaurant trade. 'We got into catering to survive,' one longstanding stallholder explained.

A stroll around this pavilion is an eye-opener. Here I saw fruit and vegetables that made me feel hungry, produce with the sensual properties we asssociate with foreign food markets – a reminder of what a varied selection of mature, highly perishable fruits and vegetables in peak condition looks like. What was striking was the high percentage produced by UK growers. Boxes of parsley with a carpet-like thickness of pile, freshly cut, tight-headed ice-packed broccoli, purple-tinged Savoy cabbages, leafy green bunches of watercress, large Golden Wonder and knobbly Pink Fir Apple potatoes, Cornish greens and purple blush turnips were a dazzling confirmation of just how impressive and appetite-whetting seasonal UK produce can be. The stands of the traders specialising in imported produce added another dimension. Crimson Pachino and green Camone tomatoes, scented Amalfi lemons, moist, unsugared Deglet Nour dates, Italian strawberry grapes, burgundy-white striped Trevisana and delicate eau-de-nil blanched chicories . . . This was produce radically different from the imports on supermarket shelves.

Charlie Hicks, presenter of Radio 4's *Veg Talk*, who works for the Covent Garden wholesaler Lenards, explained to me what I was seeing. 'There are now two trades in fruit and vegetables in the UK. There's supermarkets, where so much is inedible, unripe, all about shipping quality not flavour, and then there's wholesale markets supplying greengrocers and restaurants where you can still get great stuff.' Mr Hicks said that if he tried to sell chefs he supplies supermarket-style produce, he would be laughed out of their kitchens and rapidly lose their business. Think about the traditional Italian recipe for peaches stuffed with amaretti, for example. For this you need large, mature fruits. It won't work properly with the peaches you see in UK supermarkets. He explained:

All summer we see really nice ripe stone fruit coming through New Covent Garden because we deal with different sorts of growers. But you won't see it in supermarkets. Ripe fruit doesn't fit in with their distribution systems. They don't care about flavour, just shipping quality. Small producers can't get a look-in with supermarkets, as you have to be able to supply the whole of the

UK. Supermarkets are getting lazier and lazier in their sourcing, relying on their category managers to do all the work for them. They are incapable of handling fresh produce in the way that good wholesalers or greengrocers can.

Unfortunately for those who like to eat fruit and vegetables and are enthusiastic – at least in principle – about eating those recommended five portions a day, supermarkets well and truly control the nation's fruit and vegetables. In the early seventies, New Covent Garden was a vibrant place and traditional wholesale markets like it around the country traded 90 per cent of fresh horticultural produce in the UK, servicing greengrocers and market stalls. Since then the supermarkets have increased their share of the UK's fruit and vegetable sales to 83 per cent, the highest level in the European Union. In that process, they have shrunk wholesale and local markets.

New Covent Garden is a testament to our supermarkets' appropriation of the UK's fruit and vegetable spend. When Covent Garden Market moved from its eponymous home and became 'New' Covent Garden in 1974, it consisted of two big fruit and vegetable halls with four rows of traders or 'buyer's walks' supplying other wholesale markets, market stalls and greengrocers. Now only one hall is open.

Peter Jacobs, a retired buying agent at New Covent Garden, charted for me how this once mighty market became a shadow of its former self.

I started work in our family firm in 1948 buying fruit for other wholesale markets throughout Britain. In the traditional market trade, the seasons were an important aspect of the trade. After strawberries, in late summer the cherries and plums came in, followed in early autumn by apples and pears. These lasted until Christmas. They were then followed by southern hemisphere fruit and also some from Canada. These were known as 'Imperial

Preference' as they were allowed into the country free of duty. Fruit from other sources had to pay tariffs to protect British growers. Fruits from South America were almost unknown.

By the 1970s, supermarkets began to appear buying on the markets. At first we welcomed them as another customer. We were happy at first, delighted even. But they soon became very picky, selecting only certain sizes of fruit. As an example, both oranges and apples are graded to about a dozen different sizes. The supermarkets, with their large orders, would clear the most popular sizes from the market, leaving other traders the less popular counts. The supermarkets soon discovered our supply sources and began buying direct, quickly forcing the growers to cater for their needs. They would buy fruit direct from the docks, have it sent to their packing depot, hold it for a fortnight then reject what they didn't want. So this fruit would come back on to the market and it was flooded with substandard fruit.

But supermarkets wave a big stick, and by the 1980s they had a stranglehold. From then on they started cutting out dealing with importing boards and began to go direct to growers. By the 1990s, supermarkets controlled so much that they were sourcing from volume growers abroad. It was far easier for them to import their tonnage of apples, for example, from Chile or New Zealand than bother with English ones. They would only come to the market occasionally when a supplier let them down. I once sold a large supermarket chain 5,000 boxes of French Golden Delicious, all of one stipulated size. I organised five articulated lorryloads to send to their distribution depot and they rejected it. The lorry driver told me that they didn't even look at the apples because their own supply had turned up. This way of doing business was so different from the traditional market. It was an honourable trade where people helped and trusted one another.

In the financial year 1989–1990, New Covent Garden turned over £231 million of fruit and vegetables. A decade later that figure was just £151 million. Traditional wholesale fruit markets up and down the land are in much the same general position. Some towns and cities have lost their wholesale markets altogether. A few have got slightly busier as independent shopkeepers are forced to drive further afield to get a supply from the more thriving markets that still handle a substantial volume of produce. The bottom line everywhere is that supermarkets have done grievous bodily harm to the institution of the wholesale market, once a key structural link in a supply chain that fed the nation through independent greengrocers. Wholesale markets continue to operate for the time being, but massively under capacity. They mop up residual consumer fruit and vegetable spend and offer a limited outlet for smaller-scale growers who won't or can't supply supermarkets. They offer a home for 'Grade 2' produce – fruit and vegetables that are perfectly wholesome but are too mature, too varied, too fleetingly seasonal or insufficiently uniform to catch the supermarkets' eyes. But they depend on catering and restaurants for viability.

27

A perfect world

A sense of humour, growers and packers promised me, was the only special attribute I'd require when interpreting a supermarket's fruit or vegetable specification. This is the document, usually three to five sides of A4 paper, which growers receive from a supermarket stipulating the size, shape, colour, general appearance and presentation of the produce to be supplied. These documents are meant to be confidential but several growers forwarded them to me anyway. 'You'll have a laugh,' they said and they were right. But the humour is black. The specifications spell out our supermarkets' vision of a perfect world where all produce is groomed to beauty pageant standards. Remember the gleaming red apple the wicked queen gave to Snow White? (She should have known better than eat it. It looked like a supermarket class 1 McRed.) Or those fake ornamental fruits and vegetables you can buy as an alternative to a floral display? Think of the plastic kind that gather dust in time-warped restaurants. That's the sort of produce our supermarkets are after.

Supermarket specifications are the horticultural equivalent of body fascism, a ruthless rooting-out of all that is non-uniform, however common or normal. The truly terrifying thing about them, and the people who conceive them, is their cavalier disregard for the realities of the natural world. Not all pears mature to the same size. Grow radishes yourself and you'll harvest everything from lozenge shapes to gobstoppers. Left to their own devices, grapes don't sort themselves into bunches weighing 350 grams and tomatoes don't present themselves in neat groups of six to a stem. Plums have sticky sappy bits. Some apples have russety humps. Courgettes and cucumbers can be as curvy as the thighs of one of Matisse's models. But supermarkets want to override all that. Fruit and vegetables are not naturally amenable to supermarkets' industrial approach to their products, so they have to be reformulated to fit.

Supermarket fresh produce specifications all share broadly the same criteria. Supermarkets only really deal in what the European Union classifies as 'Grade 1' or 'Extra' produce. That means produce without any visible flaws conforming to measurements set to reflect the ideal visual specimen. On occasion, supermarkets might accept 'Grade 2' produce, say for organic fruits that cannot meet cosmetic standards because organic growers are not allowed to use pesticides applied for the sake of appearance. But several organic growers told me that they were expected to meet the same cosmetic standards set for conventional produce. Grade 2 is a more flexible standard for produce that is fine to eat, but may not all conform to size or grading standards. However, as far as our supermarkets are concerned, Grade 2 produce is generally only fit for the wholesale fruit and vegetable market since it is insufficiently manicured to meet their pernickety requirements.

Supermarket specifications routinely cover the variety to be grown, where it should come from, how it should be stored, 'quality' standards and presentation. Take tomatoes, for example. Examination of several chains' specifications made it clear that the first matter of concern is variety. Varieties must be agreed with the retailer prior to planting. One chain was explicit about what it was looking for. 'Varieties are to be selected for optimum appearance, flavour and shelf life.' There was no mention of any possible contradiction between the last two requirements. But growers told me that they had learned to interpret these requirements as 'Don't worry too much about taste as long as the tomatoes look good.'

The next criterion is size. One chain stipulated a size of 53–63 millimetres (mm) in circumference, another 47–57 mm or 57–67 mm. Whatever the chain, tomatoes had to fit within a 10mm band. (For those who struggle to envisage measurements, that is less than the nail on a girl's pinkie or about twice the length of a rubber eraser on a pencil.) In other words, all tomatoes in the pack must be more or less the same size.

Then we come to appearance, by far the most substantial section in the specifications I saw. Some chains accompany their specifications with a separate colour chart or photographic specification manual. One chain wanted the colour of the tomatoes to be within a range of 4–7 on its colour chart, another stipulates 5–7, while a third chain was even more specific, stipulating 'colour stage 4–5 aiming for stage 5'. All chains seemed to agree that every tomato should have its calyx (the green stemmy bit) attached. Anyone with experience of tomatoes can tell you that when tomatoes are ripe, the calyx detaches itself more often than not.

On the 'organoleptic' or flavour front, the tomato specifications were vague, rarely being more expansive than remarks like 'good balance between sugar and acid'. By contrast, the list of blemishes disallowed was copious and detailed. Generally these were broken down into 'major' and 'minor' blemishes and possible 'tolerances', usually 5–10 per cent, for each category. The word 'tolerances', as far as most growers are concerned, means that on a good day, and if it really needs the supply, the supermarket might just accept them; but if it wants to be difficult or has a stock of tomatoes building up, it will almost certainly use the blemishes as an excuse to reject them.

The specifications showed that growers have precious little room for manoeuvre. With any of the following 'faults' the tomatoes would almost certainly be rejected:

- more than 5 per cent of the tomatoes not uniform in size
- light scarring or blemishes
- ribbed, angular or misshapen tomatoes
- a colour of 0, 1, 2 or 7 on the supermarket's colour chart
- slightly chewy skin
- soft tender tomatoes
- tomatoes at different colour stages in the same box.

One chain delineated its dream-ticket tomato to which growers should aspire as follows. In a pack of four tomatoes, each fruit should be at colour stage 5, uniform in shape and size, 100 per cent firm with zero major or minor blemishes. Another chain sent out mixed messages concerning colour – one indication of ripeness – and maturity. The tomatoes must be 'mature enough to meet colour requirements but must not be soft and bladdery ... The development and condition of the tomatoes must be such as to enable them to withstand transport and handling and to arrive in satisfactory condition at the place of destination.'

The ability to withstand transport and handling is clearly a paramount concern. One chain spelt out what it meant by 'product life'. 'The tomato should be capable of providing an instore life of 4 days plus a customer life of 3 days. Time from harvest to arrival into depot for British grown products should not exceed 3 days ... for imported, 3 days from receipt in to stock.' In other words, the chain expects a total life of ten days for its home-grown tomatoes, adding on a couple of days more for imported ones. Another chain specified a total shelf life – from the day of packing until the 'use by' date – of eleven days.

Pity UK tomato growers – and their colleagues further afield in tomato-exporting countries – trying to make sense of this little lot. Firm but not too firm. Soft but not oversoft. Red but not over-ripe. An acid/sugar balance, but with a shelf life of eleven days, not allowing for packing or any delivery time that might involve. Red and presumably ripe, yet all calyxes firmly attached. Identikit sizes and shapes.

Looking over specifications for other produce, I saw that they had the same preoccupations, echoing our supermarkets' desire to stamp their master race template on everything in sight, even crops like onions and cooking apples which will be chopped up to be cooked. They documented our supermarkets' insistence on treating food like an industrial product that can be produced over and over and over again. The size range for dessert apples, for example, was 60–75 mm. Within that range, they had to be graded into 10 mm bands. 'Slight uneven colour outside stated range' or a 'red colour too brown' or a 'russet in the stem cavity' or '10% of fruit either too green, too yellow' or 'misshapen fruit more than 10 mm offset' could trigger rejection. The skin on Fuji apples should be 'pale yellow/green with a minimum 30% block or striped red coloration'. Heaven help any Fuji grower whose apples have only 29 per cent! Waxy fruit – a natural feature of many native English varieties – is 'not acceptable'. Minor defects should not exceed a 'maximum of 2 square cm per fruit in 10% of sample'. On potatoes the requirements were just as picky. Most chains agreed that 50–80 centimetres (cm) was the optimum size, though one wanted a tighter range of 50–65 cm. When did you last take a ruler to your spuds? Potatoes might be rejected because of 'slightly uneven grading'. If in doubt about the 'skin finish' deemed appropriate, growers and packers were told to refer to their photographic specifications. On broccoli, not only the head size was specified, but also the stalk diameter: 'stalk diameter 5cm, head diameter 7–12 cm'.

Some of the specifications for organic products were particularly exacting. Take broccoli, for example. 'To conform to EC Class 1 standards, broccoli is to be free from defects and be fresh in appearance. Heads should be fully turgid, firm and compact with a uniform, attractive blue-green colour and tightly grained. The buds must be fully closed and no bronzing. Stems to be cut cleanly at right angles. No pest infestation. Holes in the butt tolerated between 5 and 10 mm.' Another supermarket packer listed 'purpling on the head' as a possible cause for rejection.

Much space in the specifications was given to final presentation. Any fruit or vegetable might be rejected because of a 'secure but slightly out of position seal' or even an 'off centre' label. Cauliflowers had to have 'one ring of outer leaf, top trimmed at shoulder of curd [the white bit] and clasping leaves removed'.

The name of the game, then, is varieties selected for their cosmetic attributes that can offer good shelf life. Flavour is of secondary importance and true freshness of the produce – that is, produce that is ripe, mature and perishable – is an impossibility.

Suppliers explained to me the sort of horticultural practice that such specifications breed. Their philosophy is one of extreme conformity and no risk taking. Growers come up with produce that keeps the supermarket quality controller happy; the consumer is not their prime concern. Consequently most growing decisions – variety, method of cultivation, time of harvesting – are taken so as to ensure produce that meets cosmetic standards.

One carrot grower who dealt with a supermarket through a packer explained to me:

If you have some perfectly wholesome Siamese twin carrots or organic carrots that have the merest hint of entirely benign 'silvering' it isn't even worth harvesting them if your client is a supermarket. They want pretty well identical carrots. We use more pesticides than we'd like to try to meet the cosmetic standards set. Anything that reduces the appearance will increase the proportion rejected. Even so, a typical 'pack-out' [rejection] might be 35 per cent of what we send.

Another supplier commented: 'They want a perfect product that will keep for a week because they have encouraged that one-stop, once-a-week shopping pattern. But trying to make quality last a week logically leads to more pesticides, genetic modification of varieties, even irradiation because that's the only way you can hold [stock] product looking OK for all that time.' A case in point is a government-funded project currently under way at Horticultural Research International (HRI) to extend the shelf life of broccoli. Crop scientists are 'investigating the genes and individual compounds of the vegetable and looking at factors that determine why the keeping qualities of individual varieties vary' because supermarkets find that they can keep it on the shelf for only two days before it yellows and goes floppy. Already, one grower told me, supermarkets put pressure on suppliers to produce a year-round supply of cauliflowers by 'forcing early cauliflowers and growing others later and later in the year using artificial light, heat and management techniques'. I heard that research was under way with Cox's apples to see if their natural slight russeting could be got rid of.

With their specifications, as well as measures, pressure probes and finely tuned electronic grading machines that can detect even the tiniest variation in colour, size and shape, supermarkets are the main drivers in horticulture these days.

One reader wrote to me complaining that she had a good mind to report Sainsbury's to her local Trading Standards Office for advertising their nectarines and peaches as 'ripe and juicy'. 'They were rock hard,' she wrote, 'and of course, cold to the touch' – a description that probably resonates with supermarket shoppers up and down the land. But a packer explained to me such action is uncommon: UK consumers rarely complain about produce that is picked 'green and backward' or which has no flavour. (This could be because consumers think that taste is too subjective a ground for complaint or simply because they are pragmatic enough to recognise that eating quality is not part of the super-market offer.) On the other hand, he pointed out, the most common cause of rejection by supermarkets is cosmetic.

High levels of rejections or 'pack-outs' show the inherent waste built into the supermarket buying system. When Friends of the Earth surveyed English apple and pear growers in 2002, fewer than a third of respondents said that they managed to meet supermarket specifications for 80 per cent or more of their crop. Everything that is not within supermarkets' narrow cosmetic terms, the cream of the crop, is rejected, and these pack-outs are the grower's problem. A potato grower explained to me:

> Our outgrades [produce that is too big or too small] on standard potatoes may be as high as 20 per cent. With salad and baking potatoes it's worse. The ideal dimension for a salad is 30–40 mm and for bakers it's 65–80 but the variety that produces the salads is different from the one you'd grow for bakers. You can't use the same one. So you have to grow two different varieties then get out riddles and take out bands in the middle. But what do we do with the rest of the crop, which could be as much as 50 per cent? Sometimes the supermarkets will take it as a 'Buy One Get One Free' offer, which means that we are paying for it, or as a 'value pack'. Otherwise, we have to find another outlet.

It is no wonder that to avoid such waste, growers are adapting growing methods to suit supermarket specifications. The operations director of one hi-tech nursery gave this example to *Observer Food Monthly*: 'With Flavorino vine tomatoes, there would be 10 or 12 flowers on each truss but the likes of Sainsbury's want exactly eight tomatoes, so we have to prune. If we left 10 on, the top ones would be too soft and the bottom ones too green – they always ripen from the top – so the supermarkets would reject them. They complain, they warn you, and if it doesn't improve, they reject the whole batch. Since we pay the disposal costs, it pays to get it right.'

One brassica grower told me how he had fallen foul of supermarket specifications.

We were growing for a packer acting on behalf of a supermarket. We usually sent them a 40-foot lorry full of pallets of cauliflower. They sent them back two days later saying that they were rejecting them because they were not white enough. By this point they were three days old, not properly stored and beginning to look tired so it was impossible to find alternative customers for that quantity quickly enough. This happened on half a dozen occasions in the course of a season and in the end they stopped taking our cauliflowers entirely. We were left with a crop planted for them and had to leave it in the field. If the cauliflowers had been poor, we wouldn't blame the packer. The thing that was so distressing though was that they looked perfect. If you saw one, I guarantee you'd like it. We suspected that the packer just had too many cauliflowers and used the slightly creamy colour as an excuse to get out of taking them.

Several growers told me that in their experience supermarkets' computerised ordering systems were less finely tuned than they portrayed them, which led to product backing up in distribution depots, sudden shortages, changed or cancelled orders and last-minute rejections on debatable grounds.

Ginny Mayall, an organic farmer from Shropshire, told *BBC Good Food* magazine of her problems with a supermarket. 'The year before last, we were advised that the supermarket wanted bigger potatoes, so we planted a larger variety. But when it came to harvest, we were told they were too big. We ended up feeding them to our livestock and lost £30,000 at a stroke.' A packer confirmed that supermarket rejections were often arbitrary and whimsical – and gave an example of the draconian penalties (for which there is no appeals process) that supermarkets may inflict. 'Send them potatoes with three spots on and they'll reject them. The quality control people know they're fine but have been told by the buyer to reject them to cover his back. With one particular chain, if there's a problem at the distribution centre and they reject produce, then they charge you an enormous amount of money, tens of thousands of pounds as a fine.' Another potato grower said that in the past a little potato scab did not matter because it left only tiny cosmetic blotches. Now supermarkets rejected potatoes with scab out of hand.

Growers try hard to give supermarkets the perfection they demand in order to limit the likelihood of rejections, but even so they view them as inevitable.

28

Variety is not the spice of life

In UK supermarket produce sections, the concept of 'variety' has a very particular interpretation. It means that on any given day of the year, you should be able to buy as wide a range of different types of fruits and vegetables as possible, irrespective of whether or not they are in season. Anything, any time. Peaches in November, parsnips in May and so on. But there is another sort of variety: biodiversity, or genetic variety. Both at home and abroad, throughout the natural world, there are hundreds of varieties within every fruit or vegetable category. But our supermarkets are totally indifferent to all but the most commercial ones. Genetic variety doesn't suit the way they like to do business. There are, for example, some 2,000 traditional British apple varieties, of which some 100–250 are still in small-scale commercial production somewhere in the UK. But if you shop in UK supermarkets, you'll be lucky if you find any more than a handful. Bramley, Cox, a couple of weeks of Discovery or Fiesta – that's your lot, unless you patronise one of a few flagship stores with a strong AB1 profile, in which case you might get the occasional tantalising glimpse of a few boutique 'heirloom' (rare traditional) varieties at premium prices. Produce shelves are lined with fruit and vegetable varieties that have been selected by supermarkets then dictated to growers not because they taste good, or because they are nutritious, or because consumers want them, but because they are easy to buy and sell.

Take UK strawberries. Our supermarkets love one variety in particular, the accommodating Elsanta. It will emerge from cold store and juggernaut looking lush and glossy. OK, it's as crunchy as most cucumbers and its scent is, well, slight, but supermarket buyers like dealing with Elsanta and have told growers to supply it, cold shouldering more fragile and flavoursome varieties such as Royal Sovereign and Cambridge Vigour. The message has filtered down effectively; now 80 per cent of strawberries grown in the UK are of this one variety. As Tesco enthusiastically put it: 'We work with our growers to select the exact strawberry varieties we want to meet our customers' expectations as much as two years before the plants are even planted!'

Fancy a salad? Then how about a nice iceberg lettuce, pioneered by Marks & Spencer and copied by the supermarket chains, a disaster to eat but a joy to sell. One salad authority described it to me thus: 'Unless it's ultra fresh, it has a bloody awful taste. It goes bitter. It's really a cabbage but supermarkets like it because it's clean, peels off in leaves and keeps in the fridge for ages.'

Going exotic (and why not – the supermarkets have encouraged us to think that a year-round supply of tropical fruit is essential), what about a lovely Tommy Atkin mango? Whether it comes from Brazil, Israel, Venezuela, Mexico, Egypt, Jamaica, Ecuador or any other of the long list of countries supplying mangoes to our exigent supermarkets, odds on it will be a Tommy Atkin. This is an archetypal supermarket variety, developed in the twenties in Florida (that well-known mango-growing area) specifically for export. Supermarkets like it because of its excellent shelf life. It stores for up to three weeks at 13°C. It is a lovely-looking mango – for a designer of twee gift cards, that is, as its overwhelmingly green skin merging with rosy red blushing lends itself to pretty shading. Any mango grower in the world knows that there are literally hundreds of other varieties that are superior in every other respect, with infinitely better flavour and silkier, less fibrous texture. But they might be totally green or yellow, not UK supermarket-approved mango colours. They might possibly have small brown flecks or even, perish the thought, sticky bits. And we all know, because supermarkets have told us so often, how the British shopper freaks out at the mere suspicion of a brown fleck or sticky bit. More to the point, you cannot pick them 'green and backward' and transport them halfway around the world then stick a seven-day 'eat by' date on them as you can do with the ever-obliging Tommy Atkin. So what if they taste like a cross between a stunted honeydew melon and a bendy orange turnip that's languished in the vegetable rack for too long? And when customers eventually give up buying them you can wheel in Tommy's equally tasteless lookalikes, Kent and Keitt, and rebadge them as new 'tree-ripened' mangoes, upping the sale price as you go.

What about a nice juicy plum, that permanent bloody head-ache for the supermarket fruit technologist? Traditional varieties like Victoria or Marjorie Seedling, or greengage, are a nightmare to handle because they bruise easily, even if you instruct pickers to harvest them a fortnight too early and chill them into Siberian oblivion. It is much easier for supermarket buyers to tell suppliers they want a nice, firm, black California-bred Angelino. True, that tough purple-black skin and meaty yellow interior tastes of zilch unless cooked, but Angelinos show no obvious sign of age for weeks. Switch to Angelinos and your waste margins will be slashed.

A former citrus importer told me that Spanish orange growers used to send to the UK many different varieties of orange – Blancas, Oriheulas, Viciedas, Macetaras, Sanguinas and, the most popular of all, oval Jaffa Shamoutis. 'Now they send mainly Navelinas. Supermarkets prefer them because the growers can offer more tonnage and the sizes are easier to control.'

The Dutch horticulture industry has been particularly effective at providing UK supermarkets with exactly the sort of produce they want. When their identikit technopeppers became the butt of New Covent Garden jokes because of their almost cloned uniformity and consumers started complaining, wily Dutch growers obligingly developed the Ramiro pepper, 'specially grown for sweet flavour and unique appearance'. The Spanish-sounding name and the slightly more rustic, though still cosmetically perfect, appearance conjures up images of intrinsically more flavoursome peppers from sunnier climes. But though they retail for a premium, their flavour is no better than the standard Dutch pepper and each looks as perfectly imperfect (thin and pointy) as the next. As one New Covent Garden wag observed, 'Holland is not a Mediterranean country so they get quite a lot of help from the men in white coats.'

Supermarkets adore shiny modern varieties designed to fulfil the dual goals of idealised appearance and shelf life. They have energetically supported new varieties that achieve these goals – Pink Lady, for example, a blushing pink Australian-bred apple with a US patent and consequent plant breeding rights attached to it. For the privilege of cultivating it, growers have to pay a royalty for each tree planted. Another royalty is levied on the company that supplies it to the retailer. But despite this disincentive, and as a result of our supermarkets' patronage, this expensive foreign variety is now as prominent on produce shelves as traditional favourites such as Cox or Bramley.

This ruthless selection of varieties extends to all fruit and vegetables, even those that will be cut up or cooked. One carrot grower told me that to supply supermarkets he has to grow two varieties, Nantucket and Nairobi, because they look the best. But neither are especially tasty varieties; nor were they particularly suited to his soil. Another said: 'The carrots must be F1 hybrids [varieties cross-bred to produce uniform, vigorous and high-yielding offspring] because these can be teased and tweaked into yielding more even-length, uniform specimens with a crown measuring between 28 and 40 millimetres though the natural, non-supermarket carrot range is from 5 to 70 millimetres.' A potato grower confirmed that he too was unable to grow the varieties he'd like, varieties that were historically associated with his area because they grew well there. 'Some of the varieties they [supermarkets] want have shelf life but I'd never bring them home for my dinner. They have no flavour – Nadine is one example. The flavour is dreadful but they look tremendous.' A potato enthusiast explained that there was no point expecting supermarkets to take an interest in oval potato varieties, however flavoursome, because when they were mechanically harvested they wouldn't roll, and would bump and get bruised. Supermarket systems need potatoes to be round.

Supermarkets like not only varieties that look good and lend themselves to supermarket handling and distribution but also those that offer a unique selling point that adds value. Tesco researchers, for example, working with government funding, have introduced the new Supasweet variety of onion. Its selling pitch is that it can be peeled and chopped without bringing tears to the eye, because it releases less pyruvic acid (the substance that makes eyes water). 'It heralds a new era for onions,' Tesco gushed at its launch. The verdict of the resident chef in one newspaper taste test was rather different: 'virtually no flavour . . . a nice texture but that's it . . . not an onion to cook with'. Whatever the fruit or vegetable, the main driver for research and breeding nowadays is the will to reshape the natural order to fit supermarket criteria. That has created a bonanza for bland-tasting, high-yielding F1 hybrid varieties because they fit the supermarket stereotype and perform well when used in conjunction with synthetic fertilisers and pesticides. Often such varieties are genetically very similar – the Pentland group of potatoes or the Snowman/Snowflake cauliflower group, for example. Meanwhile more intrinsically flavoursome, genetically diverse and interesting varieties are disappearing from commercial production, grown only by allotment holders and keen gardeners.

We are rapidly getting to a situation where, looking at any one crop, supermarkets are feeding the nation on only a handful of varieties of any crop, picked from a possible choice of hundreds, and dictating what varieties are grown. The result is not only boring, tasteless uniform produce but a narrowing biodiversity and genetic erosion. As Alan Gear, director of the Henry Doubleday Research Association, which works to defend biodiversity, explained, 'the massive genetic spread that exists in nature is there to safeguard against disease'. The Irish potato famine is just one frightening historical example of how a country's food security can be wrecked when that natural genetic spread is eroded. But as supermarkets stamp their specifications on plant breeders and growers, our genetic base is narrowing by the minute.

29

First stop Europe

In Hradec Kralove in the Czech Republic an international war is being waged. Hradec Kralove is not some tinderbox ethnic-tension hotspot, though, just a prosperous city, the administrative capital of east Bohemia, some forty kilometres from the Polish border. But you don't have to be there for long to notice that a struggle is under way for the loyalties of the town's 100,000 citizens. The war – Tesco v. Carrefour (the French hypermarket chain) and, to a lesser extent, every other supermarket multiple represented in the city (Interspar, Kaufland, Lidl, Penny Market, Hypernova, Plus and several more) – is all around you. Skirmishes start on the trunk roads leading to the town. If you come in from the east, for example, you see a huge billboard flagging Tesco's hypermarket presence some 29 kilometres further along the route. That billboard happens to be right next to a small, discount grocery store, a juxtaposition that is clearly intentional. The message is clear. Why shop here when you could drive a little further to Tesco?

In the city itself, billboards on street lights at regular intervals plot the driver's route to Tesco, like approach lights guiding pilots in to land. It is a wholesale billboard war with a ping-pong predictability to it. If you see a Tesco lamp post, you can be sure that it will be followed a few lamp posts further on by a Carrefour one. Come into the city by train and the first thing you see when you walk into the station's arrivals hall is a huge, semi-permanent advert straddling the wall space above the exit to the city. The billboard is divided down the middle. The left-hand side has a giant Tesco logo with a list of the bus routes that take you to Tesco. On the right-hand side, there is also information about transport, this time to Carrefour.

Leave the station and step out into the station plaza, and you will see buses emblazoned with adverts for Tesco and people scurrying up and down carrying Tesco carrier bags. From this perspective, Hradec Kralove already looks like a Tesco town, but that's only because you are just a stone's throw from its central Tesco, a two-storey, relatively unobtrusive store cocooned in a grid of busy shopping streets. This Tesco is evidently well used. Its strategic position near to the bus and train stations in the commercial heart of the town makes it a handy drop-in shopping stop for 'small basket' customers. It is unrecognisable as a Tesco to anyone used to Tesco's UK stores. Since the mid 1990s, Tesco has been targeting 'emerging' central European economies, countries considered to be in transition and moving towards full-blown capitalism. By 2003, it had 53 stores in Hungary, 66 in Poland, 17 in Slovakia and another 17 in the Czech Republic. Initially, many of them, such as this store, were existing grocery or department stores rebadged as Tesco – a diplomatic, non-threatening way for the supermarket to make an entrance into a new market. Apart from a change of logo above the door, and a few Tesco own-brand lines squeezed in on shelves crammed with European branded products, Hradec Kralove's central Tesco has got pretty much the typically Czech selection of groceries you would find in any of the smaller grocery multiples that operate throughout the town. Most notably to the outsider, that means a strong showing of pork, sausages and dumplings, heaps of sourdough breads and cabbage. There is nothing very Tesco-ish about the store at all; nothing very British even, apart from the odd tin of Twinings tea. It is not like a foreign Marks & Spencer, one of those forever-England landmarks serving homesick expats or locals who go for a distinctly British offering. In this store, chameleon-like Tesco assumes a local identity.

Though this central Tesco clearly turns over a tidy sum each day, the purpose of the Tesco adverts that bark out at the citizens of Hradec Kralove is to persuade them to desert the busy new town with its small grocers and proliferation of small multiples, bypass Carrefour, which is semi-hidden in a shopping centre–cinema complex on the fringes of the new town, and head for the Tesco hypermarket, a few kilometres further out.

Visually and culturally, the zone the hypermarket inhabits is strikingly different from the characterful city. Hradec Kralove's original core, the old town, is small, neat and historic, rich in handsome Renaissance and Baroque architecture painted in pretty pastel tones. The new town, where all the action happens, is unique. It was built between the two world wars, the result of a radical masterplan designed by the father of Czech Modernism, the architect Jan Kotera, and interpreted after his death by his pupil, Josef Gocar, who developed a distinctively Czech style of architecture named Rondo-Cubism. It's a real one-off with a very strong sense of place. There is no place quite like Hradec Kralove either in the Czech Republic or further afield.

The Tesco hypermarket, on the other hand, sits on no man's land where town meets country, the outside layer of the urban onion, an anonymous terrain of roads, warehouses, car show-rooms, fast-food drive-throughs and big-box retail developments. It could be France, it could be the US, it might be Germany, Mexico, Belgium, Malaysia, the UK or Chile. Just another global retail zone, stripped of any geographical or national character. Without the language clue provided by signs, you could be any-where. But you would not feel lost, because Big Retail speaks a universal language wherever it goes, a language that increasingly we all understand. Get in the car. Park in the car park. Do all your shopping under one roof. Load up. Drive home. A one-size-fits-all formula for any country.

Out here on the shop 'n' drive strip, Tesco has a larger-than-life presence, representative of the way the chain wants to develop in Europe and internationally. It consists of a titanic blue-and-white box warehouse of a size that makes the typical Ikea seem slight, with mammoth freestanding Tesco signage picked out in red on the roof. A separate outlook tower reminiscent of a high-security camp forms another landmark, shouting out 'Tesco' and 'Nonstop' from three sides. The net effect is big, bold and attention-grabbing from all directions. There is no way you can miss it. It signals Tesco's towering ambitions. Tesco won't be satisfied to be yet another multiple represented in the already well-provided Czech market. It wants to dominate it. Its international growth strategy is 'to develop large stores in big markets where it can establish a leading position'. Tesco could realise that goal. It is already the largest hypermarket operator in central Europe even though it only entered the market in 1994.

Inside, the hypermarket is as big as a professional football pitch, a windowless barn, clean and functional with exposed air conditioning and lighting under a flat roof. There is a fifty-fifty grocery and non-food split. As well as food you can buy car tyres, washing machines, children's swings, vacuum cleaners, clothes, tools, three-piece suites and paddling pools. This hypermarket has all the departments you might expect in a UK store, plus a 'Tesco Grill': a fast-food-style food service counter with burger-bar-type illuminated displays above it, selling rotisserie chicken, pizza slices and sweet fizzy drinks. The checkouts are flanked with confectionery, packets of cigarettes and condoms. In fact it seems to stock everything that any Czech might conceivably need.

In the produce section, one British supermarket trait shines out: the fresh fruit is every bit as green and backward and hopelessly under-ripe as it would be in the UK. But otherwise, for anyone used to shopping in a UK Tesco, the selection of groceries is noticeably more varied. The Czechs eat a lot of carp and trout, and the occasional lobster, so there are several tanks with live fish swimming around. An assistant nets a fish, dispatches it discreetly behind the counter and then bags it – a practice likely to provoke an animal rights picket outside a UK Tesco, but one that won't raise an eyebrow in Hradec Kralove. The shelves show that the Czech Republic is still a nation where people cook each day from scratch: unlike British stores with aisles of ready meals and snacks, the Czech store might offer the odd reheatable dumpling, but that's about your lot.

The biggest difference of all is the preponderance of branded goods. Along with other Europeans, the Czechs like their brands. They expect, and are accustomed to having, a large choice of different brands or labels within any product category. Brand A's pickled cucumbers versus Brands B, C, D and so on. They are tuned into the nuances of different companies' offerings and more likely to be attached to certain preferred brands. This is a country where even the smallest supermarket offers an astonishing choice of ten different brands of tomato ketchups, for example, in various sizes too. European consumers expect a lot more choice within a category than UK consumers.

All this is shelf-clogging nonsense as far as UK supermarket chains are concerned: in the UK the shelves are streamlined, with pride of place given to own-label products and a smaller, carefully managed selection of the most profitable branded lines (see Chapter 22). Study the shelves in this store, however, and Tesco's stocking policy is apparent. Having dragged everyone out from Hradec Kralove to shop here, build the Tesco own-label. Make Tesco a household name. The strategy to achieve that is as follows. Maintain the range of brands that Czechs expect, but identify and then target the products that they buy most of. Have at least two Tesco own-label lines (a Value line, the standard offering and, if at all possible, a Finest offering) in every category to compete with the branded equivalent alongside, and make sure that they are cheaper – much cheaper.

Take pork and chicken luncheon meat, for example, a big seller. A Tesco Value tin costs 16.50 Czech crowns or koruna (Kc) while the branded equivalent in the same size costs 31.90 Kc. If you are after aerosol cream – a favourite for squirting on all those pancakes the Czechs consume – Tesco beats the opposition on price hands down. A Tesco Value aerosol costs 25.90 Kc and Tesco's standard offering 26.90 Kc, while the nearest branded aerosol costs 45.90 Kc. A similar comparison can be made in one product category after another. The shelves seem to chorus: 'Buy Tesco's own-label. Tesco's cheaper.'

It is hard not to get the impression that Tesco is buying loyalty from its customers, wooing newcomers to the Tesco brand by ruthlessly undercutting the opposition. The store is full of eye-popping deals. Hradec Kralove's citizens can pick up a whole frozen chicken here for about £1 and a kilo of chicken breasts or a joint of smoked pork for £2 – all own-label. With prices like these, Tesco's own-label lines are bound to steal market share. It is a strategy that has worked elsewhere. Tesco only moved into the Polish market in 1995, for example, but by 2003, own-label products accounted for 14 per cent of its sales there.

Cheap chicken certainly fulfils Tesco's mission to 'deliver unbeatable value for our customers in every market that we operate'. But how can it afford to do it? Competition between rival supermarket chains is cut-throat in the European market and margins are wafer-thin. In central Europe, Tesco has to do battle with international giants such as the French Carrefour, Belgian Delhaize, Dutch Ahold and German Metro chains. How can it achieve such low prices? Is the chicken factory-farmed so cheaply and intensively that its producer can make money as well as cut Tesco in on the deal? Is cheap poultry a loss leader with Tesco absorbing the loss to win consumers? Or is the supplier of all those small icy birds selling below cost to get a foot in the door with Tesco as it slowly but surely extends its international operations, opening up the prospect of ever larger volumes of sales?

The chickens could, of course, be sourced in an online auction, a procurement tool used increasingly in the UK to extract the best price from prospective own-label suppliers. It was developed in Europe by Tesco's Dutch competitor, Ahold. At an appointed time, a supermarket chain conducts an online auction with suppliers, who are all connected via computer terminals to the retailer. The chain takes the product with the cheapest price. It is a tough system for suppliers. The successful price has to be low, very low, possibly even below the cost of production. Quality is not the point. The secret of success is to supply a big volume of some generic, anonymous, bottom-of-the-range, own-label product such as block cheese, sliced ham or soap powder, at the lowest possible price.

All the big European supermarket players, Tesco included, are using this system, sourcing product for all their stores in one region or several countries in one fell swoop. The sweetener for suppliers is that they get a supermarket chain's listing, which is quite an achievement these days as the chains look to eliminate suppliers rather than take them on. They can also expect big orders. As these retail giants grow ever more powerful, as market analysts expect them to do, wrenching market share from smaller multiples, independents and food markets, suppliers hope to secure their business. As one own-label supplier supplying several international supermarket chains put it: 'Private label [own label] is still in its infancy in eastern Europe but we expect it to grow strongly and in due course we will be well placed to service customers more globally as they extend their international operations.'

Online auctions are just part of the package to which would-be European suppliers (usually own-label) must submit. Market analysts believe that a good part of the profits generated by all the big hypermarket players in Europe comes from hefty 'listing fees' – large sums of money paid by suppliers in return for getting their products on the supermarket shelves. Ongoing contributions are expected too: a cheque or discount from the supplier to celebrate new store openings or birthdays, or additional payments made in other thinly disguised forms, such as contributions to promotional leaflets and mailshots. They also point out that hypermarket chains active in Europe take their time to pay suppliers. Terms of more than ninety days are not unusual.

Big supermarket chains, especially when they have pan-national buying power, can dictate terms to suppliers. That is why Tesco can afford to sell the citizens of Hradec Kralove a chicken for £1, or six 185 gram tins of tuna for £1.25 or a half-kilo tin of luncheon meat for 40p. If you were a citizen of Hradec Kralove, you might well rush along to Tesco to take advantage of these fantastic offers. The Tesco mail shots that drop through everyone's doorways trumpet the deals but do not mention what has to happen to sustain them. Independent retailers and smaller multiples will disappear because they won't be able to compete. More Anytown-Anywhere retail sprawl will stamp Tesco's international brand on the landscape. Category management will diminish the total choice within product categories to the consumer, liquidating less heavyweight brands from the shelves. Squeezing the lowest price out of farmers, growers and manufacturers means that they will have to lower production costs and consequentially standards. Every cheap chicken has its hidden price.

30

Next stop the world

Once supermarkets were the rich Western world's place to shop, but not any more: they are taking over the planet. Surprising though it may seem, in Kenya, for example, about 40 per cent of small to medium-sized towns have supermarkets. In China, they are now spreading rapidly from the big coastal cities to poorer and more remote areas. Wherever you go in any reasonably populous area of the globe these days, rich or poor, you are likely to see a supermarket, or even a hypermarket, looking pretty much like those you find in Europe or the US. And whether you're in Caracas or the Comoros, Madagascar or Mauritius, Seoul or Saigon, don't be surprised to come across a Carrefour, a Costco, a Casino, a Tesco or a Wal-Mart. These days, the most successful and powerful grocers are no longer content to stay at home. They are gripped by wanderlust and firmly believe that the world is their oyster.

We're not just talking about supermarkets having a finite number of token flagship foreign stores, as is the case with Marks & Spencer, nor even relatively small-time acquisitions such as Sainsbury's purchase in the US of Shaw's supermarkets. The name of the game is to make an early entry into emerging markets and rapidly establish a major, preferably leading presence in key locations, like twenty-first-century retail conquistadors. Progress so far is impressive. 'The first wave [of supermarket development] hit major cities in the larger or richer countries of Latin America. The second wave hit East/Southeast Asia; the third in smaller or poorer countries of Latin America and Asia including, for example, Central America and Southern then Eastern Africa. By this time, secondary cities and towns in the areas of the "first wave" were being hit. The fourth wave, just starting now, is hitting South Asia and West Africa,' is how one set of researchers sum up what has happened.

The rise and rise of supermarkets in poor or still traditional parts of the world has been remarkably rapid, mostly within the last ten years. Why is that? It isn't as if people around the globe simultaneously chorused, 'I've had enough of growing my own or buying from the hawkers at the market and the family-run shops down the road . . . Let's have supermarkets!' Quite simply, retailers in foreign countries decided it was high time that these countries had them, and the rapid growth has been fuelled by Foreign Direct Investment (FDI). In Latin America, for example, supermarket growth was pretty puny when the companies were financed by domestic capital. It is thought that in the 1980s supermarkets accounted for only 10–20 per cent of food sales. By 2000, supermarkets' share had leapt to 50–60 per cent. These supermarkets are overwhelmingly foreign-owned. Global supermarket chains now account for 70–80 per cent of the top five chains in most countries in the region. What this means in practical terms is that already three out of every ten pesos that Mexicans spend on food is spent in a Wal-Mart.

Some countries in Europe have recently undergone a supermarket explosion. In 2000, only 25 per cent of the food sales in Croatia were made in supermarkets. Most people shopped in small shops and food markets. By 2002, after the global grocers moved in, supermarkets' market share rocketed to 51 per cent. Effectively, Croatia has undergone the retail transformation in five years that France or the US experienced in fifty.

The flow of foreign investment shows no sign of slowing. In the first eight months of 2002, for example, six global retailers – British Tesco, French Carrefour and Casino, Dutch Ahold and Makro and Belgian Food Lion – spent 6 million bhat ($120 million) in Thailand alone. Tesco's express strategy is to 'develop large stores in big markets where we can establish a leading position'. It seems well on the way to achieving that. An indicator of its commitment to international expansion is the fact that its largest depot is now not in the UK but in South Korea. In addition to Thailand and South Korea, it has stores in Taiwan, Malaysia, the Czech Republic, Hungary, Poland, Slovakia and Ireland. By 2003 it was the market leader in six of the eleven countries where it has established a presence and by 2003 18.2 per cent of its sales were outside the UK. In 2004 Tesco acquired a £140 million stake in a Chinese hypermarket chain and in 2003 it signed a deal to acquire a chain in Turkey.

Look more closely at supermarket chains throughout the world and even if their names don't sound foreign, you may well find that they are owned outright by a foreign company or that global grocers have a strategic financial share in them. Tesco, for example, now owns the C Two-Network in Japan while Wal-Mart owns Supermercados Amigo in Puerto Rico. And when they are not colonising new territories, global grocers are similarly mopping up shares in what they deem to be under-supermarketed markets such as Italy and Russia, where a significant number of people still use small independent shops, local chains and food markets. According to the UK Institute of Grocery Development, in 2002 Italy and Russia were 'Priority 1' emerging markets in terms of their attractiveness for food retail expansion. Every grocer still selling local salumi and cheese in Italy and every baker still making staff-of-life rye bread in Russia signals a business opportunity for global chains.

The possibility of such spectacular growth gives a clue to why a supermarket chain based, say, in Bentonville in Arkansas, or

Cheshunt in Herefordshire, wants to give itself the hassle of servicing the needs of food shoppers thousands of miles away. On their home patch, supermarket chains usually compete with one another in intensely competitive, nearly saturated markets. In the UK, for example, where supermarkets already control around 80 per cent of grocery business, there is only so much share that retailers can squeeze from one another. Seen from the perspective of the overheated European or US supermarket sector, as yet underdeveloped markets offer an alluring business opportunity. The pull is irresistible. Get richer quicker. Even if a store is at the other side of the world it can produce operating profits that will keep the investors happy. Throughout the 1990s the French chain Carrefour, for example, which has supermarkets in thirty-one different countries, made margins in its Argentine stores that were three times higher on average than those in its French ones.

Characteristically the markets targeted by global chains have very little in the way of supermarkets, and so the field is wide open, and there is potentially lots of business to be poached from small multiples and independents. Everywhere they go in the world, supermarkets set in motion a familiar process. Independent food shops and local chains are squeezed out. Wholesale and retail markets suffer, sometimes terminally. Small farmers see their outlets disappear but they aren't big enough to supply the supermarkets. The only way bigger farmers can get a look-in is by getting up to their necks in debt, tooling up to service the needs of exigent foreign chains. Before you know it, there isn't a family-owned shop in which to buy a watermelon and the farmer down the road has downed tools and gone to the city to look for work.

The lure for the global chains is not just growth prospects. What also appeals is the opportunity to strengthen their buying power by centralising buying and consolidating distribution. This is what supermarket chains mean when they talk about 'driving costs out of the system'. Think about it in straight business terms and it makes total sense. Why should a global grocer source its chicken in a high-costs economy like Britain when it can strike a much cheaper deal with poultry producers in Thailand or Brazil? Why have your cashmere spun in Scotland if you can get it done for a fraction of the price in Bangladesh? By being broad-minded about where they buy the product they put on their shelves, supermarkets can cherry-pick the best deals to be struck around the globe like bargain hunters at sale time.

The bigger supermarket chains get, the less their suppliers can expect to get paid. Commenting on the possible sale of Safeway in the UK, David Simons, a former chief executive of Somerfield, spelt out the consequences. 'If a trade buyer [another supermarket chain] bought Safeway, terms for suppliers . . . would be renegotiated down to the lowest price and a further volume discount demanded. There will not simply be a 1–2% reduction in prices [to suppliers] but 5–10%.'

If this percentage is the difference that a bit of extra national buying clout makes, just think what leverage international buying power confers. In 2003, Tony De Nunzio, Asda's chief executive, quantified the advantage. Before Wal-Mart, the biggest global grocer, took over Asda in 1999, he said, a basic pair of George jeans cost £14.99. Now they cost as little as £4. This massive reduction was courtesy of Wal-Mart's buying power. Asda was paying its suppliers 50 per cent less for denim now that it is part of Wal-Mart. Fleece, Mr De Nunzio said, was another very good example of what he referred to as 'the virtuous circle': more sales, better buying, lower prices and still more sales. Asda used to buy 50,000 yards of fleece at a time at a cost of $9 a yard. Wal-Mart buys 6 million yards at $3 a yard. There were fewer opportunities for global sourcing in the food department because more food is sourced locally, Mr De Nunzio explained, but there were still a few. Asda's bananas, for example, are now bought along with Wal-Mart's; as a result, the cost price (to Asda) is down by a fifth. Tesco too is reaping rewards from its growing global buying power. It says that over 2,500 of its 'Value' lines are increasingly being 'advantageously sourced centrally' for its eighty-eight hypermarkets in central Europe and it has made it clear that it aims to procure more products from emerging markets such as the Indian sub-continent and the former USSR satellites.

As supermarket chains become more international, their biggest suppliers – companies responsible for brands that are household names worldwide – are being left in no doubt as to who is top dog. In 2002, for example, the Dutch supermarket Albert Heijn, which is owned by Ahold, the third biggest global grocer, boycotted thirty Unilever products in a bid to get better terms. That same year, Tesco was reported to be 'naming and shaming' suppliers who it said were offering lower prices to Tesco in Europe than those they were offering to Tesco in the UK. About half a dozen of the biggest grocery suppliers were said to be on a Tesco 'blacklist'. One supplier commented at the time: 'It was made clear that they had better give Tesco better terms – or else.'

Obviously, international buying muscle gives any company a major advantage over national competitors. In 2003, the Competition Commission reiterated its finding that 'bigger multiple grocery retailers obtained lower prices from suppliers than their smaller rivals'. These lower prices, combined with economies of scale, mean that multinational chains can offer prices to their customers that purely national chains can't match. This allows them to extend their market share at the expense of UK-focused rivals. This is the pattern the world over. As one market analysis report put it: 'The worst performing companies [in the global grocers' top 30] were easier to categorise – largely domestic players.' So it is no coincidence that in the UK, the two top chains are Tesco and Asda Wal-Mart. By 2004 Tesco was the fourth biggest retailer worldwide, while Wal-Mart reigned supreme at number one.

By 2003, the Top 30 grocery retail chains accounted for 33 per cent of global food sales. Now the biggest and most ambitious among them are eyeing up the remaining 67 per cent. The ultimate goal of global grocers, irrespective of what corner of the planet they operate from, is to establish a more or less captive market in as many countries as possible while simultaneously benefiting from the huge economies of scale that flow from having suppliers at their beck and call. That's the way to enhance the bottom line.

SUPERMARKET CULTURE

31

The new community

In September 2002, Asda's Elgin branch in the Scottish Highlands notched up an astonishing supermarket first: an instore wedding. The minister of the local church married two employees in the store's cafeteria. The ceremony was broadcast over the public address system for customers to hear. Asda FM played a mix of the Asda jingle and Mendelssohn's wedding march. The bridal party wore Asda name badges.

A supermarket isn't everyone's idea of the most stylish or romantic venue for a wedding. It's scarcely what most engaged couples had in mind when they learnt that the government was allowing people to get married in locations other than the traditional church or register office. But there is a certain logic to a supermarket wedding. For years now, wanting to counter the public perception of supermarkets as soul-destroying and alienating places, supermarkets have been trying to make their stores more appealing by convincing us that they are the obvious locations for a romantic tryst. Propagating the Sexy Supermarket Story has sent some retailers' public relations departments into overdrive. On Valentine's Day 2003, for example, Somerfield revealed that a survey had found that two in five of its customers had been chatted up while doing their weekly shopping. Such a storyline is guaranteed to be taken up enthusiastically by weekend supplements short on ideas and budget yet with considerable space to fill. One newspaper even dredged up a supermarket-inspired poet to come up with a poem, 'Love Among the Frozen Peas', whose first clunky lines read:

> Our eyes met across the organic courgettes
> Where she smouldered a smile at me
> It slipped from the corner of her eyes
> Like a Buy One Get One Free.

Ever inventive, Somerfield also put up consumer psychologists to explain to journalists the new science of 'trolley-ology', the executive summary of which was 'You show me the contents of the trolley and I'll tell you the degree of availability.' A frozen ready meal for one was taken to indicate not a lonely, tastebud-challenged couch potato heading for heart disease at fifty but 'a single, potentially hot, person'; a single woman with too much salad was a 'control freak' and so on.

Asda likes to perpetuate the 'It's hot to shop' image too. It runs singles nights on Valentine's Day, when customers are encouraged to park their cars in alternate 'girl/boy spaces' (tough if you are gay, or a cyclist, or both) and linger in 'love spots' around the store. In one Glasgow Asda store, customers have been given red, amber and green badges to indicate their degree of 'availability'.

Such initiatives are all part of our large retailers' ongoing campaign to get us to spend more and more time in supermarkets, and to see their stores as the obvious jumping-off point for most of life's essential activities. Supermarkets have always wanted to be seen as more than grocers. The first sign of them slipping into pastoral garb came in the form of instore 'community notice-boards'. These provide a tiny oasis of local interest in stores that might otherwise have been stamped out by corporate cookie cutters. Whether it is a small ad for a children's party conjurer, the local mother and toddler group, that oddjobbing handyman or the hardly worn judo outfit, these noticeboards help promote the idea of the supermarket as an enabling focal point for all those little people and their myriad social interactions. By aping the traditional small ads' showcase, the local newsagent's window, these noticeboards seem to show that the supermarket is part of the local community, not something that threatens it.

In reality, however, supermarkets have been a distinctive sort of community blight. Few towns have an obvious civic centre any longer because of the neutron-bomb-type effect of superstores on traditional shopping streets. All those outings people used to make that consisted of a mixture of grocery shopping and generally sorting out their lives have become problematical. It's no longer easy, for example, to cash your pension, pick up a doctor's prescription, buy a newspaper, take back library books and do a spot of shopping in the town centre. Having been major contributors to this problem, the supermarkets are keen to step into the breach, offering their stores as the new and natural focus for community life.

They have been remarkably successful in this mission, to the extent that the supermarket has now become the new forum of the modern civic landscape, a new community village, a destination in its own right, a place to go when you don't know what else to do with yourself – as the words of Pulp's 1995 chart hit 'Common People' convey: 'I took her to a supermarket. I don't know why but I had to start it somewhere. So it started there.' As the Church's role as the pillar of the community has diminished and no one is entirely clear what its secular equivalent might be, our large chains are stepping in to fill the gap. They want their stores to become one-stop shops for all society's needs. From birth, through courtship, marriage and even until death, supermarkets are carving themselves the role of a cradle-to-grave community institution with an ever more central position in customers' lives. Forget all that twentieth-century stuff about town halls, churches, libraries, youth clubs and parades of local shops: the new social focus for the twenty-first century is a superstore and its car park. As Bill Grimsey, chief executive of the Big Food Group, which owns Iceland, put it: 'Ten years ago families would use Sunday to go to the park or take the children to a museum. Now they feed their kids on beans and toast in the cafeteria of a big supermarket.'

This idea has been taken up most enthusiastically by Asda since 1999 when it became 'part of the Wal-Mart family', the largest company on the globe. In 2002 Wal-Mart's sales equalled the combined revenue of IBM, AT&T, Procter & Gamble, Microsoft and Gillette. Nevertheless it cultivates an image as a big, happy family of consumers and workers, a community in its own right. Though Wal-Mart specialises in enormous supercentres (150–200,000 square feet) in the US, it also runs smaller stores, which it calls Neighborhood Centers and Home Town stores, where the express objective is to create a community around the local store.

Since its takeover by Wal-Mart, Asda has worked doggedly at building its community profile. In 2001, for example, it employed actors as 'greeters' to welcome shoppers to its stores and interact with them once there. In promoting social interaction it aimed to provide an antidote to the popular image of supermarkets as impersonal shopping environments, devoid of the easy, one-to-one human communication that local shops can provide, where the only chit-chat that normally passes between aisle-numbed customers and bored-out-their-brains staff is a functional 'Do you have a loyalty card?' or a wistful 'Is it still sunny outside?'

Now each Asda has members of staff – sorry *colleagues* – who wear a badge that says 'Welcome to Asda. Hi, I'm John/Janet' (or whatever name is appropriate), whose job is to welcome customers. Sometimes they take a broad-brush Happy Campers approach with a message over the tannoy, typically sounding something like this: 'Hello, I'm Mary. I'm one of your greeters for tonight ... We have some *wonderful* offers in store tonight.

Have you seen our unbelievable jeans offer? Gentlemen's jeans only £4 a pair! Who would have thought that jeans could be that cheap? So why not get along to our central aisle and have a look? Anything else you'd like to know, come and see Margaret or myself at the customer service desk. We're always happy to help. Thank you for your attention. Goodnight.' There's lots of room for improvisation. 'I like to give them the personal touch,' one greeter explained. 'If someone comes in and tells me that it's their wife's birthday or their anniversary, I'll put a message out over the tannoy and make sure everyone gives them a little cheer. If it's a really special occasion, I'll make sure they leave with a bunch of flowers.'

Asda's cheesy community doesn't stop there. Each Asda store now has an events co-ordinator to devise community initiatives. Asda offers chaplaincy and bereavement counselling in fifty stores nationwide. It has piloted 'foyer firemen' events and 'bobby lobbies' where local firefighters and police give advice on home safety and security, and other community services such as Citizen's Advice Bureau sessions and even MPs' surgeries. Asda's York store has a birth registration office. It can register up to ten births a day, and for each child registered Asda donates a mother-and-baby pampering pack. York's superintendent registrar justified its opening by saying that the existing registration office was not pushchair-friendly. 'We needed somewhere that had parking, was known by everyone in the area and was convenient, so Asda was the obvious answer.'

Terence Blacker, writing in the *Independent*, reached the same conclusion, but from a different perspective. 'The supermarket is now the undisputed focus of a local community. Whether there is a local Tesco or a Morrisons, or Asda or a Waitrose, it defines an area's style, image and personality. This is a depressing, even sinister, development. The relationship that these organisations have to the community is simple and brutal; they want to make as much money out of it as possible.'

Surely that's unfair? It is true, as the Competition Commission established, that some 'supermarket' donations to charity are funded at least partially by their suppliers. But all the supermarkets, though acknowledging that their main function is to make profits for shareholders, can still reel off lists of good works in the community. Sainsbury's, for example, can boast that it has ploughed £15 million into its computer education venture, IT Now, which provides drop-in tuition in IT skills in selected stores. Asda, meanwhile, is proud of all the money it has raised for the charity Breast Cancer Care. But as with many supermarket charitable initiatives, in this one altruism is mixed with a good measure of self-interest. In 2003, pop star Louise Redknapp's single 'Don't Give Up' was launched across the Asda FM network. It soon climbed to number five in the charts amid a massive publicity campaign, with proceeds going to Breast Cancer Care. Then the song was plunged into controversy as radio stations were besieged by listeners pointing out its similarity to the famous 'Asda price' jingle. Asda admitted that the resemblance was intentional and that the hit was co-written by the man who created its trademark theme tune, but denied that it was being used as a marketing tool.

Tesco's favourite community service badge of honour is reserved for its annual Computers For Schools scheme, launched in 1992. Tesco shoppers earned vouchers that schools could collect and use to get free computer equipment. 'Over 23,000 schools across the UK benefit from participation in this initiative,' it says. This scheme is a striking example of how a supermarket chain can help the community, yet still extract several pounds of retail flesh. Tesco shoppers feel they are benefiting their local schools every time they shop there. But in 2001 *Which?* investigated the scheme and found that the sums behind it didn't stack up. *Which?* calculated that 4,490 vouchers would provide a school with a scanner. That meant that shoppers had to spend £44,900 in Tesco to get enough vouchers to buy an item that

Tesco itself sold for £80 and which would cost it even less wholesale. A school would have to generate £208,800 of Tesco shopping to receive £1,000 worth of equipment. *Which?* did not attempt to calculate the advertising benefit to Tesco of having its vouchers and promotional material flooding into schools – in 2002 alone, Tesco distributed over 273 million vouchers for the scheme. But it noted that Tesco provided head teachers with a letter to photocopy and circulate to parents urging them to participate and suggested that schools design and distribute flyers advertising the scheme.

Supermarkets are keen on targeting young people and signing them up good and early as lifelong members of their community. Children can have surprisingly large amounts of money to spend and are not circumspect about how they spend it. Students too are likely to be the high spenders of the future. Promotions to suck them in are strong supermarket priorities. One such was the campaign Asda ran in the autumn of 2003, for example, targeting first-year undergraduates. Freshers throughout the UK received an unsolicited mailing, encouraging them to participate in a '£6,000 giveaway' using their enclosed 'Asda gift card'. Students eagerly read the conditions, thinking that Asda, in common with other companies trying to woo them, would be offering some interesting discounts or special offers, free ringbinder folders or notepads perhaps. Unfortunately not. Though '120 lucky winners' might each win £125 (hence the £6,000) by using their cards, the rest had to look to their parents. 'As a student, one of your biggest concerns will be where your next meal is coming from ... To help you out, Asda has come up with a foolproof way of persuading your parents to send more funds in your direction ... On the back of your card is a number; pass this on to your folks and they can top up your card with cash at any Asda store. Then head down to Asda and fill up your trolley, safe in the knowledge that someone else is paying! And if a little gets diverted towards a new outfit from George clothing or that new CD, who needs to know?' Oh and by the way, 'Should the Asda gift card remain active for 24 months or more, Asda reserves the right to charge an administration fee of £1 per month whilst the account remains in credit.' Far from being a straightforward sweetener to gain student custom, the gift card was a promotion designed to coax more cash from parents' pockets into Asda tills.

Nobody can accuse supermarkets of not playing a part in the community. There's no doubt that they are keen to promote their vision of twenty-first-century community life. The only problem is that they want to own, control and brand it. They want us to be lifelong citizens of a new type of community entirely, an Asda community, a Tesco community, a Sainsbury's community, a Morrisons community. Loyalty cards, such as Sainsbury's Nectar card and Tesco's Clubcard, are a systematic attempt to get us to bond with the chain and enlist us as enthusiastic members of its branded community, by dangling a number of bonuses. (Wow! 500 Nectar points generated by a £250 spend earns you a free rental movie from Blockbuster or a free McDonald's medium Extra Value Meal!) However, whether loyalty cards are an effective means of bonding consumers to chains is questionable. Some chains have scorned them, dubbing them 'promiscuity cards', because many shoppers simply take every card from every chain offering it then 'shop around'. As Waitrose's director of selling and marketing put it, 'Customer loyalty was never what it was about, rather understanding purchasing patterns and aiding category management.' The real value of loyalty cards to supermarket chains is that they are a means of gathering detailed information about buying habits, allowing customers to be targeted more effectively with tailor-made promotions. Or as Tesco prefers to put it: 'Clubcard helps us understand our customers better.'

Information gleaned from loyalty cards helps supermarkets plot their next move, allowing the new supermarket community to dovetail effortlessly with the existing structure of any area, as defined by income and class. Supermarkets study an area to decide how good a 'fit' it will be for their chain, using 'geodemographic' computer modelling. Geodemographic profiling provides retailers with an indication of the make-up of the local population which can be cross-referenced with other data, such as expenditure details from loyalty cards. Sainsbury's, for example, knows that its brand most appeals to wealthy suburban achievers, better-off executives in inner-city areas, white-collar workers in 'better off multi-ethnic areas', affluent 'greys' and comfortable 'middle agers' in mature home-owning areas. Waitrose is the chain most popular with 'wealthy achievers in suburbia', 'wealthy executives' and 'prosperous professionals in metropolitan areas'. Tesco does slightly less well than Sainsbury's with 'well-off suburbanites' but more than makes up with its success with 'affluent urbanites', 'comfortable middle age home owners', older people in less prosperous areas and 'affluent greys' in rural communities. Asda scores with 'well-off workers in family areas, skilled, home-owning workers, new home owners in mature communities and council estate residents'. Kwik Save is favoured by 'struggling families', and so on.

Supermarkets want us to be loyal Asda/Tesco/Sainsbury's-defined citizens. They have found ways to make us, in a blind, almost tribal way and according to our income, become such people, whose money flows into their tills as unquestioningly and automatically as a direct debit.

32

That's supermarket price

Can there be many adverts that have insinuated themselves into public consciousness more effectively than 'That's Asda price' (chink, chink)? The tune is as instantly recalled as a Coca-Cola jingle but the message is more focused. Usually an attractive, reasonably prosperous-looking woman, savvy and just a little bit sexy, smacks the change in her pocket to produce that now familiar coin-chinking sound that sums up Asda's message. Shop in Asda, and you'll be left with more change in your pocket. It's cheap to shop at Asda. You get more for less at Asda. Shopping at Asda allows you to spend less on food and more on everything else. Food at Asda is cheaper than anywhere else and cheap food is obviously *a good thing*, end of story. It's a clear and simple message, uncomplicated by any possibly contradictory subtext or disclaimer. It doesn't attempt to tell you anything about whether Asda offers quality, range or even value for money. The only thing that puts that contented smile on this Asda shopper's face is the thought of the money she can save.

There was a time when our larger supermarkets tried to give a more rounded account of themselves. They wanted to tell us about what good food they sold or what good service they gave. In the 1980s and 1990s, they seemed to be moving inexorably upmarket. Bragging about bargain-basement prices was territory best left to foreign-owned 'hard discounters' like Aldi, Lidl or Netto. Our indigenous chains didn't want to be seen as undignified barrow boys, scrapping over grocery business. Tesco, remember, actively wanted to get away from its traditional 'pile it high and sell it cheap' image and pull its brand upmarket.

But these days, the supermarket chains whose financial performance makes them the darlings of city analysts are those whose dominant message is low prices. Now Asda with its 'everyday low prices . . . pocket the pennies . . . more for your money . . . rolling back prices' slogans has company from Tesco, 'Where every little counts . . . Helping you to spend less every day', and Morrison's, offering 'the very best for less'. Sainsbury's, which in 1995 was the UK's leading supermarket chain, had dropped by 2003 to number three position in the supermarket superpower league table – a chilling warning that chains not sufficiently price-conscious can expect to suffer. Sainsbury's has altered its customary quality-centred message to keep up with its price-slashing rivals. It is emphasising that it is the place where 'good food costs less' and where prices are 'chopped'. Even Waitrose, with its well-heeled clientele, has a new slogan, 'Quality food attractively priced'. To put it bluntly, if you want to be a player in the supermarket first division, you have to be keenly focused on price.

In theory, this is all tremendously good news for consumers. Asda has even managed to make its relentless price cutting sound like a philanthropic mission: 'Our purpose is to make goods and services more affordable for everyone,' it says. And indeed it does seem that we have never spent so little on food. In 1958, 26 per cent of consumer spending went on food; by 1998, it was only 10.3 per cent. Supermarkets and their supporters regularly take credit for this. 'The ability of the modern British food chain to deliver increased choice at reducing real prices has been a significant contributor to improvements in living standards,' said Richard Ali, spokesperson for the British Retail Consortium.

Elsewhere in Europe, if a retailer consistently offered low prices on all food lines, consumers' first instinct might be to wonder what was wrong with the food, or suppose that prices had been too high to start with. In Europe, buying cheap food may be seen as a necessity, but not automatically as a virtue. But now in the UK, thanks largely to the price-cutting climate fostered by supermarkets, spending as little as possible on food has become a matter of personal pride. A lower bill at the checkout is seen as evidence of shopper thriftiness and wise domestic economy, even if you aren't hard up. Nationally, Britain stands out as the country that makes a virtue out of spending as little as possible on feeding itself. The proportion of our budget that goes on food has also steadily declined. In the year 2001–2002, the average UK household spent less on food than it did on transport (buying and running cars, public transport) or on recreation and culture (televisions, computers, newspapers, books, leisure services, package holidays). In the UK pecking order of life's essentials, food now comes lower down the list of spending priorities of the average household than a better car or a second television.

Is that any surprise when increasingly our supermarkets have encouraged us to think that the most important thing about food is its price? And we have implicitly been led to believe that apparently low prices at the checkout can be achieved without causing any unwelcome fallout further back in the food chain. The world, according to our big supermarkets, is a place where they can go on sourcing food for less and less, pretty much indefinitely. We have been spun the line that supermarkets are consumer champions, driving down unjustifiably high prices on our behalf without compromising on quality or safety or endangering the environment and the livelihoods of producers. Food at ever lower prices with no downside whatsoever? Everybody likes a bargain. Who could say no to that supermarket proposition?

Even consumers who suspect that it is a partial truth are happy to go along with it, in the absence of evidence to the contrary. But many smell a rat. When consumers were asked to agree or disagree with the statement 'I trust UK stores to charge the best possible prices they can to their customers', only 16 per cent could agree; 83 per cent felt that UK stores were being greedy in the prices they charged and 86 per cent thought that the fact that there were so many special offers around made them think full prices must be too high. Another market analysis report concluded that although supermarkets are generally regarded as offering lower-priced groceries than convenience stores or small retailers, this perception did not extend to fresh foods such as fruit, vegetables and meat. And indeed in 2002, when researchers from *Which?* compared prices at farmers' markets and supermarkets, they confirmed that supermarkets were charging either the same, or frequently more, for fresh food. All the fruit and vegetables sold at farmers' markets were cheaper, as were free-range and organic eggs. At one stall eggs were half the price of those on sale at the Safeway store up the road.

In June 2004, the journalist Dominic Prince, writing in the *Spectator*, decided to conduct his own investigation into supermarket pricing. He bought the same list of food items from market stalls and independent shops in his home town of Shaftesbury in Dorset and then from his nearest Tesco in Blandford. He found that Tesco charged 42.98 per cent more. He also remarked that several of the Tesco items, such as pork chops and all the fruit and vegetables, were inferior on taste grounds. 'We are all being done,' he concluded. 'We are being misled, brainwashed, cheated and we don't even know it's happening.'

Later that month, a *Sunday Times* investigation exposed how supermarket consumers buying in bigger sizes in the belief that they are more economical were being conned because supermarkets were charging up to 30 per cent more for some products bought in bulk than for the same products purchased in smaller quantities. The *Sunday Times* listed overpriced items bearing a 'bulk penalty' in Waitrose, Sainsbury's, Safeway, Tesco and Asda.

At about the same time, a mailshot for Tesco's 'Helping you spend less every day' Value campaign featuring special offers popped through my letter box. I was inspired by Mr Prince's example to carry out my own one-woman price comparison. Many of the offers were for items such as sweets or fizzy drinks that I do not buy, but I was attracted by the idea of the boldly marked 'half price' raspberries and strawberries. So I price-checked these against my local greengrocer's, only to find that the Tesco berries were roughly 100 per cent more expensive. My greengrocer's berries were fresh, prime Scottish fruits in peak condition, so at least as good as Tesco's if not better.

Then in September, the *Sunday Times* accused Tesco of raising prices on hundreds of items while at the same time claiming that it was slashing prices, effectively paying for price cuts on low-volume items by hiking up the price on bestsellers. Tesco dismissed claims that it was running a 'phoney' price war as nonsense, saying that some of its price rises were on seasonal products. But the *Sunday Times* pointed out that this scarcely applied to items like Heinz baked beans (up from 69 to 78 pence) or boxes of Tetley tea-bags (up 8 pence).

But if consumers are not entirely sure what to make of the rafts of low prices and apparent price cuts emanating from our grocery chains, supermarket suppliers are much, much clearer. When they hear those Asda coins chinking, they wince. When they hear other supermarkets promising unbeatable value to consumers, they shudder. The supermarket's price cut, they believe, is the supermarket supplier's destitution. Low prices to shoppers, they insist, are being financed not by the supermarket chains but by the farmers, growers and manufacturers who produce for them. UK pig farmers, angry at the decimation of the national pig herd by the impossibly low prices paid to farmers by supermarkets and the chains' willingness to import cheaper product from abroad, have hijacked one of our supermarkets' favourite mantras. 'Every Day Low Prices' or EDLP (now the key super-market pricing strategy), they say, really stands for 'Every Day Less Pigs': EDLP is putting farmers out of business. It's not just UK producers who are complaining. In 2002, three of the largest Spanish lettuce co-operatives claimed publicly that they were being paid below the cost of production by supermarket chains, to such an extent that the future of their industry was under threat. 'Paradoxically, these [low] prices do not filter through to the end consumer and the only result is increased margins for the retailers at the expense of the Spanish growers,' they said.

Are these claims true? Or are supermarkets just a convenient enemy whom producers can blame for everything from their own inefficiencies, through farming disasters such as BSE or foot-and-mouth disease, to worldwide economic forces? One way to probe what role, if any, supermarkets play in contributing to food pro-ducers' current woes is to look into the mysterious black hole that exists between what the producer is paid and what the super-market charges. In 2002, when the National Farmers Union carried out such an exercise, it discovered not so much a gap as a yawning abyss. It found that a basket of farmed produce, including beef, eggs, milk, bread, tomatoes and apples, typically cost £37 in supermarkets but a farmer got only £11 for it – less than a third of its retail value. Farmers got only 26 per cent of what shoppers paid for beef, 20 per cent of what they paid for pork loin and 23 per cent of what they paid for onions. Cereal farmers got only 8 per cent of the price of a loaf of bread and pig farmers typically received only 14 per cent of the final sale value of bacon.

An analysis of UK price changes, carried out in 2003 by the Liberal Democrats, using House of Commons statistics, also illus-trated this gulf. Between 1985 and 2002, the retail price of shop-ping trolley favourites – chicken, tomatoes, eggs and potatoes – rose by a whopping 47 per cent while farmers saw a rise of only 12 per cent for their produce. In the seven years from 1995 to

2002 (just as the big supermarkets' price war was hotting up), this disparity seemed to intensify. Checkout prices were up 21 per cent but farmgate prices were up only 2 per cent. Andrew George MP, the Lib Dem shadow Food and Rural Affairs Secretary, didn't pull his punches. 'Somebody must be making money here, and it isn't the farmers. People are paying more for their food, yet British farmers are not getting their fair share. The record of these four items is indicative of a wider trend, adding to the pressure that puts farmers and growers out of business while the supermarkets profit.'

Looking at one of these four items, potatoes, I asked a grower to give me an instance of the differential between what he was paid and what a supermarket might charge. 'The mark-up on my ordinary potatoes is about six to seven times but salad potatoes can be much more. Last season I only got £100 a tonne for waxy salad potatoes and they were selling for over £2,000 in the store,' he told me.

The mystery of supermarket milk prices has raised eyebrows too. It costs the dairy farmer on average 21 pence to produce a litre of milk on the farm, yet the farmgate price for milk, dictated by the supermarkets, is below the cost of production – at only 18.5 pence. It is generally understood that milk processors take about 4 pence on every litre. Meanwhile, you won't find a litre of milk on sale in supermarkets much below 42 pence. So, if you follow the arithmetic, you can see that somebody is raking in a bucketload of money from the white stuff, and it isn't the farmers. The Milk Development Council claims that while farmers' margins on milk have slumped over the last decade and processors' margins have remained roughly the same, retailers' margins have shot up.

Supermarkets defend themselves against charges of profiteering by saying that a price comparison between farm gate and supermarket shelf is too crude, and that only a fraction of the mark-up they put on products turns into profit once all their costs are paid. Some products go through a long and complex food chain before reaching supermarket shelves, with processing, packaging and transport all adding on costs. Post-BSE, for example, a welter of regulations has placed huge additional costs on abattoirs and processors, which all affect the cost of meat.

However, research that takes into account processing and other costs does suggest that supermarkets are doing disproportionately well out of deals with suppliers. In 2003, Banana Link, an organisation that campaigns to improve the conditions of banana producers, looked at how much of every £1 spent by UK consumers on loose Ecuadorian bananas went to each link in the supply chain. Bananas are the number-one contributor to British supermarket profits and third in terms of sales volume after lottery tickets and petrol. It found that plantation workers got 1.5 pence, plantation owners got 10 pence, the international trading company got 31 pence (which included a 5-pence EU tariff), the ripener distributor got 17 pence, while the retailer (supermarket) took 40 pence. A similar pattern emerges with other foods. For every pack of Zimbabwean mangetouts sold in UK supermarkets, the producer gets 12 per cent of the retail value and the supermarket gets 45 per cent, which is more than all export, packaging, air freight, handling and import charges put together. The same applies to fresh vegetables sent from Kenya to the UK – those neatly trimmed baby corns, miniature asparagus, green beans and so on. Producers get 14 per cent of the retail value, while supermarkets take 46 per cent. This phenomenon is not just restricted to imported produce. It is estimated that supermarkets make a retail margin of 36 per cent on UK top fruit (apples, pears) while the grower sees only a 16 per cent return.

As price competition between the big chains has intensified in recent years and low price has become king, suppliers have found what they consider to be already depressed prices squeezed even further. Most consumers think that when a supermarket cuts its prices, it must be cutting its margins to give them a better deal. Supermarket suppliers see matters somewhat differently. They widely believe that it is they who are funding the supermarkets' much-trumpeted price cuts. 'When retail groups [supermarkets] determine that they wish to implement a price reduction or promotion, they seek to recover the cost from their suppliers, thereby maintaining their gross profit margin,' one supplier told the Competition Commission. Several suppliers told me that supermarket price promotions, such as 'Buy One Get One Free' or 'Multibuys' sound good in theory for the supplier, offering the prospect of more sales, but rarely produce any real benefit in practice. 'If the supermarket sells something on promotion one week, all that happens is that shoppers take advantage and stock up on it, which means that they buy less of it in subsequent weeks,' one supplier explained. Patrick Holden, director of the Soil Association, summed up the effect of promotions as follows: 'All the suppliers tell me that they have higher sales during the promotion but no long-term net gain.' Nevertheless, such promotions allow supermarkets to score brownie points with the consumer by offering them a cheap deal and are generally popular with consumers, although some more sceptical shoppers do wonder whether they are really saving money in the long run, or whether they are just being encouraged to spend money sooner than they otherwise would have done.

The run-up to Christmas is a traditional period for supermarket price cuts. Some chains like to send out mail shots trumpeting low Christmas prices. As a result, pressure on suppliers to cut prices then and maintain them through the hard-up months of January and February can be intense. In November 2002 Sainsbury's, for example, wrote to suppliers asking them to try to cut costs by 5 per cent and pass on the savings to Sainsbury's in the form of lower prices. This caused consternation amongst suppliers, who already regarded their margins as well and truly pared to the bone. The *Financial Times* translated Sainsbury's plan to 'help' suppliers drive their cost base down by 5 per cent as 'cut your prices or else'.

Even big international brands complain publicly about supermarkets' 'commoditisation' of products, warning that the supermarkets' obsession with price is driving value out of the UK grocery market and could cause permanent damage. Artisan producers have for some time been complaining that price cutting is cheapening the value of their products in the eyes of consumers and making it harder for them to charge what they need to earn a decent living. How can they keep going, they ask, when supermarkets' loss leaders make products priced at a sustainable and fair price look like a rip-off?

Most of this goes over the heads of shoppers wheeling their trolleys round stores, bombarded with prominent signs on products that scream out 'Why pay more?' or 'Wow! That's amazing!' Most of us are inexorably drawn to the supermarket 'hot spots' such as shelf ends with their eye-grabbing, price-slashing deals. Increasingly, such offers may include non-food items. As one market analysis report concluded, 'A competitively-priced non-food offer provides a halo over the rest of the offer and supports the price perception that the food offer is also keenly priced.' Best-selling books are candidates for supermarket price cutting. Supermarkets offer popular titles at massive reductions. The average book price in a supermarket is £4.50, compared to £7.45 elsewhere. How are these prices financed? According to the *Bookseller*, supermarkets demand massive discounts from publishers – as high as 65 per cent through distributors. 'If this situation continues,' the *Bookseller* noted, 'supermarkets could soon be selling books more cheaply than high street booksellers can buy them from publishers.' By the end of 2003, some publishers were threatening to walk away from deals with supermarkets, even if that meant saying no to the prospect of high-volume sales. They felt that the discounts demanded by supermarkets, combined with rocketing levels of stock ordered by them and then returned, made supermarket deals uneconomic.

Traditionally, though, the most aggressive price promotions are conducted on 'known-value items' (KVIs) – food lines such as milk, bread, baked beans and bananas. KVIs are core grocery lines and weekly staples, products that are considered to be most price sensitive. Supermarkets call them 'traffic generators' because they have to be purchased frequently. They figure that consumers' price awareness is partial and our impression of value for money is largely formed by a few benchmark items. So supermarkets price-cut ruthlessly on KVIs while hiking up margins on items that nobody has a clue about. Higher prices on non-KVIs can be used to 'cross-subsidise' losses on KVIs. Who has any idea what South African grapes should really cost ? Or own-label focaccia, for that matter?

Cheap bananas, though? That sounds great, doesn't it? Until you hear what the people who grow them have to say about it, that is. In 2003, the Windward Islands Banana Development and Exporting Company gave the Competition Commission an illustration of what KVI cost-cutting had meant for its producers: 'A decision by Asda in 2002 to award its entire business to a single banana supplier – Del Monte – was followed by a banana price war which still continued, creating hardship across the spectrum for banana producers.' As the Prime Minister of St Vincent and the Grenadines, Ralph Gonsalves, put it, 'What is at stake is not just the sale of a few thousand boxes of bananas but the future of the banana industry and the livelihood of thousands of small producers and the economies of the Windward Islands.' The Windward Islands banana growers said that because their bananas were produced in an environmentally friendly way, and workers were better paid than is typical in the global banana industry, they could not compete in a price war against countries producing bananas more cheaply. Bananas that had cost £1 a pound the year before were now selling at 85 pence but sales had not risen as a result of the price cut. In effect, Windward Islands banana growers had been hit twice, first by falling prices and then by the loss of a major customer.

Banana Link has also catalogued the consequences of the present banana price war for people in 'competitive' banana zones: falling wages (below a living wage), casualisation of the labour force, worsening social benefits (such as maternity pay) and an onslaught against organised labour (trade unions). Banana Link alleges, drawing on information from industry sources, that suppliers to one major chain saw the price they were paid for a box of bananas slashed from £11 at the end of 2001 to around £7.75 by the summer of 2003, as the chain sought to preserve its profit margins while cutting the retail price.

UK banana wars demonstrate that rival supermarket chains appear effortlessly to co-ordinate their KVI price-cutting activities. If one cuts, they all cut. Each wants to be seen to be as cheap as competitors on these vital products which consumers compare. But heaven help producers on the receiving end of UK supermarkets' KVI 'price co-ordination'.

British bakers have first-hand experience of it. There have been times where UK supermarkets have set the price of sliced bread so low that farmers have found it cheaper to feed to their stock than animal feed. In 1999, when supermarket white sliced bread was being sold for as little at 7 pence a loaf, independent bakers claimed that this price didn't even cover the cost of flour. By then, the independent craft baking industry was already looking lean. In 1996, when major multiples cut instore bread prices by 30 per cent to capture a bigger share of the bread market, their prolonged price-cutting had caused a wave of bankruptcies and closures amongst high-street bakers. Supermarkets were selling for 50 pence crusty loaves that looked the same as those that sold for 80 pence on the high street. Dubbing the practice 'predatory pricing', independent bakers argued that however chuffed some consumers might be with their cheap loaves, supermarkets were selling them below cost to grab market share. De facto, supermarket instore bakeries' share has increased dramatically over recent years to account for 18 per cent of all bread sales, largely at the expense of the high-street craft baker, whose share has dropped to around 7 per cent or even less, depending on the statistics you look at. By sheer force of capital and market pressure, supermarkets have devastated the UK's craft baking industry.

Another British staple, baked beans, was the subject of the most aggressive price cutting ever witnessed in the UK. Throughout the early 1990s, a 420-gram tin of beans cost between 16 and 19 pence. Then a supermarket 'baked beans war' started, and the price dropped first to 9 pence and then to an astonishing 3 pence, when the hard discounter Kwik Save slashed its price in 1996, quickly followed by Tesco. The direct consequence was factory closures and loss of jobs. 'We literally could not can fresh air for the price they wanted to retail it at ... the cans were costing us more than [that],' Nestlé told the Competition Commission. Nestlé closed its Crosse & Blackwell canning operations and withdrew from that area of business.

The human cost of supermarkets' quest for ever lower prices from suppliers was hammered home again in September 2003, when the House of Commons Environment, Food and Rural Affairs Committee reported its findings on casual labour in agriculture and horticulture. MPs blamed the supermarkets for fostering an environment that allows gangmasters to recruit foreign casual workers to pick fruit and vegetables for a pittance. 'Gangmasters told us that suppliers are often heavily reliant on individual supermarkets and could not therefore risk antagonising their major customer by trying to negotiate over price or why produce was being rejected. The main variable cost that suppliers have is the cost of labour. It follows that they will seek to reduce this cost when their costs are under pressure.'

More coins in our pockets? Wow! But who put them there? And what did it cost them?

33

Take our word for it

Do you ever find yourself standing in a supermarket, wondering whether to buy the chain's own-label product or a branded equivalent? Our large supermarkets really want you to pick up that own-label product. They aspire to having around 50 per cent of what they sell under own-label. They want consumers to behave like groupies, following a pre-ordained script reminiscent of the brainwashed mums featured in television commercials: 'I always shop in Tesco/Sainsbury's/Asda/Safeway/Morrisons/ Somerfield, etc., and if I can I Buy Own Label.' They would like us to shake off any urge we might feel to review the relative merits of equivalent branded products and instead put blind trust in the all-round unbeatable quality of their own-label offerings.

Own-label food was pioneered in the UK by the non-supermarket food retailer Marks & Spencer. It created the highly profitable idea of St Michael as an overarching own-label brand, one so exacting that it made all other quality marks or brand assurances redundant. 'If it's good enough for St Michael it's good enough for me.' Since then the large supermarket chains, though they have never succeeded in putting their brands up there with St Michael in the UK consumer's mind, have cut themselves in for a slice of this action. Supermarkets love the idea of building up default loyalty to their brand, a kneejerk response that doesn't enquire too much about where the product comes from and how it was produced: a 'take our word for it' concept of quality. This is the beauty of own-label from a supermarket's point of view. It says to us that we really don't have to know anything much about what we buy – just that it comes from that chain. When a supermarket sells us own-label, it sells us not just a product but the notion that there is only one chain that supplies it.

There are other reasons why supermarkets love own-label. Right away, it thwarts any potentially invidious price comparisons. If consumers are so minded, they can trot round other chains comparing prices of branded lines. With own-label products, on the other hand, all that matters is that they appear to undercut any branded equivalent. If one chain's own-label lasagne seems to be rather more expensive than another's, it can cite superior ingredients or a different recipe as a plea in mitigation. Own-label lines also strengthen the supermarkets' ability to beat branded suppliers down on price with a 'Give us your product for £x or we'll replace it with own-label' negotiating stance.

Own-label can also be used against suppliers in a more ruthless way – by copying them. With the exception of chilled prepared foods, which were developed by the supermarkets trying to copy Marks & Spencer, supermarket own-label products have traditionally been imitations of best-selling brands. In extreme cases, they have looked so much like them that consumers might confuse the two. Asda, for example, was forced to change the packaging of its Puffin chocolate biscuit because it was very similar to United Biscuits' Penguin. Likewise Sainsbury's changed the design of its Classic Cola after protests by Coca-Cola. Most brands, however, are not confident or powerful enough to challenge our supermarkets in this way. They just have to cross their fingers and hope that a supermarket won't pay them the ultimate compliment of copying what they do. When 100 brand managers were questioned in one survey, more than half said they had seen their brands closely copied by retailers, and eight out of ten had lost sales as a result. By this mechanism, supermarkets use own-label to cash in on popular branded lines without incurring the costs of developing them. Some companies say that supermarkets have encouraged them to spend money trailblazing a branded product to see what sales it attracts, like a pilot line. If it sells well, and the company builds demand for it, the supermarket brings out an own-label equivalent. As one supermarket expert noted: 'In grocery products, retailers have very strong relationships with captive suppliers and can imitate a new brand within a very short time. They will sell it at a significantly lower price than the brand, eating into its sales and possibly putting downward pressure on price.'

One supplier told me about his experience:

We had this very successful product with a highly distinctive unique selling point. We were overwhelmed by orders for it from one supermarket chain so we decided to also have it made by another company under licence to increase capacity. After about a year the buyer started muttering that the product wasn't lasting long enough, to which our reply was 'Why not reduce the shelf life?' but they delisted it anyway. Then the chain started selling a very similar-looking product under a different name, made by the company that we had licensed. It had the same unique selling point but it was made with cheaper ingredients and chemical additives. The supermarket chain had been in cahoots with our licensee and colluded in the removal of the original product and its replacement with another (inferior) one it could sell more cheaply with no acknowledgement of our role in creating its unique selling point. We protested and withdrew our licence from the company. The chain was surprised we had demurred: it expected us just to accept it, and thought we were just being petulant. It punished us by delisting a further two of our products, so we ended up supplying it with only two out of the initial five.

Dave Hammond, managing director of Shetland Smokehouse, explained to me why he had vowed never to deal with British supermarkets again.

We had developed a range of restaurant-quality, chef-prepared chilled fish soups. We spent 4–5 years investing in a new system of packaging with a clear can with a metal lid which kept the contents tasting fresh. We had been supplying it to both Safeway and Waitrose for more than a year and were just about to wash our face financially after all the investment when they both turned round and told us they were delisting it for their own label. Safeway gave us just six days to get the product off the shelves. The products looked like ours but the ingredients were inferior. They had been downgraded to such an extent that I wouldn't have fed it to my dog. They charged the same for the own-label soup although it clearly cost a lot less to produce. Consumers were getting a £1.00 product in £1.99 packaging. They lifted our product and packaging, benefited from all our research and development work. It cost us a five-figure sum and five jobs. It was pretty gut-wrenching. This is what supermarkets do. They use small companies as cheap new-product development and look to us for innovation then use their own muscle to capitalise on it. They purport to extend consumer choice when in reality they are denying it, denying the public access to proper food.

Another advantage of own-label from the supermarket point of view is that the profit margin on own-label products is generally greater than on branded ones. The high proportion of own-label sold by UK supermarkets – anything from 40–60 per cent depending on the chain – is often one of the reasons given to explain why British supermarkets make higher profits than foreign chains, for whom own-label is characteristically around 20 per cent of sales. By bringing suppliers into their fold, supermarkets automatically tighten their control on their supply base.

That enables them to increase their margin, more often than not, by re-routing some of the supplier's profit into the supermarkets' own coffers, and makes own-label suppliers the most malleable and vulnerable of all supermarket suppliers.

Currently, the large supermarkets are trying to compete with one another on price without in any way reducing their profits. To fund this perpetual price war, they put own-label suppliers under constant pressure to come up with ever lower prices. Several of the large multiples are introducing what is known as 'open-book costing' with own-label suppliers. The suppliers have to open their books so that the supermarket can understand their costs and work out ways that they can be reduced. Many suppliers believe that this is being used as just another mechanism to drive down the price the supermarket pays.

Another tool to achieve lower prices, developed by the supermarkets, is the online auction system. Also known as 'e-auctions' or 'e-tenders', these allow the supermarket to play off would-be own-label suppliers against one another and thus drive down price. Suppliers know that they can lose all their business with a supermarket at the click of a mouse. They may be tempted to offer an unrealistically low price just to secure the business. Having won the business at the auction, they then have to work out how to make it pay. When *The Grocer* asked supermarket buyers whether they thought that online auctions were a better buying tool than the old system of sealed bids, 88 per cent said yes. Suppliers, on the other hand, saw them as 'blunt instruments with which to bludgeon incumbents and commoditise the supply base'. Despite the unpopularity of these auctions, 100 per cent of supermarket buyers questioned said that they were 'here to stay'.

Branded suppliers operate at arm's length from supermarket control. Unlike own-label suppliers, they have a small measure of security in the anxious world of supermarket retailing. When a product has a name – Hillside's Welsh Lamb, Sunny Orchard

Fruits, Mrs Blogg's Weekend Bakes, Organic Century Harvest and so on – the farmers, growers and producers behind them have a public face with the consumer. If consumers like what they get, the chances are that they will come back looking for more, creating a demand that the retailer may find hard to ignore. When fighting to keep their product on supermarket shelves and bracing themselves for the next round of supermarket demands, branded suppliers can console themselves with the thought that if, at the end of the day, the supermarket delisted them, it could be held to account by aggrieved consumers badgering store managers and customer relations managers to find out what happened to their favourite lines. They hope and pray that even if a buying department wants to clear them off the shelves, they can count on their visibility with the public to make it think twice. As one confectionery supplier explained, 'The major brands are in a much stronger bargaining position than own-label suppliers as the multiples have to stock them because of consumer demand.'

Own-label suppliers are faceless and anonymous as far as consumers are concerned. If a supermarket decides to change the company that makes its own-label pizza, or ditch one grower to make way for another, the change is not evident to the customers who buy the product. One co-operative explained: 'We used to pack our vegetables in our own bags with our own name but the supermarkets didn't want customers coming and asking for them by name because then they [the supermarkets] would have to buy them from us. But when they're in the chain's bags, they could be from anyone. We always wanted to get our name featured but they wouldn't do it. They didn't want their producers to have any power.' Every supermarket own-label sale automatically builds the retailer's brand, not the supplier's. Own-label is another mechanism by which supermarkets keep the retailer–supplier power balance tilted firmly in their favour.

Does the consumer get a better all-round deal from supermarket own-label, though? In the 1970s and 1980s when supermarkets first started expanding the number of own-label products they stocked, consumers saw them as cheap and cheerful no-frills lines. Many manufacturers were known to be producing both their own branded product and a supermarket lookalike own-label equivalent. Supermarkets were happy if consumers believed that when you paid more for branded products, you were simply paying through the nose for better presentation and clever marketing. Supermarkets promoted the idea that the quality of the product was no different and that it might even be coming from the same supplier. Supermarkets always presented own-label as the chain simply using its buying clout and no-nonsense approach to carve out a better deal from suppliers on the consumer's behalf. Not everyone was totally convinced though, many consumers remaining true to their favourite brands, adamant that a bowl of Kellogg's corn flakes tasted better than the own-label equivalent or that the own-label washing-up liquid didn't last as long, and was not as kind to the hands, as mild green Fairy.

Nowadays, in a climate of e-auctions, open-book costing and constant pressure to lower prices, for many suppliers it is not possible to sustain the prices demanded by the supermarkets as well as maintaining quality. One supplier told *The Grocer* that it had abandoned its own-label programme because battles over price with the multiples meant that it was 'turning out a much inferior product'. Another said that it had taken the same action. 'We found we could no longer make any money out of own-label ... It was driven by price, not quality, and it now appears the consumer may be tiring of own-label and declining product quality could be one reason.' Further illustrating the decline of quality of own-label products is the claim by suppliers of confectionery, ready meals and household goods to Sainsbury's in August 2003 that the multiple had 'asked them to grade down quality to match Asda and Tesco on price'. One confectionery supplier said that Sainsbury's had told him that its quality was too high to compete on price with Tesco and Asda and consequently it was 'product tiering' its whole own-label offering into high-quality, standard and price-fighting ranges, 'taking quality out at all levels'. This process is otherwise known as 'value engineering', an industry term for looking at ways to use cheaper ingredients.

When you pick up own-label, although the packaging looks smart, it may not live up to its promise. The people who produced it are probably getting less and less out of doing so, because they are being squeezed on price so that the supermarket can undercut branded equivalents and match other chains' prices while maintaining its overall profit margin. Own-label suppliers do not even have the consolation, as branded suppliers do, of feeling proud because some consumers like what they do. Increasingly they are treated as anonymous, dispensable workhorses to churn out product – a product that the supermarket sources as a commodity but sells to the consumer as if it was up there with the best in its league.

34

Safety in numbers

Shopping in supermarkets gives us a certain sense of security, of safety in numbers. We tend to believe that if we were going to encounter a dodgy piece of meat, or a potentially dangerous or fraudulent product of any sort, this would be more likely to happen at a market stall, a roadside burger bar, a school or hospital canteen – not on our supermarket shelves. Supermarkets tell us they have rigorous quality standards that embrace food safety issues. Tesco, for example, says that its 'technical and quality standards are always very high to ensure we always deliver customers safe, high quality food' while Sainsbury's says that 'food safety is paramount to Sainsbury's and we are committed to the highest standards in this area'. We know that big institutions have a lot to lose if they get it wrong. We would like to think that supermarkets have constructed an impenetrable firewall around the food they sell. In the words of one market intelligence report, 'The multiples must be seen as keepers of food safety and standards. If this slips the chains will be vulnerable.' Consumers already have their doubts. In an ICM poll carried out for the *Guardian* in 2003, only 39 per cent of respondents said they trusted supermarkets to give them reliable information about the safety of food.

From speaking to suppliers, it became clear to me that supermarkets set great store by auditing schemes, conducted by either official or external bodies that embrace food safety and check that a product is what it says it is. Farmers, growers and manufacturers told me that they are expected to sign up to a number of quality assurance schemes – usually at their own expense – so that in the event of anything going wrong with a product there would be a paper trail to show that neither they nor the supermarket had been negligent.

In the spring of 2003, my eye was drawn to a news article about soup. Asda had recalled a batch of vegetable soup because of concerns that the cans might explode as a result of being overfilled. Product recall notices appear in newspapers on a regular basis, and with me they rarely earn more than a passing glance to check that the product affected is not in my larder. But this one captured my imagination, even amused me. The image of an erupting fountain of Thick Country Vegetable Soup was spectacular and faintly ludicrous, like something out of a comic strip. True, a soup explosion could have been very nasty indeed for someone, and not just because their kitchen walls would almost certainly require repainting, but no one appeared to have been hurt. And Asda was keen to make amends. Customers should throw away the affected tins, it said, and save the labels for a refund. All's well that ends well.

But that recall got me wondering whether the products on our shelves were as safe as we would like to think. I started looking out for product recalls. I discovered that in the two months before the exploding soup warnings, Asda had issued recalls on two other items. 'Despite rigorous quality control procedures a quantity of Asda French set yogurts may contain small pieces of metal.' That sounded a lot less funny than the exploding soup, and Asda's offer of 'a full return or replacement' seemed somewhat inadequate in the circumstances. Its apology for 'any inconvenience caused' didn't seem to do justice to the potential gravity of the situation either. Yogurts, after all, are frequently eaten by toddlers with very small throats. And then there were the Asda Extra Special Totally Nuts Cookies that had been incorrectly packaged in Extra Special Belgian Cookie boxes. Although the latter were labelled with a 'may contain traces of nuts' warning, Asda was clearly worried about potential consequences for nut allergy sufferers who, in their haste to scoff the cookies, might not remember to check the small print. Tesco's recall of fruit muesli was in the same mould, necessitated by the 'inadvertent' inclusion of nuts and seeds.

It began to dawn on me that there was a constant trickle of product recalls emanating from our large supermarket chains. There were the hot dogs withdrawn by both Asda and Lidl in 2001 'because they carried a small risk of giving people food poisoning'; Asda talked of 'a small risk of bacterial spoilage'. Furthermore, the Lidl cans were 'at risk of exploding'. That same year, Asda, Morrisons and Sainsbury's all recalled tins of gooseberries because they might contain 'levels of tin that exceed statutory limits'. In 2003, a batch of Morrisons' own-label salad cream was recalled because 'a small number may contain pieces of glass'. Glass was also the concern when Tesco recalled batches of Vegetarian Four Nut Cutlets 'due to possible contamination'. Later in 2003 Morrisons also had a problem with four different own-label soups: cream of mushroom, cream of chicken, cream of tomato and vegetable. In this instance the warning simply read that 'tests have identified a packaging fault which may affect the high standard of the above soups'. There were no hints as to what that might mean for consumer health or safety.

I noticed that recalls invariably came with assurances that only specific batches were affected. 'No other products or codes affected' was a phrase that appeared frequently. It certainly made me feel a whole lot better. These recalls, it seemed, were worrying but understandable one-offs. Unfortunate things do happen in food production. Bits drop off equipment, glass cracks. They're the retail equivalent of hairgrips and drawing pins dropping into the family dinner. I couldn't get too steamed up about it. The alacrity with which supermarkets issue recall notices could be favourably interpreted as a sign of their extreme vigilance, or less favourably as indicative of a sincere desire to avoid legal action. Non-supermarket retailers are often affected too; recalls are not an exclusively supermarket problem. Supermarkets loomed large in product recalls, though, because they supply some 80 per cent of the food Britain eats.

But then there were the bigger, more deeply troubling scares that often affected several chains simultaneously. In March 2002, the Food Standards Agency issued a warning about batches of shrimps and prawns from South-East Asia. Its tests on 16 out of 77 samples had tested positive for 'illegal and unacceptable residues of nitrofuran drugs'. Nitrofurans are banned in the EU because of concerns including 'a possible increased risk of cancer in humans through long-term consumption', the Agency explained. Companies involved were co-operating with the Agency and had issued recalls. The list included Sainsbury's, Tesco, Safeway, the Co-op and Iceland.

A product recall with even longer tentacles was necessitated by Sudan 1. This is a dye, normally used for industrial purposes in solvents, petrol and shoe polish but banned in food. It had turned up in chilli powder. 'Because Sudan 1 may contribute to the development of cancer in people it is not considered safe to eat at any level and independent experts advise that intakes should be as low as possible,' the Food Standards Agency explained. This discovery started hitting the headlines in August 2003, when batches of Cirio brand Arrabbiata sauce that had been on sale in Sainsbury's and Waitrose were recalled. In the following month, Bertolli's Pesto Rosso was recalled, as were three Safeway and four Sainsbury's pasta sauces. By October, Asda's Chinese chicken curry with egg fried rice had joined the recall list, as had Morrisons' chicken tikka masala. The penetration of Sudan 1 in food products was not confined to supermarkets. A number of independent brands not stocked by supermarkets as well as products sold wholesale to catering and small retailers were affected too. The presence of Sudan 1 in so many foods spoke volumes about the British fondness for chilli heat. But it also showed that several supermarket chains' safety standards were not fail-safe. As with nitrofuran residues in prawns, the problem had been picked up by EU surveillance agencies and the Food Standards Agency, not the supermarkets.

The permeability of some leading chains' safety standards was most starkly demonstrated in August 2003 by the case of Denby Poultry Products in Derbyshire. Four men working for this company were found guilty of diverting unfit meat into the food chain. The court heard how at the company's pet-food processing plant the gang had received from slaughterhouses waste that was either condemned or intended for pet food, butchered it, then passed it on as legitimate poultry meat. Denby's extensive output found its way not just to the usual suspects – institutional caterers and takeaways – but to Sainsbury's, Tesco, Asda, Waitrose and Kwik Save.

What was most alarming about this fraud, apart from the fact that it had involved a substantial tonnage of unfit poultry over a period of a year or more, was that it had come to light through tip-offs from an informer which were then followed up by the local environmental health authority and the police. Unlike the product recalls mentioned above, in this case no warning bells had rung in supermarket surveillance systems. Indeed supermarkets had been unaware that all was not well with certain products until it was brought to their attention by the police. Needless to say, product recalls swiftly followed the discovery.

When BBC 1's *Food Police* programme reported on the case later in the year, the response it got from supermarkets involved was not reassuring. Sainsbury's, whose own-label chicken paste was affected, and Kwik Save both said that all their meat ingredients came from officially approved sources. Tesco and Asda said that they could not be held accountable for every branded product in their stores. Waitrose made no comment. It sounded as though the supermarkets involved were renouncing responsibility. Many viewers were left wondering how the safety standards of some chains could have been so thoroughly compromised by such a dangerous and unsophisticated fraud. As Professor Hugh Pennington, one of the foremost UK experts on food poisoning, told the BBC, 'I am surprised that supermarkets have been conned by criminals. There are clearly loopholes in the systems operated by supermarkets.'

Every year, of course, UK supermarkets sell hundreds of thousands of tonnes of safe and wholesome food. Products that do not fit this bill, and which are consequently recalled, represent only the tiniest proportion of the food they sell. But these particularly worrying episodes underline the fact that even leading supermarkets' food safety defence systems are more porous than consumers might like to think.

to the origins of their food', Sainsbury's started putting photographs of British farmers on packaging. Predictably, those chosen to smile out at the public all farmed organically. It might be some time, I reckoned, before the habitually publicity-shunning personnel of intensive farming offered themselves up for mugshots. Captions such as 'Hi there. I'm Bill, the guy who keeps thousands of chickens in a stuffy, windowless barn!' Or 'Meet Sally. She checks your farmed salmon for sea lice!' don't have quite the right ring.

If you look at our big supermarkets' promotional material, you could be forgiven for getting the impression that they were terribly serious about encouraging small (often organic), native and preferably local producers. In the last year or two, supermarkets have formed 'local sourcing' and 'regionality' teams, who are keen to introduce us to suppliers who rear lamb on windswept, seaweedy shores, make handmade cheese with time-honoured techniques and manufacture puddings to a traditional family recipe in a cosy farmhouse kitchen. Depending on the food category, you can expect visual props: a nautical oilskin and an Arran polo neck for the salmon farmer, a shepherd's crook for the lamb man, a dinner-lady hat and shiny copper pots for the pudding person. Forget any image you might have of supermarkets churning out vast volumes of food from factory farms and kitchens: supermarkets would like us to think that an ever more significant proportion of the business they conduct is with small, artisan producers working down muddy country lanes lined with hedgerows and dry stone dykes.

And it all sounds so damn delicious too! By the time I'd finished briefing myself on all the goodies from local producers that were theoretically available in supermarkets, I was drooling. I was heartened to read about Safeway's Lancashire tomatoes, advertised in local papers when in season, its Kentish apple trial scheme, which, if successful might be rolled out to other counties. In Northern Ireland Safeway you could buy local favourites like

Tayto crisps and Denny sausage, and at the appropriate time of year Safeway would sell Northumberland lamb in Northumberland. Somerfield's Celtic Pride Lamb and West Country beef sounded yummy and I was itching to try Asda's Lakeland Sausage and Arran ice cream, and sink my teeth into Waitrose's organic bread from Long Crichel Bakery in Dorset. The extent to which supermarkets were trying to satisfy customers' desire for local food seemed to know no bounds. Sainsbury's had launched supplier development programmes, aimed specifically at small suppliers, in both Wales and the south-west of England. Asda had a Best of Wales and Best of the Lakes range, not to mention 'Local choice' gondola ends. Tesco had announced its intention to open regional buying offices in Scotland and Wales to 'seek out and source more local products for customers'. Somerfield had a Local Life logo too.

All this sounded as though it should add up to a cornucopia of more local/regional choices for the consumer. So what were we to make of the survey by Mintel, 'Attitudes towards buying local produce (2003)'? This survey had found a 'considerable degree of frustration among shoppers who appear to be willing to buy British but are unable to do so because the produce is not stocked by their retailers. Almost one third (30 per cent) complain that British produce is not always available; specifically (21 per cent) point the finger at supermarkets for not stocking enough British-grown fruit and vegetables and 11 per cent claim that these same retailers do not carry enough British meat.' Mintel commented, 'there is no indication of any direct support (among most supermarkets) for locally sourced produce'. Forget local, it seemed: many shoppers were still struggling to buy British in UK supermarkets.

It was back to the drawing board. How could we nail this one? I sent a questionnaire to the nine leading supermarket chains, plus non-supermarket food retailer Marks & Spencer, asking them what percentage of all their food lines, both dry and fresh, in a typical store were locally produced, defining this as produced within a thirty-mile radius. Any chain could group together all its local initiatives and specialist products and draw up a portfolio that suggested nationwide sourcing and availability. The acid test was what was available to customers in their nearest store. A rough percentage would help give a sense of our supermarkets' commitment to local products. The thirty-mile measure was not plucked from the air. Waitrose had told me that it used this measure 'because this is the distance that most people consider local . . . travel any further out of your area and the word "local" becomes meaningless'. Fair enough, though I had decided to be lenient and allow for a certain amount of slippage between 'local' and 'regional'. As long as an initiative seemed broadly in keeping with the general spirit of encouraging things local, I did not intend to be pedantic about the odd twenty miles here or there.

Even so, our supermarkets seemed to have inordinate difficulty in coming up with a straight answer to a relatively simple question. The best response came from the family-owned chain Booths in the north-west of England. It told me that 25 per cent of produce sold comes from 'within Booths Country' – Lancashire, Cumbria, Yorkshire and Cheshire. That was quite a bit more than thirty miles, obviously, but a spot check of a Booths store in Preston confirmed that its shelves contained a notable number of local/regional lines. Anyone actively looking for local food in Booths had quite a few choices, and not just in produce. I could instantly see why Booths had won in 2003 a prestigious Radio 4 Food and Farming Award as Best Retailer, in recognition of its strongly demonstrated commitment to local producers.

But what did the others have to say? Precisely nothing, in the case of both Tesco and Sainsbury's, who, despite being given three weeks to reply with weekly reminders, did not respond. Morrisons said that it wouldn't be able to supply me with 'that sort of information'. Safeway sent several pages of information on regional produce and local initiatives, but when it came to talking percentages it was not keen. 'A lot of the buyers are coming back to me saying they wouldn't be happy releasing such sensitive information given the current situation Safeway is in,' reported an apologetic press officer. Safeway was up for sale at the time but it was hard to see why this should prevent it from answering the question.

Waitrose had quite a lot to say on the theory of local produce. In addition to setting the thirty-mile criterion, Waitrose felt it was important that local foods should be authentic and be produced by small suppliers with strong links to the local economy. But it preferred not to talk cut-and-dried, even rough, percentages. 'This is not a numbers game, nor is it tokenism,' it said, leaving me none the wiser. Food writer Lynda Brown then carried out a spot check in a Waitrose in Marlow, Buckinghamshire, and reported the ensuing dialogue as follows.

Q. 'I've heard that Waitrose is selling local foods. Do you have any in this branch?'

A. from a shelf stacker: 'I don't know, I haven't heard anything about that.'

A. from the manager: 'No, we don't have any here. Waitrose are introducing them gradually, so we might get some in the future.'

Marks & Spencer directed me to its forthcoming 'M&S farmers in their local stores' events. M&S growers were being invited to 'adopt' their local M&S and participate in 'Meet the British Farmer and Grower' events in flagship stores. But M&S did not offer any percentage or figures for local lines in a typical store. 'There isn't a typical store especially as many of our stores are in city centres,' it said. I was left confused. Did they mean that a city-centre store couldn't have local lines? Draw a thirty-mile radius around any city and you could net a substantial number of local products if you were so minded. I was thinking of all the independent bakers, sushi-rollers, fruit juicers, sandwich stuffers, hummus makers, chocolatiers and so on who operate in London alone, and that wasn't even reaching out to the Home Counties. But Somerfield felt that 'in urban areas such as London and the South East there are few local products available'. This perceived conflict between local and urban underlined my impression that, to some chains, 'local' seemed to mean twee, heritage food, a nostalgic counterpoint to the main business of food retailing, not a new and promising way forward in itself. Somerfield also said that 'in some stores we have a percentage of local foods' but didn't say what this was.

Some chains were game enough to quantify the number of local products they stocked. Asda said that it had over 1,000 regional lines (mainly in Scotland and Wales) and 579 local products. Given that UK supermarkets now stock an average of 26,000 food lines, and Asda stores are bigger than most rivals', 579 local products nationwide sounded like a drop in the ocean. The Co-op said that it did not define local as being within thirty miles. 'We would consider local as regional i.e. Scotland, Northern Ireland, Wales, South West, South East, etc. Based on that definition, less than 1 per cent would be sourced locally if one takes a national average. However in Scotland or Northern Ireland the all store average is about 5 per cent.' I tested the Co-op's estimate by popping into my nearest Co-op to ask the manager what local products he stocked. Over the windows were emblazoned four words: 'Fresh, Natural, Value and Local'. The manager tried to be helpful but was somewhat stumped. The 'local' referred to the location of the store, he said; it was local to the area, as opposed to a suburban, out-of-town store. He could think of only one really local product – a pizza made by a company in the same city. In a nearby Sainsbury's Local store, it was apparent that a similar definition was at work since it stocked the same sandwiches, fizzy drinks, alcohol, cigarettes and convenience foods you would find in any Sainsbury's Local. Anyone naively assuming that the chain's prominent use of the word 'local' meant that locally sourced food would be on sale would have got the wrong end of the stick.

None of this research left me convinced that supermarket 'local' initiatives were either deep-rooted or well established. The suppliers I spoke to seemed downright cynical about these initiatives. Supermarkets, they said, were cultivating a Panama-hat-and-canvas-awning image that promotes a nostalgic image of food production that could be used to create a halo around many more product lines than it naturally encompassed. A grower described to me her experience of a photo shoot with a supermarket chain to produce images that would be used in its promotional literature. 'They turned up with those straw wicker baskets that make you think of country markets and asked us to pose picking the fruit and then putting it into the baskets. Our farm is actually quite modern and hi-tech. We don't ever put the fruit in straw baskets. But they were determined to show us filling the baskets because this is the image they wanted to portray to customers. It's a very successful strategy, it gives the supermarket a nice image, a warm glow.'

Others spoke of their difficulty in getting listed. 'Smaller suppliers can't get into supermarkets. They go on about local produce, maybe in a very small and select way for some fancy pots of honey, but unless you're prepared to put in an offer to a packer that you'll supply them for a year and give them prepared added value lines, you can't get in,' said one vegetable grower. Another larger supplier explained to me why local sourcing and supermarkets were strange bedfellows. 'Producers have to be able to offer a critical mass before it makes economic sense for supermarkets to deal with them. Supermarkets can actually find it easier to source product abroad from big global suppliers than have to rely on local producers. By their very nature, small-scale, local producers simply cannot come up with enough standardised product in enough guaranteed quantity. Small producers are inevitably marginal to any large retailer's activities.'

This point was hammered home when a Soil Association survey found that some major supermarkets were importing organic food from abroad when they could be buying from UK organic farmers. The survey was conducted during November and December 2003, a period chosen precisely because UK home-grown organic produce is widely available during these months. The survey showed, for example, that only 23 per cent of the organic pork on sale in Asda was from UK farms, while in Tesco only 47 per cent of the organic beef was British. In Safeway only 13 per cent of the organic cauliflowers, and in Asda only 19 per cent of the organic onions, were home-grown.

Supermarkets know that potentially many of their customers will be alienated by the uniformity of the selection of food they can buy in any supermarket up and down the land. By introducing some local lines and making them high profile, supermarkets can tap into shoppers' latent emotional desire for something qualitatively different. They therefore need local producers, marginal or not. For this reason, one food retailing futures report has predicted: 'Global sourcing by supermarkets will increase . . . [but] this trend ironically means new chances and opportunities for "local jewels".' So perhaps our shelves will be studded with local foods over the next couple of years as supermarkets uncover one gem after another. Time will tell. In the meantime, consumers can judge for themselves what supermarket local food adds up to by going into their nearest store and making a list of local lines. In all but the most exceptional stores, the back of an envelope should suffice.

36

Race to the bottom

If you are a journalist, an awful lot of bits of paper arrive on your desk highlighting supermarket 'make the world a better place'-type initiatives. Collectively, these could give the impression that our supermarkets are among the most ethical companies on the planet. But although the promotional literature lends itself to quick soundbites, when such initiatives are examined more deeply – a difficult task since critical detail, as opposed to public relations spin, is frequently lacking – they are usually very piecemeal. Sainsbury's, for example, seemed to be looking for press coverage when it drew to my attention its new website which allowed consumers to trace all UK organic fruit and vegetables back to the farm. 'The move heralds a new era of transparency and traceability in the organic food chain,' the press release chirrupped. But what about transparency in the non-organic food chain? Why should it be more opaque? When I asked Sainsbury's press office to answer some straightforward questions such as 'What percentage of meat and poultry in your ready meals comes from UK-reared animals?' it was not forthcoming. In fact, it was unable to give me any response, despite repeated requests.

You can't blame supermarkets for trumpeting their successes and keeping quiet about less impressive aspects of their trading behaviour. Everyone likes to load their curriculum vitae with achievements that show them in the most flattering light. Clearly, our supermarket chains are not adverse to a little corporate halo polishing when the opportunity arises. But the fact remains that whether it is the treatment of third-world producers, the welfare of animals, the working conditions of supermarket employees, the environment or public health that concerns you, edited feel-good highlights do not help to gauge a chain's overall behaviour.

Supermarket 'good works' leave lots of questions unanswered. If a chain sells Fairtrade bananas, for example, can we assume that it has stopped selling *un*fairly traded bananas? When a super-market gets a splash in the media for its new promotion of healthy food for children, does this mean that it has cut back its promotions of *un*healthy foods to children? Do we hear more about admirably ethical behaviour from certain chains just because they are more adept than others at spinning stories to the media? And when supermarkets win prestigious-sounding awards, are they worth the paper they were written on or have the criteria been diplomatically watered down or confidentiality agreements signed to ensure that supermarkets would play along with them?

Are some chains genuinely more socially responsible than others? Most supermarket chains now sell Fairtrade coffee, for example, albeit not in all their stores. Yet the Co-op is the only one committed enough to switch its entire own-label range of instant and ground coffee to Fairtrade, even though the Co-op is paying two and three times more for its coffee. Would others be so willing?

If chains sign up to laudable charters or schemes, we might infer that they make efforts to see that they abide by their prin-ciples, but that may not be the case. In 2003, Tesco, for example, was forced to admit that it had been selling 'Outdoor Deluxe' garden furniture made from illegally logged hardwoods from the Indonesian rain forest. For as little as £25, Tesco's customers could buy their very own chunk of endangered forest. Yet since 1995 Tesco had been an enthusiastic signatory to a charter run by the UK arm of the WWF, the global environment group, which was designed to protect ancient, internationally threatened forests. Tesco defended itself by saying that it had not 'knowingly bought the timber from illegal sources', leaving consumers and environmentalists wondering how good its checks were. How much of supermarket behaviour is Dr Jekyll? How much is Mr Hyde?

The most systematic attempt to date to track UK supermarkets' progress towards a greener and fairer food system was Race to the Top, a grouping together of organisations by the International Institute of Environment and Development in 2000 to conduct an annual external review of supermarket performance in seven key areas: environment, producer relations, worker welfare in stores and supply chain, local sourcing, biodiversity, animal welfare and public health. It was a constructive, middle-of-the-road project. Seasoned opponents tend to dismiss supermarkets as a bunch of baddies and hurl stones at them from a distance; the opposite reaction is to uncritically accept supermarkets' own assessment of their performance. Race to the Top was a measured, patient attempt to set up a positive, progressive dialogue between supermarkets and the rest of society. Organisations backing it represented a wide range of civil society interest or 'stakeholder' groups: English Nature, the Royal Society for the Protection of Birds, the Fairtrade Foundation, the Marine Conservation Society, the National Federation of Women's Institutes and many more. The project involved cross-checking data provided by supermarkets through external surveys of stores and suppliers as well as commissioning research. The generally optimistic idea was that supermarkets and interest groups could work together to identify shared goals, assess performance against agreed indicators and so measure progress. For chains that were truly on the side of the angels, this was the perfect opportunity to show it. But within three years the project was as good as dead. What happened?

Problem number one was that some chains seemed to have an allergic reaction to the idea of external, third-party assessment, viewing it as an unwelcome precedent, either as a point of principle, or because they feared that it might be picked up by government and eventually lead to a regulatory scheme. UK supermarkets are used to judging themselves and accustomed to a very light regulatory touch. Most of them are keen to keep it that way. Supermarkets are already twitchy about the government's Food Industry Sustainability Strategy, which sets out to tackle issues such as pollution, litter, waste, food miles, transport and energy use and will incorporate 'challenging key performance indicators' for all the food industry, including retailers. What chain needs external regulators breathing down its neck?

Six major chains, however, agreed to partipate – the Co-op group, Iceland, Marks & Spencer, Safeway, Sainsbury's and Somerfield. Throughout 2001, discussions aimed at encouraging participation continued with Asda, Tesco, Waitrose and Morrisons, but to no avail. Without the participation of Tesco and Asda – the two biggest UK supermarket chains – Race to the Top was already looking shaky.

Throughout 2002, supermarkets were asked to fill in detailed questionnaires detailing policy and practice on key issues – the sort of nitty-gritty information needed to allow an objective assessment of performance. Methods were also developed to assess supermarkets from the outside, such as surveys of how suppliers judged the fairness of supermarkets' trading practices. But compromises were made to keep participating chains on board. In response to retailers' concerns about methodology and potentially negative publicity, it was agreed that no scores or league tables would be made public, only 'Best in Class' assessments.

By 2003, however, Iceland, Marks & Spencer and Sainsbury's

had withdrawn, citing 'lack of critical mass' – the absence of Tesco and Asda – as their primary reason. Race to the Top only had three participants left: the Co-op group, Safeway and Somerfield.

A non-supermarket participant gave me an assessment of why this constructive initiative had come to naught:

> It became clear that a number of major chains do not support the notion that they should be transparent and open to external review. Some supermarkets' ideas of accountability are very limited. They are often confined to the management of risk and image. There is a wide divergence in corporate philosophy between PLC chains like Tesco and Asda on the one hand, and the Co-op on the other. City investors don't care about companies' social responsibility credentials, and price competition instigated by Asda following its acquisition by Wal-Mart is increasingly drowning out social, environmental and ethical issues, creating a 'Race to the Bottom'. This price pressure is making supermarkets even more wary of making what they consider to be 'non-essential' investments that don't contribute to the bottom line in the short-term. In practical terms, supermarkets are also decreasingly able to respond to ethical issues posed by external groups because they are in the process of culling the kind of technical staff who would provide data on sustainable performance.

I ran this analysis by supermarket experts. No one was surprised that Race to the Top had broken down. 'Supermarkets are basically controllers,' explained one insider. 'They don't like to be controlled.' I learned that key personnel in several chains charged with advancing ethical policy objectives in a practical, as opposed to tokenistic way, had been made redundant in a bid to cut costs. There was no career ladder for those working on the ethical side of supermarket activity, they stressed; that area was more of a sleepy backwater.

Others underlined the extent to which supermarket top brass are slaves to the Stock Market and how even the slightest negative nuance in the financial press – that a chain's performance is slipping, say, or the mere mention of words like 'ailing' – is enough to stampede them into rash, short-term judgements that might prove unwise in the longer term. 'What they most dread is that their share advice on the Stock Market slips from "hold" to "sell". This compromises their offer to customers and the emphasis on financial delivery affects the chain all the way down to the buying floor,' explained one senior supermarket executive.

The fate of supermarket executives who do not deliver to the Stock Market is well recorded. For instance, Sir Peter Davis, then Sainsbury's chief executive, was nicknamed 'the Billy Bunter of food retail' by the *Sunday Times* 'Sharewatch' column for delivering 'weak' sales and 'anaemic' profit growth. The *Guardian*'s City Editor noted that Sir Peter had 'spurned the Every Day Low Prices strategy pursued by Tesco and Asda' and that his successor, Justin King, an ex-Asda and M&S man, was known to believe that 'Sir Peter had made a strategic error by not focusing, first and foremost, on checkout prices'. On Mr King's appointment, Sir Peter, who was to stay on as Sainsbury's chairman for a one-year transitional period, promptly signalled a U-turn on his pricing strategy, promising to cut prices sharply for consumers. With this sort of pressure to deliver almost immediate results to investors, it is no surprise if broader corporate social responsibility issues get left behind. As Carlos Criado-Perez, chief executive officer of Safeway, put it: 'We try to do business ethically, but we also want to do what is best business for our shareholders.'

A supplier summed up why Stock Market-listed chains are not wired up to put ethics first:

The supermarket CEO is a man with two heads. One head is looking east to the City of London, to shareholders and pension funds, and he has to deliver a better share price. It doesn't matter if he already makes perfectly respectable amounts of money. He is judged on his share price. The other head is looking to his customers. To them he has to convey this warm, cuddly, glowing, caring image otherwise they won't come into his stores. One side of supermarket behaviour is all about pure commercial profit, the other side all ethical and inclusive. So you get this lovey dovey message expressed at board level then filtered down through the marketing department, telling customers about how the chain is doing all sorts of nice things. But there is no commercial power behind it. The marketing and commercial departments simply don't connect. The marketing creates the spin while the commercial side of the operation is empowered to deliver to the Stock Market.

SUPERMARKET FUTURE

37

Retail domination

By September 2003, when Tesco announced its six-monthly profits, it was able to boast that more than £12 out of every £100 spent on the UK's high streets now went into its tills. 'This huge figure,' commented one city editor, 'shows how Tesco has been transformed from a pile-it-high and sell-it-cheap grocery business into a vast retailing machine which dominates UK shopping.' Not that Tesco's share of the grocery market was flagging: for every £100 spent on groceries in the UK, Tesco got £18. But its overall retail success was attributed to what supermarkets and market analysts refer to as the 'non-food' sector. Tesco had 'expanded into new sectors ranging from prescription medicines to furniture, DVDs, books, banking and fashion', the editor said, 'and the strategy is clearly working'.

Two months earlier, Asda had pulled off the historic coup of overtaking Sainsbury's in UK supermarket rankings to become Britain's second largest supermarket (based on total sales) after Tesco. Asda's lead over Sainsbury's was fuelled not by grocery sales – Sainsbury's still commanded 15.5 per cent of the grocery market compared to Asda's 13 per cent – but by non-food. Sainsbury's poorer performance was widely interpreted as evidence of its slowness to expand into the non-food market, which commands significantly higher margins than food.

Tesco and Asda's success underlines the fact, now widely acknowledged, that our large supermarket chains are moving up a gear. Nowadays, with only lean pickings left to be stripped from the independent grocery sector, and efforts to compete on prices in a bid to eat into rivals' market share putting their food profit margins under pressure, supermarkets aren't content with cornering the nation's grocery spend. Their chosen avenue for development is to extend their operations into newer, non-grocery territory – any area where they think they can make more money. As one market commentator put it, 'of every £5 additional operating profit to be collectively attained by the grocers [supermarkets] in 2007, we expect £4 to be derived from non-food sales'. By 2007, non-food sales at supermarkets are expected to jump by 71 per cent to £20 billion.

Hence the ever-expanding list of non-grocery goods and services on offer from UK supermarkets. These include:

- birth registration
- mortgages
- insurance (pet, car, house, travel, life)
- post office
- wills
- prescriptions
- Internet service provision
- flu jabs
- blood-pressure testing
- spectacles, contact lenses, eye tests
- nail bars
- nutritional advice
- Internet cafés
- alcoholic drinks
- coffee bars
- newspapers and magazines
- bank accounts
- crèche
- bureau de change
- credit cards
- flowers, plants and bulbs
- clothing and footwear
- electrical goods
- videos
- jewellery
- food supplements
- books
- hairdressing
- garden equipment
- tools

- car wash
- diabetes monitoring
- photo developing
- cash machines
- bouquet delivery
- dry cleaning
- land-line domestic phone provision
- kiosks for downloading music on to CDs
- cigarettes
- healthy-living zones
- beauty shops
- electricity and gas provision
- travel agents/websites
- stamps and post boxes
- paint
- key cutting
- glass hire
- financial loans
- body-mass index testing
- petrol

As the extensiveness of this list suggests, there is not a provider of goods or services whose business our large supermarkets aren't after. The newsagent, the florist, the garden centre, the chemist, the bookshop, the beautician, the off-licence, the dry cleaner, the health food shop – any retail outlet, independent or chain, is fair game. Our largest supermarket chains have become multi-tasking retail monsters with voracious appetites, looking for larger and larger stores to accommodate a higher proportion of non-grocery items. The sky is the limit. When Tesco announced its record profits in September 2003, Tesco's deputy chairman, David Reid, was clearly hungry for more. 'It's not good enough. We have got only 5% of the non-food market. We have 18% of the grocery market and there's 90% of the non-food market to go for. And we are up against overpriced high street stores. There's a lot left to go for.'

So confident is Asda about the lure of its George clothing line (jeans start at £4) that it has opened two stand-alone high-street George stores in Leeds and Croydon. These are trial stores for a possible 'roll out' of further high-street stores. By November 2003, Sainsbury's was getting its non-food act together, in the form of its Jeff & Co range featuring faux fur-trimmed sweaters and wine lace embroidered underwear with matching stockings;

and Tesco was reported to be 'eyeing up Matalan', the discount clothing retailer, for a possible takeover. 'Things really are changing, and fast. The big three [Tesco, Asda and Sainsbury's] are nipping at the heels of high street retailers in terms of emulating catwalk trends, and it goes without saying they are wiping the floor with them on price. Florence+Fred at Tesco have pastel cashmere blend turtlenecks for £8, a price that seems impossible to beat . . . The battle for my heart and mind has been won,' purred one enthusiastic fashion editor. Such is Tesco's success with its value-conscious Florence+Fred and Cherokee ranges that at the end of 2003 it decided to test a more upmarket Finest clothing range.

In other non-food fields, supermarket progress is already impressive. In 2002, one in every five music albums sold in the UK was bought in a supermarket. Only 6 per cent of books are currently sold in supermarkets but their share of individual best-selling titles can be as much as 80 per cent. 'It is nearly impossible to get to number one without the support of Tesco in particular,' one publisher told the *Bookseller*. By 2003, Tesco alone was selling more chart CDs than HMV. Asda aims to be the third or fourth largest optical retailer by 2005. Following its acquisition of the T&S chain of convenience stores in 2002, Tesco was within a hair's breadth of having market leadership in UK news and magazine retailing. By September 2003, Tesco was selling more medicines and toiletries than Boots and Super-drug together and had shifted more copies of the latest Harry Potter book than WHSmith. Shortly afterwards, when it launched its new Tesco Mobile (mobile phone) venture, Tesco said that it hoped to sign up two million customers. By that point it was already leader in mobile phone airtime sales with 12 per cent of the market for vouchers and etop-up. Tesco has also teamed up with Lastminute.com in a travel website joint venture.

Understandably, many companies in many retail sectors are becoming worried about supermarket encroachment on to their territory. In August 2003, for example, Oddbins ran a press advert showing an oppressed-looking food shopper pushing a supermarket trolley. 'Amazingly, we are not yet required by law to buy everything in supermarkets. Good news – because a lot of our wines are so rare and cheeky that supermarkets haven't even heard of them,' it read. Oddbins clearly wanted shoppers to stop and think before automatically loading up with supermarket wine. The Thresher off-licence group made its anxiety explicit when later that year it told the Competition Commission that the supermarkets used predatory pricing techniques in order to put specialists out of business. 'Following success with butchers and bakers,' it said, the specialist off-licence and the drinks category were now 'firmly in their sights'. The supermarkets' abuse of market dominance would inevitably result in 'the end of the specialist drinks retailer', said Thresher. 'Already, over 3,000 off-licences had closed since 1997 under these marketing practices.' By 2003, supermarkets controlled 65 per cent of UK wine sales and Tesco was selling one out of every five bottles of wine bought in the UK.

In the autumn of 2003, when Marks & Spencer suffered a 6 per cent plunge in its share of the back-to-school clothing market, this was attributed to its losing sales to supermarket rivals, Asda in particular. And sure enough, by August 2004, Marks & Spencer had lost its crown as the UK's largest clothing retailer to Asda. One market analyst interpreted BHS boss Phillip Green's interest in buying Safeway as a sign of concern amongst high-street non-food retailers. 'In the longer term, clothing could become the preserve of supermarkets, making life much harder for the likes of BHS. No wonder Green is keen to get his hands on one of the chains as he can see the threat round the corner.'

By the autumn of 2004, it was clear that Tesco and Asda's move into non-food areas was eating into other major retailers' profits too – and big time. Once a stalwart of the high street, WHSmith announced its worst financial performances ever, a state of affairs attributed widely to the supermarket squeeze. It was a similar story just along the high street at Boots, commented one City editor. 'Like WHSmith, Boots has been savaged by the supermarkets encroaching on its traditional health and beauty business.'

The supermarket superpowers are going head to head with big institutions too – building societies, insurers, utility providers and banks. 'There is high demand for home, motor and travel insurance, partly because of the sheer convenience,' Asda's finance director David Rutley pointed out. An indicator of the chain's keenness to incorporate financial products into the whole Asda package is the fact that it has trained its call-centre staff specially. 'We have invested a lot of time to make sure people there sound and feel like Asda colleagues [staff] and it feels like shopping at Asda.' Checkouts in all Asda stores have also been altered so that leaflets advertising financial products can be displayed alongside other 'impulse' items. Why not just pop an insurance policy into your trolley along with the weekly shop?

Supermarkets even have their eyes on the professions. Tesco, for example, is looking at extending into legal services and Sainsbury's has said that it is 'open to opportunities'. One day soon, shoppers may be able to pick up a divorce or buy a house along with their chicken korma and washing powder. In July 2003, the Lord Chancellor, Lord Falconer of Thoroton, announced his intention to shake up legal services in England and Wales. He highlighted the need for different ways of providing services, opening the way for what he dubbed 'Tesco law', whereby instead of having to go to a high-street solicitor, people could consult lawyers teamed with tax advisers and accountants to offer a one-stop legal shop all under a supermarket roof. 'Our concern,' responded the Law Society, 'is that new entrants (such as supermarkets) might cherry pick the more profitable and less complex areas of work, threatening the viability of established local firms that offer a full range of services at the heart of their communities.' In other words, if you are after a divorce or conveyancing, supermarket law shops would want to know you. But if you had an immigration problem, or you were in debt to a catalogue company, or you were a protagonist in a protracted landlord–tenant dispute, they might not.

The dream ticket for the big supermarkets is that whatever we might want or need, whatever we might have to write a cheque for, our reflex action is to look to them to provide it. They are excited by a vision of loyal consumers leading a thoroughly supermarketed life – with their chain's logo firmly emblazoned on it. In this vision, we wake up in a house bought, sold and mortgaged through a supermarket. All our heating and hot water are provided via that supermarket. Our phone land line and any Internet hook-up or mobile phones are too. Our house is furnished from that supermarket. Our clothes come from it, and if they need dry cleaning, we drop them off there. All our food and drink, needless to say, is bought there; likewise all the books and papers we read, videos and DVDs. Any trouble focusing on these, and we just pop on our supermarket spectacles. The whole shooting match – including freezer breakdown cover to safeguard all those supermarket ready meals – is insured through the supermarket. The dog is too. (Tesco already has a nationwide number for pet insurance in every phone directory.) Our garden is sown with supermarket bulbs, the grass mown with a supermarket-bought lawnmower. Bouquets of flowers and greetings cards for life's various celebrations and commiserations all come from the supermarket. Our car is financed through the supermarket. We make sure of filling it up at the supermarket's petrol pumps so as to collect more points for when we shop at the supermarket. We get advice about vaccinations and anti-malarials and sort out our travel plans at the supermarket, and we get our holiday snaps developed there on the way back. If we are feeling peaky, or just slightly hypochondriacal, we can make full use of the supermarket's instore pharmacy, healthy-living zone and shelves stacked with supplements, or we can submit ourselves to a battery of health checks. After we stock up on crisps with that bumper fifty-packet box of assorted flavours that's on promotion, we can pay to have our body mass index calculated on the way out. If the prognosis is bad, we can even write our will on the spot just in case we don't make it any further than the car park. What with all these goods and services on offer from our chosen supermarket, in the fullness of time it might make sense for us to open an account with the chain to consolidate all our various purchases into one monthly direct debit – a supermarket package payment.

Does that sound deadly boring – alarming, even? It is rapidly becoming a reality.

38

Big day out

I was on the train reading a newspaper when an article caught my eye. A new pocket-sized guide to the worst places to live in the UK had just been published, a 'Crap Map' of Britain, and sitting there at number twelve in the top fifty was my destination, Stockport. Never having visited Stockport before, I wasn't in a position to say whether it merited this ignominious designation, but I was surprised. It might be a dump as far as the editor of *Crap Towns* was concerned, but at Hazel Grove, just five minutes from the centre, it had the most advanced Sainsbury's in the country. 'A ground-breaking customer focused store constructed from a customer wish list exercise' no less, with a range of technology and services 'never seen before in the UK'. Did this editor never do any food shopping, I wondered?

Walking into the car park of this Sainsbury's, I was surprised again. It was a large store, some 40,000 square feet, but not the Asda-sized mammoth I'd expected. It looked more like a Las Vegas architect's ever so slightly futuristic take on a classical temple, or a ritzy resort hotel in Cancun, all curvy arches, pillars and pediment in dazzling white and soft Tuscan gold, warmed up with Sainsbury's favourite hot-orange lettering. Digitally remove the concrete car park out front, insert sweeping lawns or a hilltop setting, and you could send a postcard home. Well, almost.

The press blurb had made it sound like the *Tomorrow's World* of grocery, full of 'Thunderbirds are go' gizmos and little twenty-first-century luxuries that would 'make life taste better'. No, not valet parking, but it did have a staff-monitored system designed to ensure for once that disabled shoppers and mothers with small children could park, and quick-shop parking places with a twenty-minute electronic countdown ending in flashing red 'embarrassment lights' for the overstayers. It had personal shoppers to scuttle up and down the aisles deciphering your shopping list while you lounged around in a Starbucks-style Internet café with comfy sofas and Austin Powers chairs, staring at plasma screens broadcasting everything from football matches and meal ideas to adverts for Sainsbury's financial services, while the kids ran amok in the Kid's Zone above. There was a petrol-station-forecourt-sized Quick Shop for when you only wanted a carton of milk and one lemon, or a hasty lunchtime sandwich. There were airport-style 'easy checkouts' where staff would pack your shopping. You could even play at being a checkout assistant yourself at the self-scan, fast-track checkouts reserved for VIPs, otherwise known as Nectar cardholders. Better still, there were customer ambassadors who would inspire you with ideas about what you might cook that night.

Inside, this cutting-edge Sainsbury's was strangely disorienting. It was like an industrial warehouse, its innards – silvery ducts and conduits, prefab roofing, lighting gantries – all out on display. With its pearly floor, steely grey gondolas and shelving, being in it was a bit like being lost inside a giant shiny cube made from aluminium foil. The fruit and vegetable section that usually greets shoppers had been pushed back into the store and the entrance led into an area filled with non-food items: CDs, DVDs, bouquets of flower and so on – a shifting of priorities that signalled Sainsbury's goal of catching up with Asda and Tesco in this higher-profit sector.

Thereafter the store was divided into two distinct areas. Going with the flow, I first found myself strolling through a clutter of asymmetrically arranged counters: a salad bar, fishmonger's, butcher's and so on. I was on a stage set, a 'retailtainment' zone that was meant to give that 'This is not really a supermarket but a farmer's market' effect. Staff were kitted out with pork-pie hats to look the part and attention had been paid to appropriate window dressing. Fruits, for example, were displayed in 'American ends': rustic-looking cane baskets filled with straw – an idea copied from the US. A fairly humdrum instore bakery had been reinvented as a 'naked bread' counter with unwrapped bread displayed in wicker baskets in the manner of a small craft bakery. This was the most interesting part of Hazel Grove: the zone where you were meant to ooh and aah and get carried away with impulse purchases, also known as 'splurchases', from 'hero departments' that would inject some excitement into the supermarket shopping experience. The rest of the store had a more familiar layout, parallel rows of rather daunting shelves where you might drift on autopilot, picking up the drearier, less glamorous necessities of life.

The net effect was a mish-mash, a soup of contradictions. A faux farmer's market in a big box warehouse, seasoned with a dash of cappuccino cool. People and props whose apparent role was to inspire customers with ideas – but whizz them out the exit in record time. Hazel Grove seemed to be saying, 'Come to a supermarket that is not really a supermarket. Stock up here and pretend that you aren't doing your shopping at all, just popping in for a skinny latte and a motivational chat with your personal cooking coach.' Predictably, the bad news for Stockport was that Hazel Grove was destined to be out of date almost from the moment it opened, as nothing stays still in supermarketing. But Hazel Grove does demonstrate the dynamic that is driving the development of stores: hi-tech meets Olde Worlde.

In 2003, various consultants were asked to visualise the supermarket of the future for a design competition. One entry in particular attracted attention. Like Hazel Grove, it was technology-driven but retained some traditional, more sensory aspects of food shopping. The format centres around a café hub, occupying 60 per cent of the store space. Café hubs are what are known as 'dwell time areas', which reinforce the idea of supermarket shopping as a leisure activity. From here customers are hooked up to a main computer via a flat-screen computer monitor or 'link table'. They sit here with handheld personal digital assistants (PDAs), programmed to personalise their shopping experience, looking at pictures or lists of products on a screen as they travel down electronic aisles. If they buy tomato soup, for example, the PDA will also show them three similar products or alternatives. A sort of 'If you like this then you might like that' device. It will flag up special offers too. It will know what sort of products you like because it can communicate with your loyalty card, which in turn can communicate with radio frequency identification tags (RFIDs), small chips the size of a grain of sand. Using 'latent semantic indexing' – that is a picture, collated over time, of an individual's shopping habits – this technology can be used to target shoppers with customised information.

If customers never want to leave the hub, that's fine. But for the more traditional shopper – the quaint old-fashioned type who likes to sniff a melon or palpate an avocado – there are still food 'galleries' rather like display cabinets where customers can peruse the products. 'We did talk about getting rid of them [food displays/shelves] but people like them, so we kept them, albeit in a dumbed down way,' explained the designers. For that same reason, this supermarket of the future also embraces a tradition of the past in the form of market stalls to 'bring back the older, more sensory aspects of buying'.

In this vision of the future, supermarket shoppers can forget about ever having to see or physically handle food, or any other products, during a shopping trip. The same applies to walking round stores putting shopping in a trolley. That is done remotely at a distribution warehouse and the shopping is then delivered to a designated pick-up point, a bit like shopping at Argos. And there are no checkouts either. The table console doubles up as a personalised checkout.

If all this sounds like the product of an overheated imagination, it most definitely is not. Elements of this design are already being tested out by the German Metro supermarket group in its Future Store in Rheinberg, which opened in May 2003. Here, customers still have to stretch their legs outside the café, but then they pick up a tablet PC or 'personal shopping assistant' (PSA) and slot it into the front of their trolley. This gizmo then guides them through the store, leading them at the touch of a button to the aisle they want, giving them helpful information about the products and allowing them to self-scan purchases. 'Intelligent scales' digitally image and weigh any fruit or vegetable, cross-referencing it with pictures in a database, and print a label. There are information terminals where you can scan, say, a piece of pork, and get ideas about how to cook it and what wine might go with it. Plasma screens run adverts that are changed from time to time at a touch of the stock controller's PDA. A supermarket chain in Austria and Germany, Aktiv Markt, is already doing a roaring trade with special '50-plus' stores aimed at capturing the 'grey-Euro'. Germany's Federal Statistics Office predicts that by 2050 pensioners will account for half the population. Gearing their stores to the needs of this growing segment of the population gives supermarkets a whole new list of features to add to the modern mix, such as extra-loud announcements for the hard-of-hearing and shopping trolleys with folding tables for shoppers to rest on.

Irrespective of whose vision of the supermarket of the future you look at, 'instore marketing' looms large. Research shows that 75 per cent of all purchase decisions are made in the store at the 'point of purchase' or PoP. Why spend your advertising budget on expensive broad-brush media advertising campaigns when you can target customers more cheaply and effectively as they are deliberating over what to buy? As Nestlé Rowntree's marketing director Andrew Harrison put it: 'Supermarkets have replaced TV as the delivery channel for the mass audience. If I want to get my message across to 70% of British households it is obviously going to be more cost effective to run display ends in major retailers than to purchase overpriced breaks in a soap.'

Plasma screens flashing up adverts, promotional videos and specially designed PoP gondola ends that combine advertising with the storage of stock are all techniques that retailers know can influence customers' last-minute buying decisions, and they have been experimenting with ways of using them. Marks & Spencer, for example, has trialled its 'Chillovator', designed specifically for the merchandising of strawberries, described by M&S as 'a chilled hot spot for impulse purchase'. In 2003, Tesco trialled its digital advertising network, Tesco TV, in stores in Cambridge and Surrey. This consisted of a series of 42-inch plasma screens hanging from the ceiling along the main horizontal aisle, mini-screens attached to the top of shelves and a back-projected screen at the entrance. The number of screens depended on the store size, with the Bar Hill Extra store outside Cambridge getting the largest number, about seventy. Sainsbury's quickly followed with pilots of eye-height shelf-edge digital advertising in stores in Wigan, Chiswick, Winchester and Beaconsfield. Each store had about fourteen screens carrying messages from ten brand manufacturers. Larger screens over the meat and fish counters showed adverts such as Jamie Oliver demonstrating what to do with a particular meat or fish. In the US, the Safeway chain has tested trolleys equipped with screens that track customers' progress through stores and target them with specific advertising based on loyalty-card data.

Increasingly, major supermarkets expect their suppliers to carry out research and development into innovative ways of marketing their products in stores. For example, the Greenery, a supplier of vast amounts of Dutch glasshouse-grown peppers and tomatoes to UK multiples, has come up with the concept of the salad 'octagon':

> The octagon is an eight-sided island unit that can be designed to accommodate ambient and chilled core and convenience salad products, enhanced by a variety of features such as:
> – eye-catching surfaces (reflective glass, light panels, lit graphics)
> – interactive monitors (with web cams to talk directly to the 'Store Salad Chef' about meal ideas, or to growers about their produce)
> – complementary products, such as salad dressings, croutons, herbs and spices, plus recipe books, relevant utensils and equipment
> – recorded film loops (about varieties, growing, serving ideas of food personalities and star chefs presenting their choices, tips and recipes to camera)
> – 'market fresh' and 'best buy' chalkboard panels
> – triangular rotating 'today's recipe ideas' panels (like the large, constantly changing high street poster sites)
> – nutritional/health information panels.

Optional extras suggested include uplighters 'to add drama to the overall fixture and greatly increase the appeal of fresh produce lines', fragrance in the form of 'haze systems' that impart 'enhanced mouthwatering smells', projected light washes and sounds, such as bird, wind and water effects, to give background to the salad section. Another radical suggestion is to place a greenhouse around the salad section where shoppers can 'pick' their own fresh produce. Who needs farm shops?

Designers, IT consultants, marketers – there are teams of clever, well-paid people pooling their skills to come up with new ways to get us to spend more in supermarkets. This endeavour has gone way beyond the old supermarket techniques of placement and presentation. Once it was good enough just to know that customers tend to walk clockwise round a store or that products sell best at eye-level, on gondola ends and in the middle of aisles. It isn't rocket science, for example, to figure out that you will sell more sweets if you put them in 'hotspots' next to checkouts through which a captive audience of small children must pass. Supermarkets already know all the tricks in the book, from lighting produce with special bulbs that make all colours appear vibrant to using mist-generating humidifiers to keep everything looking fresh. They are past masters at laying out an apparently vast, but essentially fake variety that makes mesmerised shoppers reach out and grab the first product that sits up and says hello; 'Buy One Get One Free', 'Multibuy', 'Get 33% More For Free' and so on. But all this is Stone Age stuff. What we are facing now is a new generation of ultra-sophisticated, hi-tech stores, a brave new world of retailing where a Big Brother chain knows all about you as you walk in the store – likes and dislikes, a full list of purchases going back for years – and can target you with instore marketing and special offers designed to tickle your fancy.

In the future a trip to the supermarket could be like an outing to a retail theme park, a destination expedition for all the family that makes the high street redundant. With more gizmos than an entertainment arcade, multiple mini-cinema experiences and all the interactive opportunities you might expect in the most commercially driven modern museum to keep reluctant spouses and grizzly kids amused, the store will be a place where at least half of what is on sale is non-food, offering vast expanses where customers can hang around for hours at a time, soaking up the retailtainment and spending lots of money. The process of selecting goods and then paying for them will be speeded up by fast-track checkout systems and streamlined payment methods that liberate shoppers from the clunky grind of shopping and leave them freer to spend more money faster.

Shoppers turned off or simply bamboozled by the barrage of

'visual noise' will have their shopping choices effectively drip-fed them in the form of tailor-made meals and suggested lifestyle packages heavily influenced by the promotional spend of the biggest, most powerful suppliers. 'You bought Luxury Beef Stroganoff last time you shopped. But you haven't tried it yet along with our own-label "Better Than The Rest" luscious fruity Australian Shiraz currently on "Buy Six Bottles Get One Free" promotion . . . Along with our own-label Tarte Citron you've got a meal that tastes as good as if you had made it yourself – so why bother cooking? Be good to yourself. You're worth it . . . Oh, by the way, check out our great-value insurance quotes (special premiums for those who sign up today) . . . And with Halloween coming up fast, we have fantastic offers on children's fancy dress costumes – they make super Christmas presents too . . . Why not surprise your loved one with a bouquet for Valentine's Day? It's never too soon to make things easy on yourself by ordering early . . .'

Those stubborn consumers who still feel the need to retain some sovereignty over their shopping baskets or who just can't hack a celebrity chef on a plasma screen yacking away in their ear will be left with the reassuring nostalgia of the mock farmer's market supplemented by a few carefully stage-managed food-handling opportunities – the retail equivalents of the touchy-feely installations you get in museums to enliven rooms of dusty artefacts.

39

Tesco world

For years, the actress Prunella Scales, who played the bargain-hunting Dotty in television adverts, was the amiable public face of Tesco, Britain's biggest supermarket chain. Dotty was a character to whom people could relate, a demanding, price-conscious granny who kept the chain on its toes but always emerged well pleased with her purchases. She epitomized the image that Tesco wanted to project: that of an unthreatening, mainstream chain, not too posh like Waitrose or Sainsbury's, not downmarket like Morrisons or the foreign 'hard discounters', Lidl, Aldi and Netto. As Tesco itself put it, 'We have worked hard at developing a business model where "everyone is welcome" – we are able to serve all types of communities with our different ranges from Value to Finest foods, and with our different formats from large to small.'

But towards the end of 2006, Tesco faced a major embarrassment when the actress came out publicly in support of independent traders by backing a campaign to save her local Northcote Road in Battersea and keep big-name stores – such as Tesco – out of the area.

Ms Scales's defection from the Tesco camp seemed symptomatic of a change in the British public's attitude towards supermarkets, and Tesco in particular. Nowadays, even many people who like to use supermarkets are increasingly dismayed and dumbfounded by the number of seemingly surplus-to-requirements Tesco stores which are multiplying through the country. As Ms Scales remarked, 'I'm not against supermarkets, but I don't think they should take over.' By the beginning of 2007, there was evidence that other people in Britain felt the same way in the form of seventy-five active campaigns opposing Tesco's plans to build or expand stores.

In a parallel trend, a whole new family of words has entered common usage: take your pick from the nouns 'Tescoization', 'Tescofication', 'Tescopoly', 'Tescoland' and 'Tescoworld' and the verbs to 'Tesco' or to 'Tescofy'. These terms usually crop up in the company of words such as 'outrage', 'backlash', 'protest' and 'takeover'. In fact, words with a Tesco prefix have shot into use along with 'McWorld' or 'Walmartization' as all-purpose, derogatory terms which can be applied in many different contexts to sum up the elimination of competition by an over-dominant player. The MP Iain Duncan Smith, for instance, made an impassioned speech warning against allowing a small minority of charities to become too dominant. 'Too many Tescos means that the small chaps miss out,' he said. Other commentators complain about Google's 'Tescoization' of the internet, or Waterstone's 'Tescoization' of bookshop sales.

When applied to individuals, such terms can be used to describe a growing number of British consumers. Sean O'Grady, writing in the *Independent*, offered this definition:

> There must be people out there now whose lives have been completely 'Tescoed'. By which I mean that they will buy their groceries there, their newspapers, their lottery tickets, cut flowers, seeds, car care products, CDs, DVDs and basic electronic products. When they've done that, they'll pick up leaflets and get themselves Tesco home insurance, Tesco pet insurance and Tesco breakdown cover. Then they can apply to have all their gas and

electricity supplied by the company and can top it all off with a Tesco mortgage. The supermarket that ate Britain? You bet.

When applied to an area, Tesco terms describe the chain's over-bearing, super-sized presence. 'How does Tesco get away with it?' asked Jonathan Glancey, the *Guardian*'s architecture correspondent. 'Britain's most profitable and ubiquitous supermarket chain is rapidly expanding, with 1,900 outlets in this country alone. In city centres everywhere, Tesco branches are breeding like shrink-wrapped rabbits. Where once we had a church in every village, town and city, now we have Tesco with its Extras, Metros and Expresses.'

The imagery of an unstoppable behemoth crops up with increasing frequency. The *Guardian*'s city editor, Julia Finch, calls Tesco 'a retail juggernaut'. One south-coast resident campaigning against a further Tesco superstore put it less diplomatically: 'Tesco is rampaging through Hove like Attila the Hun.' Up and down the land, campaigners fighting against the chain's expansion share similar sentiments.

An exaggeration? Hardly. Tesco has managed – with no significant interference or intervention from the powers that be – to take control of almost 32 per cent of the nation's food spend. By 2006, one out of every eight pounds spent in shops in Britain – not just on food, but on all retail goods – was spent in Tesco. The chain is almost twice the size of both of its nearest rivals, Sainsbury's and Asda Wal-Mart. It nevertheless dismisses any talk that it may be approaching a monopolistic position and seeks to dispel fears that it is becoming too powerful, addressing the growing resentment over its expansionist activities by putting its defence across on its website, 'Talking Tesco'. '94% of the population has access to three or more supermarket fascias over 3,000 sq ft within a 15 minute drive of their home – that's great choice for the vast majority of people,' it says.

But in certain population centres, there is no doubt that Tesco looms worryingly large on the retail scene. Locations that have been well and truly 'Tescoed' include Southall and Truro, where the chain controls 57 per cent of local food spending, along with Swansea (54 per cent), Inverness (52 per cent), Twickenham and Perth (both 51 per cent). By the autumn of 2006, Tesco was the dominant supermarket in 81 out of Britain's 121 postcodes – up from 67 in 2005 – and held second place in 24 out of the remaining 40 postcodes. In a growing number of locations, there are almost no independent shops left and the typical shopping option consists of a 'choice' of a Tesco Extra, a Tesco superstore, a Tesco Metro and a couple of Tesco Express convenience stores.

Tesco plays on its development from its humble roots as a market stall, through its 'pile it high, sell it cheap' phase to Britain's largest grocer. 'From small beginnings,' it says, 'Tesco has grown to be the UK's most popular supermarket and one of British business' great success stories by fulfilling people's expectations to have safe, nutritious, quality food at affordable prices. We have maintained our popularity by listening to customers and responding to their needs.' Its defenders argue that anti-Tesco sentiments signal a 'small is beautiful' antipathy to successful businesses. In the words of one business commentator: 'There is a political-correctness bandwagon that has it in for Tesco, which is utterly pathetic. Why should we crucify a company for being bloody good? It isn't Tesco's fault that other retailers aren't as good as it is.'

Tesco likes to portray itself as a plucky little British company grown a little bigger, because it knows that its ever-expanding scale could help harden attitudes against it. This theme appears in its advertising. Take this advert that appeared in weekend supplements and magazines for one of its cheeses:

Cornish Blue.
From a little farm in Cornwall.
It won our 2004 British Cheese Challenge.

And now we sell it in over a hundred stores.
But don't worry . . .
It still comes from the same farm.
It's just not so little any more.

This advert is typical of how Tesco wants to appear familiar and unthreatening but behave like a big player. Tesco is actually a fiercely ambitious corporation with both national and global ambitions. It is intent on dominating the UK grocery market and non-food retail market by crowding out rival chains. A reflection of the scale of its ambitions is the fact that by the end of 2006 Tesco was seeking planning permission to create the biggest ever UK hypermarket, by extending its store in Purley, in south London, from 82,000 to 139,000 square feet. At that time, Asda held the British record for the biggest supermarket with its store at Milton Keynes, which has a floor space of 110,000 square feet. Plans for stores of these North American proportions underline how Tesco is rapidly becoming Britain's Wal-Mart. And by growing its global empire through Eastern Europe and Asia, it intends to go head to head with Wal-Mart. Sales outside the UK now account for nearly a quarter of Tesco's total revenues. 'Over half of Tesco's selling space is now outside the UK and the population of markets we operate in adds up to more than two billion people, representing more than half of the world's wealth,' it boasts.

On the home front, both rival supermarket chains and non-supermarket retailers are worried by its ballooning growth. As one retail analyst put it, 'Tesco's inexorable progress is a competitive threat to almost every other retailer.' In the past, British supermarket chains were happy to be part of a generic supermarket bloc. But nowadays, other chains are seeking to distance themselves from Tesco and its growing unpopularity. Breaking the unspoken rule that supermarkets never criticize each other in public, in 2006, Sainsbury's warned the Competition Commission that Tesco could have up to 43 per cent of the UK grocery market by 2010 if the commission did not take action to curb its growth, a suggestion dismissed by Tesco as 'supposition on supposition'. Asda Wal-Mart expressed similar sentiments. In his predictions for 2007, the editor of *Waitrose Food Illustrated*, William Sitwell, joined the anti-Tesco posse, envisaging that the coming year would see 'more of a move against Tescoisation'.

Variations on the same question are now being posed with increasing frequency, not to mention urgency. How big can Tesco become? Will there come a point when Tesco thinks that it has enough stores? Will it ever be satisfied? Tesco's own business plans suggest that the answer is 'no'. Tesco's recent expansion into its high-street Express format, which was fuelled by its acquisition of the T&S group of small convenience stores, has given it a highly visible city-centre presence. But Tesco is hungry for more. In 2005, its Corporate Affairs Director, Lucy Neville-Rolfe, told the All Party Parliamentary Small Shops Group that the chain would see doubling the number of Express stores in Britain by 2015 as 'a sustainable rate of growth'. This would involve adding another 600 Express stores to its portfolio over the next ten years. The chain has similar plans for developing its super-size Tesco Extra format. The proportion of floor space taken up by these hypermarkets more than tripled between 2003 and 2006. If the same rate of growth continues, Friends of the Earth calculates that the number of Tesco Extras will have tripled to 300 by 2015. Tesco itself has stated that it anticipates 'opening a further 20 Tesco Extras a year'.

How does Tesco do it? The chain itself argues that it never bullies its way into communities and always consults local people before opening a store. It says that it will 'only proceed where we are confident that local people will support it [a new store] by shopping there'. But Tesco's idea of public consultation does not seem to allow the community to say 'no' to a Tesco store. In reality, Tesco has become adept at exploiting the weaknesses in the planning system that favour multiples over independent stores. As a result, there is a growing belief in Britain that it has become almost impossible in practice to oppose the opening of a new Tesco store, and that even if councils initially reject Tesco's planning applications, the chain just keeps coming back, again and again, until it gets its way.

This was precisely what happened when plans by Tesco and its partner, Mercian Developments, for a store in Bridgnorth in Shropshire, were rejected by the High Court. The developers were quoted in the local press as saying 'we will be resubmitting an application ... we are not going to sit down and take what happened.'

In a similar episode in Carlisle, Tesco wrote a letter to members of the planning committee at their home addresses after taking the council to appeal for failing to decide in favour of an application regarded by councillors as going against their plans for the city. It was a move that prompted MP Eric Martlew to protest: 'It's just another example of Tesco using its massive power to bulldoze its way through. It is turning from a giant into a monster.'

Tesco's persistence in opening new stores, and extending old ones, in the face of tooth-and-nail local opposition is dispiriting for communities throughout Britain. In the words of a local resident of Shaftesbury, a Dorset market town which was the site of a campaign against a Tesco development: 'These guys are professionals and are in for the long haul. They have plenty of experience from around the country in winning planning permission – from PR campaigns in the local press to planning experts and expensive lawyers. What can we, a bunch of amateurs, do to stop them?'

Like other supermarket chains, Tesco knows how to work the planning system to get what it wants. Supermarket chains, by virtue of the enormous resources they have at their disposal, now have more power than local councils. A mixture of carrot and stick comes into operation. Supermarket chains can coax local councils into altering their long-established development plans to allow new stores, by changing the designation of an area from residential to retail, for example, or by dangling the carrot of 'planning gain' by agreeing to pay for community facilities such as sports grounds or social housing.

Increasingly, chains such as Tesco are engaged on a charm offensive. Tactics include setting up local 'community' websites supporting a new store, writing letters to councillors and making heart-warming small gifts and donations to local charities. The *Daily Telegraph* has reported seeing a 'battle plan' prepared by Tesco offering 'strategic advice on how to best promote developments and Tesco's interests in all local, regional, national and UK governments'. It reported that this document contained, amongst other things, advice on building networks at a local level, draft press releases, letters and petitions, and advice on how to 'sell' developments to the local community.

The supermarket stick comes into use if councils don't play along. Councils face the prospect of a potentially ruinous legal bill if they oppose Tesco's plans and Tesco appeals. In Allerton, south Liverpool, councillors twice rejected Tesco's proposals for a store extension, mainly on the basis that it would mean building on playing fields. Tesco appealed against the council's first decision and the appeal allegedly finally cost the council £500,000. According to the *Liverpool Daily Post*, Tesco told planners that it would withdraw the appeal if the council approved its second set of plans.

Tesco's success in opening new stores has been aided by its dogged acquisition of potential sites for new stores. By the spring of 2006, Tesco owned 58 per cent of the unbuilt-supermarket sites in the UK, some 185 sites – more than all its rivals put together. Tesco insists that the term 'landbank' is misleading, preferring to refer to it as a 'pipeline' of potential new sites. It defends the extent of its land development portfolio. 'We build stores of different sizes, often in deprived areas and on contaminated land others won't touch and parcel together sites so we can invest in town centres, always taking risks on planning approval,' it says.

But Tesco's rivals are adamant that it has established a stranglehold on possible development sites and stifling competition. Sainsbury's, for instance, has complained that Tesco's high level of market share in some areas 'restricts consumer choice and creates the potential for future consumer harm'. It warned that this situation was 'likely to worsen on current growth trajectories and landholdings' and has called for Tesco's 'landbank' of undeveloped sites to be sold off.

At the beginning of 2007, there were murmurings that the Competition Commission, in yet another probe into UK supermarkets, might eventually force Tesco to sell off some of the sites it has acquired, a move that Tesco would oppose with all its might. At the same time, the government seemed keen to press ahead with plans to 'ease' planning rules in England on the sale of green belt, in line with the recommendations of the Treasury-commissioned Barker Review. The recommendations, if adopted, would make it easier for supermarket chains to build on land next to towns and cities, and make it easier for Tesco to obtain planning permission for sites already in its development portfolio.

On its current track record, there seems little or nothing to stop Tesco becoming bigger and bigger. As they say in the US, you ain't seen nothin' yet. Should we be worried, or should we just sit back and embrace the multiple Tescos lining our high streets and crowding our suburbs? Naturally, Tesco wants us to feel comfortable with its rapid growth. 'Britain is changing,' it says. 'Shopping habits change as lives change. As life has become busier and more complex, and living costs more expensive, Tesco has helped make shopping simpler, more convenient and affordable. Customers have rewarded us with their loyalty.'

But how many British consumers actively said 'yes' to a Britain carpet-bombed with Tesco stores? How many of us really want to see more run-down shopping parades filled with charity shops and tanning parlours where the greengrocer's, chemist and butcher's used to be? Do we really want citizenship of a country where there is no real food culture and just a supermarket culture centred around just one chain – Tesco? Tesco isn't just responding to consumer demand: it is actively reshaping society and building Tescoworld to suit its own needs, rather than the wider needs of communities in Britain. We may have given our loyalty to Tesco, even by default. But just like Dotty in those Tesco adverts, it is never too late to withdraw it.

Supermarket solutions

PERSONAL SOLUTIONS – EVERY LITTLE HELPS

If the supermarket superpowers' grip on Britain's shopping basket bothers you, you can do something to confront it personally.

Support non-supermarket shopping alternatives wherever you can

Swap some of your business to independent outlets. Revisit independent food shops and think about what proportion of your shopping you could transfer to them. Buy your newspapers in newsagents, buy your wine from wine shops, use the local pharmacy for prescriptions and so on. Every sale diverted from a supermarket helps independents flourish. Use them or lose them. If consumers took even 5 per cent of their shopping from supermarkets and redistributed it amongst independents, it would make a huge difference to the non-supermarket sector. Don't worry if you can't swap the lot. Just remember Tesco's own words, Every Little Helps.

Think twice before you shop in a supermarket

If you jump into the car automatically and go to a supermarket every time you need a newspaper or a carton of milk, begin asking yourself if each trip is strictly necessary. Is there not a smaller independent outlet that can provide what you are after?

By shopping in smaller shops like greengrocers and butchers you will also reduce the amount of unnecessary packaging you have to dispose of because fresh foods from small shops are generally less over-packaged than their supermarket equivalents. Think of all the money you will save because you won't be picking up other items you don't really need, which is usually what happens every time you make yet another unnecessary supermarket trip.

Ask yourself if you actually like supermarket shopping

If the answer is no and you don't find that supermarkets 'make life taste better' or 'lighten your load', the next question is, 'Are you a masochist?' Why keep on doing it? Set about thinking how you can inject some food shopping pleasure – and variety – back into your life.

Cut the number of trips you make to a supermarket

If you usually visit a supermarket weekly, try making that fort-nightly. If you go fortnightly, cut that back to three-weekly and so on. Try to find other sources for your groceries. Cheer up your life by renouncing the tyranny of the once-a-week, one-stop shop. Enliven your cooking and eating habits. Begin to savour the pleasures to be had from getting back in touch with non-supermarket food and shopping.

Get informed about alternative shopping possibilities

When did you last check out your nearest independents? Perhaps they are better than you think. Some of the small shops that have survived the supermarket onslaught are pretty damn good. Why pigeonhole them as purveyors of the occasional real-food treat? What about local farmers' markets, box and mail-order schemes? Some independent shopkeepers now operate home-delivery schemes. Ask them what the possibilities are. There are many more than you might think.

Destroy your loyalty card

Why carry around in your wallet a permanent plastic advert for grocery giants? Do you want to be a supermarket-defined person? Do you want the big retailers to know all about you and your buying habits so that they can target you more effectively? Ceremoniously destroy any supermarket loyalty or finance card you have been carrying and pledge your loyalty instead to anyone offering an independent alternative to supermarket monoculture.

Press for change

Look at www.tescopoly.org. This is a campaigning website which explores ways of opposing new stores and extensions, reports on supermarket-related news, and discusses social, economic and environmental issues around supermarket development. It offers a wealth of material for anti-supermarket campaigners.

POLITICAL SOLUTIONS

Cap the size of all new supermarkets

Smaller stores don't have the same neutron-bomb effect on the local area as big ones. The government could set an upper size limit on all new supermarkets, as there is in the Irish Republic.

Tighten up planning law

The government could make it much harder for supermarkets to build extensions and get permission for longer opening hours. As supermarkets replicate like mutants all over the UK, it's time for government to focus on the concept of need. Do we really need any more new supermarkets? Who is going to decide when saturation point has been reached? Society, or the supermarkets themselves?

Appoint a supermarket regulator

Supermarkets are over-powerful and under-regulated. It is time for a watchdog to worry them into acting responsibly. Give him or her something solid to get his/her teeth into. A tightly worded, legally binding code of conduct which offered the protection of anonymity for complainants and a requirement for contracts to be given to suppliers would be a start.

Tighten up competition law

How long are we going to let supermarkets get away with persistent below-cost selling and price flexing in order to see off the opposition – often an independent? Clamp down on these unfair practices. The French and the Irish have done it.

Tax them more

Charge supermarkets for their acres of parking spaces. Free parking lures shoppers from independent outlets to supermarkets, encouraging car use. If supermarkets want to offer free parking, make them pay a tax for every space they offer.

Make them take back the waste they generate

To reduce the mountains of excessive, supermarket-generated food packaging building up in landfill sites up and down the land the government could make it mandatory for supermarkets to take back packaging waste and operate refundable deposit schemes on bottles. As the Irish government has done, it could legislate to cut waste by making all retailers charge for plastic carrier bags.

Reduce rates paid by independent food retailers

Rate relief could be extended to independent shops. Priority rebates could be given to high-street shops trying to compete with edge-of-town superstores and city-centre convenience-store formats run by supermarkets. Local business rates could take into account the wider benefits to the whole community of having a thriving network of small, independent shops.

Supermarket responses

In the course of researching this book, a number of suppliers I interviewed expressed concerns about how supermarkets conduct their business. Most of these suppliers were only prepared to talk to me on a non-attributable basis because they feared repercussions if their views/grievances were made public. In these circumstances, it seemed only fair to give supermarkets an opportunity to have their say. So, in order to give a balanced view of the relationship between supermarkets and suppliers, I asked each of the top ten UK grocery retailers to complete a questionnaire (see page 335). This précised the concerns raised with me by supermarket suppliers and asked the chains to state whether or not these reflected their business practice.

What follows is each chain's response. Some of these have been minimally edited and abbreviated in the interests of readability. Safeway, the Co-op, Waitrose and Booths all addressed the specific questions as put. Tesco, Asda and Sainsbury's did not answer the questions specifically but offered a covering statement or relevant information. Morrisons and Marks & Spencer declined the opportunity to respond. Somerfield was unable to respond within the time given (five weeks).

TESCO

'We understand that good supplier relationships are critical in delivering for our customers. In turn, our understanding of our customers is beneficial for the suppliers who choose to work with us and we believe that we have some of the best partnerships with our suppliers in the industry. Ensuring suppliers are treated fairly is an important issue throughout the retailing industry and there are rules and regulations by which we have to work. We do conduct tough negotiations with our suppliers, but they are also fair negotiations. Our commercial teams are thoroughly trained to ensure they comply with the Supplier Code of Conduct and we are actively helping in the code's review, currently being undertaken by the OFT. We believe this hard work is bringing benefits to both suppliers and Tesco. We would take any specific complaint very seriously and deal with it correctly through the appropriate channels.'

ASDA

'We are particularly proud of the partnerships we have developed with our agricultural and food suppliers in the last few years. We are committed to buying British wherever possible (subject to availability, quality, and food safety) and increasing the volume of British meat, dairy and produce that we sell to our customers. To illustrate that fact, 90 per cent of the fresh food we sell that we can source from Britain, we do source from Britain. We are also committed to extending the range and volume of home-grown produce we sell to our customers. In April we launched a "Buy British" campaign under the banner "Good, Honest Value – Celebrating Home-grown Produce", with the aim of increasing sales for our farmer suppliers, whilst educating customers about where their food comes from. Sales of British products have increased significantly as a result, for example we have doubled the amount of Ayrshire potatoes we sell in our thirty-four Scottish stores. We believe no multiple retailer is doing more in the area of local sourcing at the moment. This year we were extremely proud to be shortlisted for the BBC's Food and Farming award for best national/regional retailer. We were praised by the judges for our approach to local sourcing, which has seen £1m worth of local products sold each week in our stores. And our local sourcing programme is no mere PR stunt – it's at the heart of how we operate. We have a dedicated local sourcing team whose sole aim is to identify local products and work with small suppliers to enable those products to reach our stores. The team enlists the support of regional food groups as well as our own customers and colleagues to discover what the essential local brands and delicacies are in each area.

'In September 2002, Sir Donald Curry, chairman of the Government's Policy Commission on the Future of Farming and Food, called on farmers and retailers to follow ASDA's lead at the launch of Plumgarths, a pioneering partnership with a local Cumbrian food park. The initiative has been a launch pad for a range of projects to find local products from small suppliers for all 265 ASDA stores.

'ASDA's commitment to offering everyday low prices (EDLP) is supported by, and helps enhance, good relationships with our suppliers. Delivering EDLP requires us to work together with suppliers to achieve the common goal of increased sales. Removing high low pricing, i.e. buy one get one free offers etc., also ensures that our suppliers can plan their businesses more effectively, helping reduce their costs whilst removing unnecessary hassle from the supply chain.

'Recent farming initiatives that help to demonstrate how we work in partnership with our suppliers are:

Extending growing seasons

This year we extended the growing season for new, baby and salad potatoes by 10 weeks, and became the only retailer to halt foreign imports of carrots by extending the growing season from 46 weeks of the year to 52.

Increasing the number of farmer suppliers on cost-plus contracts

The core of our potato and carrot grower base is now on Cost Plus contracts. Cost Plus is an exclusive contract between ASDA, its suppliers (e.g. Fenmarc and Taypack) and a select group of dedicated British potato and carrot growers. It is designed to deliver sustainable year-on-year returns by taking growers away from the boom/bust cycle associated with the wholesale marketplace. Production costs are reviewed annually with the whole of the Cost Plus grower base. Cost Plus prices are set at the start of each season. They are not linked to external market prices; therefore when prices fall on the open market, farmers on the scheme do not suffer. Instead Cost Plus prices are based on the "true" cost of production.

ASDA Pork Link

Pork Link encourages producers to supply heavier, leaner pigs, and aims to reduce farmers' costs by between 5p and 10p per kilo. The scheme, set up in August 2002 in conjunction with Grampian Country Pork and Grampian Pig Producers (Scotland's largest pig marketing cooperative), started with just one Scottish farmer. It now boasts over 35 producers supplying more than 3,500 heavier pigs into the Grampian Buckie plant each week. Farmers on the scheme get paid within 48 hours for their pigs. In addition, farmers who are making the transition to breeding heavier pigs are offered interest free loans to ease cash flow problems.

Lamb Link

In conjunction with Welsh Country Foods in 2002, we set up ASDA Lamb Link to help British sheep farmers. Lamb Link now has 2,800 members, all of whom get paid within one working day for their lambs. In addition, lambs are collected direct from farms, saving the Lamb Link farmer time and hassle. ASDA has paid out nearly £250k in bonuses to farmers in the first full year of the scheme. We are now handling approximately one million lambs a year and sales of ASDA British lamb are up by 20% year-on-year.'

SAINSBURY'S

'Sainsbury's is committed to developing and maintaining mutually beneficial relationships with our suppliers and have carried out extensive work at a local sourcing level to help suppliers grow their businesses. There are several announcements on our corporate website – j-sainsbury.co.uk – to this effect such as 3rd June 2003 and 6th August 2003. There is a specific section of our website *http://www.j-sainsbury.co.uk/csr/suppliers.htm* which deals with our relationship with our suppliers – click on the "corporate social responsibility section" and then "suppliers" – which will provide the information you need. In particular you should look at our code of practice which covers many of the policies to which you refer in your questionnaire.'

This detailed twelve-page code of practice for Sainsbury's buyers incorporates the Office of Fair Trading Code. The key principles are transparency, fair dealing, balance and clarity of communication.

Points covered by this code particularly pertinent to my questionnaire are:

- that a buyer's responsibility is to conduct fair but effective trading relationships
- that there should be no undue delay in payments to suppliers
- that there should be no unjustified payments sought from suppliers for consumer complaints

- that suppliers should have advance notice of new or changed terms, and the more important the term affected, the more notice should be given
- that buyers should never unilaterally impose cost price changes or retrospective reductions
- that buyers should only debit supplier invoices when they have a strong argument with supporting evidence that money is owed to Sainsbury's, their senior manager has agreed and the supplier has been forewarned
- that although listing fees are considered normal practice in some retail sectors, buyers should never demand them as a precondition to a trading relationship
- that buyers should not oblige suppliers to contribute to costs or make a lump sum payment or to agree to a discount
- that buyers should use their best endeavours to agree in writing with a supplier what principal factors in their dealings would be likely to amount to negligence or default on the part of that supplier
- that there should be no changes to supply chain procedures without reasonable notice or compensation
- that suppliers should not predominantly fund promotions
- that if a supplier raises a query regarding sample charging, negotiations should be on a case-by-case basis.

SAFEWAY

Late delivery and returns

'The rules on failure to deliver/late delivery are clearly laid down in para 16 of our Standard Terms and Conditions of Trading. In all cases, Safeway may deduct from the cost payable to the supplier any costs we have incurred as a consequence of this failure. This would include the loss of profit to Safeway, but not the total sales revenue. However, we also reserve the right to cancel or vary the order as a whole. A lot will depend on the circumstances e.g. the seriousness of the shortfall/delay/failure and supplier's track record to date. Penalties are not automatic. Serious customer complaints and returns are covered in para 27. This commits us to giving the supplier full information so he can investigate the complaint. If, as a result, we reasonably believe the supplier is responsible, we will charge him for the administrative costs of handling it plus the cost of any compensation paid to the customer.'

Sampling

'Suppliers who want to hold sampling sessions in our stores usually meet the costs themselves (i.e. staffing time and products) but we don't charge them over and above this amount. Usually they also provide their own staff to run the sampling, so there is no question about whether it happens or not. Whatever outlay a supplier incurs for sampling is usually more than covered by the additional sales generated. If, however, it is the retailer's job to execute the sampling then clearly he must do so.'

Promotions

'Promotions are usually negotiated in detail between the relevant member of our trading team at head office and the supplier concerned. These would form part of the buying agreement covering the particular order or series of orders. Our normal practice is to ask suppliers to meet some of the costs involved – how much depends on the size and length of the promotion, the margin involved, the expected volume increase and so on. This is negotiated well in advance. The point about promotions is that the vast majority generate very big increases in volume sales (anything between 100% and 400% depending on the product and the level of discount). While this obviously benefits the retailer, it's very helpful to the supplier because in a mature market volume growth of this size drives scale economies and reduces unit production costs. Hence the enthusiasm of most suppliers for promotions. We do not charge for shelf-edge barkers.'

Imposed discounts
'Imposed discounts are certainly not our policy.'

Buyers' behaviour
'Our approach to supplier relations is governed by the OFT Code of Practice, which has been fully incorporated into our Terms and Conditions of trading. Every one of our 2000+ suppliers received a copy, as revised by the Code in 2002. Every member of our training team was given training in the observance of the Code, which we take very seriously. It is general practice throughout the industry for people in both buying and many other roles to be bonused on performance. In our case our buyers are given sales and profit targets on an annual basis. No sensible manager would approach the issue in the way which has been described to you. In a highly competitive market like ours, buyers obviously try hard to achieve the bonuses but it is not a question of threatening and bullying them. The fact that we bonus sales as well as margin performance emphasises the importance of longer-term market and brand development as well as short-term tactical initiatives on pricing.

'In an organisation the size of Safeway, with a product portfolio of 35,000 lines, over 2,000 suppliers and over 200 buyers/trading managers, it is clearly impossible for us to monitor their performance and behaviour day by day. If a supplier has reason to make a complaint, the procedure for doing so is laid down in our terms and conditions. Regrettably, virtually none of our suppliers has made use of the Code's provisions since it came in to effect in March 2002. The reason is their apparent fear of "reprisals" if they complain. While I understand this anxiety, it really is unjustified. Our larger suppliers would not in any case make use of the Code. Whenever they have an issue with us they would simply pick up the phone.'

Suppliers' contracts

'Para 16.3 of our Terms and Conditions specifies that once a supplier has accepted an order from us, we can only change or revoke it with the supplier's agreement. If we were to do so, it would only be for very important operational reasons. It is far more common for suppliers to fall short on their side of the contract, e.g. late delivery, failure to supply the volume required, quality issues. Para 16.5 states that it is an essential and funda-mental term and condition that the supplier consistently makes delivery by the time and date stated on the order for delivery. If we end up with too much product in stock, especially if it's a fresh product, we would sell it through at a reduced price. It sometimes happens that a supplier will ask us to help him sell through a stock overhang which he has got because the yield of the product (e.g. strawberries) has been particularly strong during the season. There is usually a fair amount of give and take in a trading relationship.

'In certain commodity categories the number of our suppliers has declined over the past years due to rationalisation within the supply base itself as processors and packers drive for greater scale economies and a conscious decision on our part to concentrate more on suppliers who are reliable and perform consistently well. There will be further rationalisation as and when we are acquired by Morrisons. Added-value products, especially ready meals and other convenience foods, are likely to remain the fastest-growing area of the food market. Product innovation is the driver of growth, so suppliers in this area tend to specialise in added-value lines. As we have good, innovative suppliers in these added-value categories, we tend to have a long-term relationship with them.'

Year-end financial pressure

'There is usually some additional pressure towards the end of a financial year. The same applies to suppliers who are public companies like us. There is give and take. The payment period for suppliers' invoices is specified in the individual buying agreement but our general rule is 30 days. This may occasionally be varied by mutual agreement.

'We do not as a rule seek to negotiate retrospective payments towards the end of our financial year. The only circumstances in which contractual changes are negotiated retrospectively are where the sales volume materially exceeds the levels forecast by both the supplier and ourselves. In such cases we would seek either to reduce the agreed price or increase the agreed discount. Paragraph 14.3 of our terms and conditions covers this point.'

Miscellaneous

'In the ready meals and allied categories, the main source of innovation over the past twenty years has been and remains the retailers' own-brand ranges. Branded manufacturers have tended to copy us, not the other way round. In other categories, retailers offer own-brand alternatives to manufacturers' brands. These may be cheaper but do not have the brand strength of the manufacturers' product. Own-brand alternatives have been around for many years and enhance consumer choice. Complaints on this score from manufacturers are somewhat disingenuous.

'It is very dangerous to generalise about suppliers. A very large proportion of what we sell is supplied by a relatively small number of manufacturers with strong brand names and well-established global operations or "must-have" brands. We have no option but to stock them and the notion that we can "exploit" them is absurd. Suppliers who supply own-brand products are more dependent on us. "Exploitation" is a pejorative term which completely fails to recognise the underlying mutuality of our relationship. Many of our suppliers have enjoyed decades of very profitable growth through their business with us. Most of our supplier relationships have evolved into long-term partnerships.

'The top twenty UK food manufacturers have reported an average net margin to sales of 11–12% compared with the top five supermarkets' average of 5%. Those who are strong in added-value ranges are generally doing well. The main area of mixed fortunes is undifferentiated commodities where brand loyalties are weak and the long-term trend is downwards. So there is constant pressure on costs and margins and the retail market is very competitive.'

MORRISONS

Morrisons told me that 'Our policy is that we don't become involved in individual questionnaires' but that it would be more than happy to provide me with a copy of its company information pack and annual report. This information pack, called 'This is Morrisons', does not cover Morrisons' relations with suppliers. The annual report did have one page on Morrisons and social responsibility. The only indirect reference to the chain's relations with suppliers was under the heading 'fair and ethical trading': 'In 1994 we were among the first major food retailers to sell fairly traded goods and in keeping with our commitment to fair and ethical trading we again supported Fair Trade Fortnight, with strong offers on our range of Fair Trade products. We remain committed to the implementation of our ethical trading code and our work in this regard is continuing.'

MARKS & SPENCER

Marks & Spencer said: 'As we do not class ourselves as a super-market we would like on this occasion to decline your offer to participate.'

CO-OP

Late delivery and returns

'It is not Co-op policy or practice to fine a supplier if it fails to deliver or is late in delivering a product.

'As part of our own-label contractual agreement there is a clause that covers customer dissatisfaction and complaints, which are handled in great depth by our technical department in liaison with our suppliers. Detailed information is provided on such complaints to the supplier involved both at the time of receipt and in summary format. Complaints are also reviewed to ensure that they are relevant and they are discussed with suppliers where concerns are raised.'

Sampling

'We do not charge suppliers for store sampling. We would not approve of such actions. Suppliers provide free stock for sampling but we do not charge for such sampling.'

Promotions

'We would normally attempt to negotiate a fully funded pro-motion with our suppliers, but this is not always achieved and we fund many promotions ourselves. It must be borne in mind that the majority of promotions are supplier initiated, espe-cially in the case of branded products. Overall our suppliers contribute to a promotional fund towards the cost of point of sale and advertising material, as part of the wider promotional package.'

Imposed discounts

'It is in the suppliers' interest to have the delisted line removed from store shelves as soon as possible to make room for their new product, and any assistance they can give is accepted but not mandatory.'

Buyers' behaviour

'Suggestions of a "bullying" culture have been made in many commercial negotiating and buying arenas – the grocery sector is not unique in this respect. Within the grocery sector itself, any such approach is slowly being replaced by one of category partnership between buyer and seller, which is seen as more constructive and mutually beneficial.

'As far as the Co-operative Group is concerned, our approach to this issue is clearly laid out in our Code of Business Conduct.

'We encourage the adoption of partnerships but cannot rule out isolated failings in this respect – whenever we identify such failings we take action to avoid any repetition.

'Wherever possible we seek to resolve disputes in a calm, rational manner, but it does, of course, take two to negotiate – we do not underestimate the power of the multinational suppliers who sometimes adopt bullying tactics to secure business with supermarkets.

'We do not offer bonus incentives to buyers, or make threats to sideline or dismiss them if targets are not met – these are not part of our business ethos.

'We have required our buyers to comply with this code since it was launched, despite the fact that this was targeted at the big supermarkets and we are not strictly required to adhere to it. We hold regular workshops to ensure it is being followed.'

Suppliers' contracts

'We have a signed agreement with all of our own-brand suppliers, which states clearly that there is a thirteen-week notice clause for cancellation of supply applicable to both parties.

'Our buyers are not permitted to pass on the financial conse-quences of overordering to suppliers. If we have a firm agreement on quantity, then we will honour that agreement.

'As we gradually move out of superstores into convenience units, we do not have the need for such a wide range of sup-pliers, although we have seen a steady growth in small local suppliers.

'We do encourage suppliers to develop value-added process lines and we do give them contractual assurance.'

Year-end financial pressure

'We do not put such pressure on suppliers in the form of rebates or withheld payments. We do not permit such practices which are contrary both to the OFT's code of practice and indeed our own supplier's code of conduct. We are not aware of any recent instances where this has happened.'

Miscellaneous

'We support the BRC code relating to "me-too" products, but will always seek to develop our own-brand range without deliber-ately imitating other branded products. In many cases, our own-brand products have taken a lead in their particular market and led to imitation by branded suppliers. In the case of product labelling, our own-brand range adheres to strict industry-leading policies that ensure clearly described products and avoid any confusion over the value of the product. Where issues are raised, they are readily investigated and addressed.

'Scale and leverage can always be abused, but not all suppliers are at risk in this respect, especially the multinationals who can exert their own dominance. As a relatively small supermarket, our leverage gives us limited advantage.'

The Co-op also referred me to its Code of Business Conduct, a twelve-page document, part of which deals with relations with suppliers. Adherence to this code is a condition of employment for anyone who works for the Co-op group. It summarises the Co-op's policies and procedures and explains how these tie in with its values – openness, honesty and social responsibility.

In relation to suppliers, it explains that the Co-op seeks to build partnership with suppliers, developing relationships built on trust. In particular it points out that the Co-op:

- makes available written terms of business
- undertakes to pay suppliers on time, according to agreed terms of trade
- uses effective business planning techniques when estimating orders
- seeks to establish clear lines of communication
- never uses its purchasing power unscrupulously
- works with suppliers to secure decent working conditions and better living standards for those involved in its supply chain
- encourages suppliers to reduce their environmental impact.

WAITROSE

'Our relationships with our dedicated farmers and growers are based on a genuine spirit of partnership embedded in the constitution of the John Lewis Partnership which states: "The Partnership's relationships with its suppliers must be based, as with its customers, on honesty, fairness, courtesy and promptness. It looks for a similar attitude throughout its supply chains. The Partnership values long-term relationships with its suppliers."

'We have demonstrated an unparalleled ability to work in

partnership with our suppliers to achieve major innovations in the food market. Waitrose promotes quality British foods from quality British farms, and has long been commended for its support of farmers, many of whom have worked with us for over thirty years. Waitrose has a long-term commitment to British agriculture, and farmers supplying Waitrose can be sure of a fair price that reflects the costs of production. Waitrose operates over twenty livestock producer groups – and is the only supermarket to do so. Through these groups, farmers benefit from close communication and connection with the market. Waitrose provides its farmers with clear specifications and a guaranteed market for quality stock. Waitrose sells 100% British beef, pork, poultry, salmon, trout, milk and cream all reared/produced through our producer group structure. In addition the Leckford estate, our own 4,000-acre Hampshire farm, produces a diverse range of products for Waitrose customers, including apples, mushrooms, poultry and wheat for flour.

'The Waitrose Locally Produced range represents a breakthrough for small producers wishing to supply a multiple retailer, but unable to support a whole store network. In developing this range, Waitrose aims to respond to customers' desire for high-quality local products by featuring distinctive foods with local provenance, integrity and, in many cases, tradition. If producers can only supply one branch of Waitrose, we are still happy to hear from them, and in many cases, products from the Locally Produced range are only available in a handful of shops.

'Should producers selling to Waitrose under the Locally Produced scheme wish to grow their businesses with us, we are happy to help them make this happen. Similarly, if Locally Produced suppliers are happy to maintain the size of their existing business, we will support that decision too. At Waitrose we believe in the partnership approach to doing business, and we build long-term relationships with our producers, whatever their size.' Waitrose also provided a number of case studies of suppliers, all of whom expressed a positive attitude towards working with Waitrose.

Late delivery and returns

'It is not Waitrose policy to fine a supplier if it fails to turn up or is late. We do have a clear-set policy detailing when lorries need to arrive, with contact details of those the delivery driver should contact should he or she be delayed. A warning will be given to drivers who fail to arrive or are delayed without reason or contacting Waitrose, and we may take a view to fine a persistent offender if deemed necessary. Regarding returned product, Waitrose will only charge a supplier for loss of sales if deemed absolutely necessary. We take an adult approach to this situation and appreciate that it is a two-way relationship between supplier and retailer and both parties can make mistakes.

'90% of customer complaints are dealt with in-branch. Waitrose believes that customers who approach a branch with a problem should be dealt with there and then and leave the branch satisfied with the outcome. Only if customers decide to write to head office regarding a complaint (one in ten) will a supplier be charged. The charge made is £25.'

Sampling

'All suppliers are offered the opportunity to sample in Waitrose branches. How and when this is done is decided by both buyer and supplier. Suppliers wishing to sample in Waitrose branches agree to pay for a tasting table, and a demonstrator to manage the sampling. Should a problem arise at the branch and the tasting does not take place, the tasting is always rescheduled on a mutually agreed date.'

Promotions

'No supplier is forced to promote its product. Large suppliers who wish to run a promotion are charged a fee that reflects the cost of carrying out that promotion. Promotions involve producing literature, delivering that literature and auditing the promotion to ensure all elements of the promotion are true and upheld. The cost and charge is variable according to the demands of the supplier. Smaller suppliers are not likely to be charged and a buyer will take a view and make this decision in conjunction with the supplier.'

Imposed discounts

'It is not Waitrose policy to charge a supplier for delisting a product. Waitrose does not approve of this behaviour.'

Buyers' behaviour

'Waitrose does not bully, issue delisting threats or blacklist suppliers. With just 3% market share, the Waitrose approach to doing business is different and based on truth, integrity, honesty and open communication. It is a partnership approach. Because Waitrose is co-owned by its staff (Partners as they are known), there is no pressure from the board room or the city and the whole culture at Waitrose is very different and majors on building long-term relationships with suppliers to get the very best food and drink at a price that reflects the true costs of production.

'All Waitrose Partners are paid a salary, and each year, are given a bonus as a percentage of that salary. Last year, every Partner was given an extra 10% of their annual salary as a bonus. No additional bonuses are available to buyers, or any Partner, as incentives in any situation. Again, because we are all co-owners of the business and are not driven by the stock market, there is not the pressure to drive cost prices down and to set unreasonable targets, attached to buyer penalties.

'Waitrose was not investigated by the OFT prior to the introduction of the code of practice, and as such does not need to comply with it. However, Waitrose has always operated a policy of responsible sourcing with strict ethical standards imposed on buyers' behaviour and relationships with suppliers. This policy, we believe, goes beyond the OFT code of practice although buyers are required to read and be aware of the OFT's requirements.'

Suppliers' contracts

'Waitrose will aim to give at least three months' notice to terminate a supplier contract. In the case of primary producers, the notice period could well be in excess of twelve months. Waitrose is aware of the pressures faced by producers and suppliers and after careful discussion and negotiation, a decent notice period will be agreed.

'Buyers will never charge suppliers for over-ordering. Waitrose will always honour the volumes agreed with the supplier at the beginning of the agreement. How we do this will be agreed by negotiation between buyer and supplier.

'Waitrose is not trying to reduce the number of suppliers, or producers. We are, however, aiming to consolidate deliveries into our central distribution centre – without compromising the face-to-face contact we have, on a regular basis, with our producers. We aim to make delivery into our distribution centre more efficient, while maintaining the producer network we have developed over many years.

'Waitrose has a reputation for excellent service, but also for its wide assortment. As such, Waitrose does encourage the development of own-label value-added lines to add interest to that assortment. This is always a collaborative exercise between buyer and supplier, which will be open to negotiation from both sides. With just 3% market share, Waitrose cannot, and would not choose to, take a mass-market approach to business and any agreement will be discussed and agreed, and re-negotiated if required. There are no surprises.'

Year-end financial pressure

'Waitrose would never demand rebates or withhold payments from suppliers. Since Waitrose is not a public quoted company, we are not looking at the city to determine our decisions, but instead, we consider the needs of our customers and producers. In fact, Waitrose considerations toward its producers and suppliers extends beyond this and in some cases, Waitrose has supported producers during their set up. For example, Peter Chandler grows a mix of apple varieties near Canterbury in Kent, including Tentation, for Waitrose. Waitrose sponsored the growing of this variety on Peter's farm by paying for the tree stakes. Similarly, we don't want our producers to go bankrupt when times are difficult, so we support them within competitive boundaries, and involve farmers in realistic discussions on price. During the foot-and-mouth crisis, Waitrose guaranteed to support its dedicated farmer suppliers by keeping the prices paid to them unchanged from those paid before the outbreak of foot-and-mouth disease.'

Miscellaneous

'Waitrose does offer an excellent range of own-label products but believes that it is essential to provide our customers with choice. Waitrose does not deliberately copy branded products and we believe there are many authentic branded products that are interesting and add to our assortment, without the need to create an own-label version. In the case of the Waitrose Locally Produced range, all of these products (produced no more than thirty miles from the local Waitrose shop) are sold under their own brand. We believe this is important and would not copy a product if an authentic branded product already exists.

'With only 3% market share, Waitrose could not possibly

dominate, or exploit. Nor would we wish to. Waitrose buyers aim to build long-term relationships with suppliers so we understand their market, their business and the challenges they face. It is not uncommon for a Waitrose buyer to stay within his or her department for more than twenty years. This way they not only get to know the people producing the food and drink we sell, but also, they have exceptional product knowledge allowing meaningful relationships to develop between buyer and supplier, but also the very best product on Waitrose shelves.'

BOOTHS

Late delivery and returns

'When we place an order with a supplier we give them an expected delivery date and ask them to confirm direct with our warehouse if they can deliver on that date or arrange an alternative one. Having confirmed a delivery date we expect them to deliver on that day or to contact us to give reasons as to why this is not possible. If they do not do this then we send them a warning letter and if it happens again, within a five-month period, we invoice them as a contribution towards the costs involved to our company by a supplier missing a reserved booking slot.

'If a customer returns a product because of a quality issue, the customer is automatically refunded. This complaint, and the customer comments, are automatically passed on to our supplier asking them to carry out an examination, contacting both us and the customer with their findings. If there is a fault with the product we charge the supplier for the cost of the product together with an administration charge for handling the complaint.'

Sampling

'If we arrange sampling of a product we charge the supplier the cost of the samples and for a contribution towards the labour costs, as the demonstrations are carried out by our own staff. If such a sampling is agreed we guarantee that they take place.'

Promotions
'We do invoice suppliers as a contribution towards the costs of all advertising material, in our stores, which is directly linked to a product. All promotions, including multi-buys, are partly funded by suppliers. The extent depends on how deep cut the promotion is and all details are agreed with the supplier before the promotion takes place.'

Imposed discounts
'We never ask a supplier to contribute towards the cost of discontinuing another company's product to introduce their line.'

Buyers' behaviour
'One of the attractions of being a buyer with Booths is that we are not big enough to bully suppliers and our policy has always been to work with suppliers, both large multi-nationals and small local suppliers, to our mutual benefit. Bullying would not be a good tactic to be used by Booths nor is it allowed.

'Whilst the buyers at Booths have a number of KPIs (key performance indicators), none of them are linked to salaries. Any bonuses paid are linked to company performance and not individual targets.'

Suppliers' contracts
'We place orders with suppliers in good faith and they are therefore never cancelled without good reason and acceptable notice. Cancellation of orders is very rare.

'All orders are placed in good faith with our suppliers, although if we were in an overstocked situation we would obviously bring it to the attention of the supplier and hope that we could come to some arrangement. This, however, is negotiated with our suppliers and they are not dictated to. In an ideal world, it makes financial sense to reduce the number of suppliers. However this is not a policy, and our first aim is to supply the products we believe our customers require irrelevant of how many suppliers this involves.

'Value-added lines are popular with our customers and therefore suppliers are encouraged to develop them wherever possible. However it is unlikely that these would be produced purely for Booths because of the volumes involved.'

Year-end financial pressure
'Our buyers are not put under any pressure towards our financial year-end and therefore suppliers are never put under any additional pressure at this time. Neither would rebates be requested from a supplier at any time and then calculated retrospectively.'

Miscellaneous
'We are mainly a branded house and our presence in own-label is relatively small. It is not a policy to quickly copy brand leaders under our own label. We would definitely agree that the dominance of the major supermarkets allows them to exploit suppliers. In many instance suppliers try to pass on these costs to independent retailers. Just as there is a suggestion of large retailers bullying suppliers, the same happens in reverse with large suppliers trying to bully retailers especially in the independent sector.'

QUESTIONNAIRE SENT TO UK SUPERMARKETS

Late delivery and returns
1. Is it your policy or practice to fine a supplier if it fails to deliver or is late in delivering a product? If so, how is the fine calculated? Some suppliers have suggested to me that they are

charged for the value of lost sales revenue, rather than loss of profit. Is that your policy?

2. Is it your policy to charge suppliers when a product is returned to you by a customer? If so, is such a charge imposed automatically or are safeguards in place to ensure the fault with the product was a fault for which the supplier was responsible? Some suppliers have suggested to me that insufficient information is provided to them about the details of customer complaints so that it is impossible for them to tell whether the problem is one for which they are responsible.

Sampling

3. Is it your policy or practice to charge suppliers for in-store sampling of their product? If so, do you ensure that in fact such sampling takes place? One supplier of stone fruit I talked to said that a percentage charge was imposed on sales of his product by the buyer as a product sampling rebate but that no sampling ever took place. Would you approve of such actions?

Promotions

4. To what extent are in-store promotions (such as buy-one-get-one-free offers) paid for by suppliers? Some suppliers have complained to me that stores rarely contribute to such promotions, and when they do it is only a small proportion of the cost. Suppliers have also complained that they are required to pay around £500 for shelf labels (sometimes known as 'Barker Cards') which promote their products. Is this your practice?

Imposed discounts

5. One supplier complained to me that he was asked to pay a delisting fee towards the cost of discounting a line which was being discontinued in favour of his product. Is that your policy? Is it behaviour of which you would approve?

Buyers' behaviour

6. Many suppliers have complained to me of bullying tactics by buyers and of the existence of a bullying culture. They complain of threats by buyers to delist or blacklist them if they do not co-operate with the buyer's demands, leading to a climate of fear. Would such methods be allowed in your company? Are you aware of instances when bullying has taken place? What is your policy on managing relations between buyers and suppliers?

7. Suppliers also complain that the bullying culture is contributed to by bonus incentives offered to buyers and of threats to sideline or dismiss buyers if targets set by management are not met. Do you offer such incentives or make such threats? If so how do you ensure this does not lead to undue pressure being put on suppliers?

8. Many suppliers complained that the OFT Code of Practice (introduced after the Competition Commission Report of October 2000) has not improved buyer behaviour. Do you require your buyers to comply with this code? Do you have internal codes of practice (such as a supplier care code) in place to ensure that bullying does not go on? What are your procedures for ensuring that codes of practice are followed?

Suppliers' contracts

9. Some suppliers have complained to me that orders placed with them are cancelled at unreasonably short notice causing the supplier to suffer serious financial consequences. Is this a practice which you would permit or condone? What is your policy on periods of notice for cancellation of an order?

10. Another complaint was that buyers sometimes order too much of a product but then pass the costs of that overordering on to the supplier. What is your policy on this? Are buyers permitted to impose the financial consequences of overordering on suppliers?

11. Is it your current policy or intention to reduce the total number of suppliers that you use?

12. Are suppliers encouraged to develop value-added processed lines? If so, do you give the supplier any form of contractual assurance as to the longevity of your requirements?

Year-end financial pressure

13. Some suppliers have complained to me that they are put under particular pressure towards the financial year end, either by buyers requiring further rebates which are then calculated retrospectively for the whole year or by payments being withheld until after the financial year end. Would you allow either practice? Are you aware of any instances where this has taken place?

Miscellaneous

14. Some suppliers have expressed concerns to me that innovative products supplied by them are quickly copied by supermarket 'own-label' products. Do your own-label products deliberately imitate products with which they are designed to compete?

15. Would you agree with the views expressed to me that the dominance in the market of the major supermarkets allows them to exploit suppliers?

Notes

1 Forgotten people

3. 'Sainsbury has got electric sliding door...': Laura Barton, *Guardian*, 11 June 2003

4. Decline in local grocers 1950/1990: Barton et al, *Shaping Neighbourhoods*, Routledge, 2000

4. DETR survey: 'The Impact of Large Foodstores on Market Towns and City Centres', October 1998

4. Cirencester, Fakenham and Warminster: Select Committee on Environment, Transport and Regional Affairs Second Report on the Environmental Impact of Supermarket Competition, 2000

5. Impact of Tesco on neighbouring retailers in Hove: *The Grocer*, 27 September 2003

5. DETR Select Committee: Select Committee on Environment, Transport and Regional Affairs Second Report on the Environmental Impact of Supermarket Competition, 2000

5. How supermarkets kill off town-centre shops: ibid. and 'Ghost Town Britain Report', New Economics Foundation, December 2002

6. The Institute of Grocery Distribution, Taylor Nelson Sofres, the Office of National Statistics and the Meat and Livestock Commission Statistics: MeatFax 20, Meat and Livestock Commission, 2003

6. Decline of butchers: ibid.

6. Fishmongers' market share: 'The Crisis in UK Local Food Retailing', Centre for Food Policy, Thames Valley University, July 2000

6. Specialist shops closing at rate of fifty a week: 'Clone Town Britain Report', New Economics Foundation, August 2004

6. Office of National Statistics small businesses 1994–2001: National Statistics Office, Small Business Service, Statistical Bulletin

6. No single independent food store by 2050: V.W. Mitchell and S. Kyris, 'Trends on Small Retail Outlets', Manchester School of Management, 1999

6. £10 spent in local food initiative is worth £25 to the local economy: 'Neighbourhood Shopping in the Millennium', University of Nottingham Business School, October 1998

6. Job losses: 'The impact of out-of-centre food stores on local retail employment', National Retail Planning Forum, April 1998

7. Majority of supermarket employees are part-time: Keynote Supermarkets and Superstores Report, 2002

7. English villages left without a shop: *Daily Mail*, August 2000

7. Rural shop closures: *The Grocer*, 31 March 2001

7. Newsagent closures: *Financial Times*, 24 January 2002

7. Convenience store figures and predictions: Institute of Grocery Distribution, 'Convenience Retailing 2001 The Market Report'

7. 'The supermarket groups are running businesses . . .': Seth and Randall, *The Grocers*, Kogan Page, 1999, page 274

8. Average family food shopping weight: Select Committee on Environment, Transport and Regional Affairs, Second Report on the Environmental Impact of Supermarket Competition, 2000

8. 'The large amounts of free car parking . . .': ibid.

8. Tax on out-of-town parking: 'Ghost Town Britain Report', New Economics Foundation, December 2002

2 Trolley towns

11. Asda's Dundee planning application: *Evening Telegraph*, 25 August 2003

12. Morrisons' Dundee planning application: *Evening Telegraph*, 27 November 2003

13. Terence Blacker: *Independent*, 1 November 2002

14. James Millar: *The Grocer*, 14 December 2002

14. Effect of Sainsbury's on Bourne: letter from Mrs M. Cullen, 7 September 2002

14. Closure of Midlands Co-op, Thurmaston: *The Grocer*, 15 November 2003

14. 'The tipping point': 'A Lethal Prescription', New Economics Foundation, August 2003, page 2

3 Small basket

16. 'The small basket' and 'competitive challenge': talk by Siemon Scamell-Katz, MD ID Magasin, Meal Solutions Conference, 30 June 2003

17. Average shopping visits 1998/2003: ibid.

17. 'C' stores growing in popularity: Harris International Marketing survey, *The Grocer*, 1 February 2003

18. Brian Logan: *Guardian* G2, 11 March 2003

18. The latter is reported to have caused drops in business of 30–40 per cent

for other local shops: 'Ghost Town Britain 2 Report', New Economics Foundation, December 2003

19. 'The Food Continuum': Giles Quick, MD Consumer Panels, Taylor Nelson Sofres, Meal Solutions Conference, 30 June 2003

19. Price flexing: Competition Commission Report on Supermarkets 2000, volume 1, pages 87–90, paras 2.394–2.409

20. Somerfield and Co-op on price flexing: *The Grocer*, 1 March 2003

20. The *Observer* investigates prices: *Observer*, 20 April 2003

20. Two distinct markets: Competition Commission Report on Supermarkets 2000, volume 1, page 18, para 2.26

21. Richard Hyman: *The Times* Business, 31 October 2002

21. Alldays and T&S acquisitions: ibid.

21. 'Tesco had done a land grab . . .': *Daily Telegraph*, 2 November 2002

22. Tesco Express opening one a week: *The Times* Business, 17 November 2003

22. Bill Grimsey: *The Grocer*, 5 July 2003

4 Working the system

24. Policy planning guidelines for supermarkets: Competition Commission Report on Supermarkets, 2000, volume 1, pages 45–6, volume 2, pages 266–9

25. Irish planning law: 'Dempsey confirms planning caps on retail development': Irish government press release, January 2001, and *The Grocer*, 23 August 2003

26. 170 supermarket planning applications: Competition Commission Report on Safeway 2003, page 232, table 5.29

5 Sugar daddies

27. 'At the end of the day . . .': Seth and Randall, *The Grocers*, Kogan Page, 1999, pages 218–19

28. Planning gain: Colin Breed MP, 'Checking Out the Supermarkets', House of Commons, 2003

28. Synergies and out-of-town developments: *The Grocer*, 31 May 2003, page 28

28. 'Sometimes the value of the land . . .': ibid.

28. Wimbledon FC/Milton Keynes/Bletchley's new stadium: www.stadium-mk.co.uk/welcome.htm

29. 'Regeneration projects . . .': *The Grocer*, 31 May 2003

30. 'Everyone Asda have a hobby': *Metro*, 19 August 2003

30. Space sweating and mezzanines: *The Grocer*, 5 July 2003

30. Internal building work does not require planning permission: 1990 Town and Country Planning Act, Section 55, subsection 2

30. *Dow Jones International News* on mezzanines: just-food.com, 17 February 2003

31. Mezzanines and 'Asda Wal-Mart is making a mockery . . .': Friends of the

Earth press release, 8 May 2003 and briefing 'How Supermarkets Avoid Planning Controls', July 2003

31. Asda's Sheffield mezzanine: *Hansard*, 21 October 2003, column 225
31. Sainsbury's Richmond extension: *The Grocer*, 19 June 2003
31. 'Planning approvals have not stopped...': *Daily Telegraph*, 2 November 2003

6 Pimlico v. Sainsbury's

32. Simon Jenkins: *Evening Standard*, 21 November 1997
33. Pimlico FREDA: 'Submissions to Former Victoria Bus Depot Local Inquiry', November 1997
35. John Prescott's calling-in of Sainsbury's Wilton Road proposal: *Sunday Telegraph*, 30 November 1997, and letters from Tim Yeo MP to Rt Hon. John Prescott MP, 24 November and 19 December 1997
36. Superstore near Richmond: *Sunday Times*, 16 November 1997
36. Relaxing planning regulations: 'Labour Boost for Out-of-town Shops', *Mail on Sunday*, 20 July 1997

7 Giving us what we want

39. 'They have voted with their feet...': Seth and Randall, *The Grocers*, Kogan Page, 1999, page 258
40. 2001 Radio 4 poll: *The Grocer*, 7 November 2002
40. Shoppers' dissatisfaction: Verdict, 30 January 1999
40. NOP poll: New Economics Foundation press release, 16 May 2003
40. Jamie Oliver and Sainsbury's: *The Grocer*, 14 June 2003
40. Jamie Oliver's favourite shops: *Observer Food Monthly*, June 2003
41. Terence Blacker: *Independent*, 20 January 2003
42. Mimi Spencer: *Observer Food Monthly*, June 2003
43. Colour-coded salads: *The Grocer*, 23 November 2002
43. Colour-coded cheese: *The Grocer*, 14 June 2003
44. Safeway and 'Frozen For Freshness': just-food.com, 12 May 2003
44. Tesco's meat cooking research: Matthew Fort, *Guardian* 'The Way We Eat Now' special, 10 May 2003
45. Safeway and The Best: Safeway press briefing, 31 March 2003
45. Radio 4 *Food Programme*: 'Grapes', 13 October 2002
46. 'A prime example is French Green Golden apples...': letter from Mr P. Jacobs, 7 September 2002
46. 'The UK customer...': *The Grocer*, 3 May 2003

8 Feeding bad food culture

48. Matthew Fort: *Eating up Italy*, Fourth Estate, page 98
49. Richard Ali: *The Grocer*, 19 April 2003
50. Terry Leahy: *Observer* Business, 13 April 2003

50. 'The Marks & Spencer sandwich . . .': Seth and Randall, *The Grocers*, Kogan Page, 1999, pages 129–30

51. One sandwich company supplied nearly a quarter of UK multiples' sandwiches: 'Sandwiches are a breadwinner for Hazlewood Foods', *Food and Drink Business*, 18 May 2000

52. Rowley Leigh samples Marks & Spencer ready meals: *Financial Mail*, 23 November 2003

52. Matthew Fort: *Guardian* 'The Way We Eat Now' special, 10 May 2003

53. 'Alongside work . . .': Safeway news release, 16 October 2002

53. 'I certainly wouldn't bother . . .': *The Grocer*, 9 November 2002

53. Sainsbury's Blue Parrot Cook Club: Sainsbury's press release, 18 June 2003

53. 4,000 hours of food programmes, etc.: talk by Giles Quick, MD Consumer Panels, Taylor Nelson Sofres, Meal Solutions Conference, 30 June 2003

54. Twenty minutes to cook a meal: *Sainsbury's Magazine*, May 2003

54. Eight minutes to prepare a meal: 'State of the Art in Food', Cap Gemini/Ernst & Young, 2002

54. 'People who are proficient in cooking . . .': Keynote Ready Meals Report, 2001

54. The Best: Safeway press briefing, 31 March 2003

54. Somerfield's 'Cheats Dinner Party': *Somerfield Magazine*, November 2003

54. Sainsbury's Christmas dinner: Sainsbury's press release, November 2003

55. 'Well-off young couples . . .': 'Supermarkets £1bn Move Upmarket', *The Scotsman*, 29 November 2002

55. Elizabeth David's boeuf bourguignon, *French Provincial Cooking*, Michael Joseph, 1960

56. Beef bourguignon ingredients: details from pack purchased 6 June 2003

56. Tesco's Finest advertisement: *Guardian*, 4 October 2003

56. Bombay Brasserie meal kits: *The Grocer*, 26 April 2003

9 Why it all tastes the same

58. Ken Hom's test, *Guardian* G2, 23 April 2003

59. Chilled meals suppliers: Keynote Ready Meals Report, 2001

59. Uniq: Annual Report 2003

60. Sub-branding: Keynote Supermarkets and Superstores Report 2002

62. Sainsbury's 'round-the-world voyage': *Sainsbury's Magazine*, May 2003

62. Sainsbury's 'American-style mini battered chicken fillets': purchased August 2003

62. Antonio Carluccio denounces supermarket Britalian food: *The Grocer*, 4 September 2004

63. 'Authenticity is not necessarily what people want . . .': *The Grocer*, 9 November 2002

63. British consumers spend £7,000 a minute: Datamonitor/*Sun*, 21 November 2003

63. Jonathan Meades: *Independent*, 16 May 2002

10 Fresh is worst

64. Decline in vegetable consumption: National Food Survey 2002
64. Jonathan Meades: *The Times*, 22 February 2003
65. Salt in Asda own-label foods: Asda press statement, 28 January 2003
65. Food Standards Agency findings on salt in Asda own-label foods: *Guardian*, 10 June 2003
66. Sainsbury's/NHS guided tours: just-food.com, 11 March 2003
66. Sainsbury's/Kellogg's/British Dietetic Association initiative: Eat 2b Fit, 2 May 2003
66. Waitrose sponsorship: Kid's Cookery School Annual Report 2002, page 7
66. Food Explorers education packs: Waitrose Food Explorers leaflet
67. Friends of the Earth survey: FOE press release, 19 November 2003
67. Funky Food Factory: *Somerfield Magazine*, November 2003
67. Food Explorers: www.waitrose.com/food explorers
67. Blue Parrot Café: www.sainsburys.co.uk/healthyeating
67. Safeway KIDS 'I'd like . . .' range: Safeway press release, December 2003
68. Lynda Brown: interview 18 November 2003
69. 'You might expect . . .': *Food Magazine*, October/December 2003
69. Sainsbury's, Tesco, Somerfield spurn government five-a-day logo: *The Grocer*, 5 April 2003
70. Phil Daoust: *Guardian* G2, 8 September 2003
71. 'Hero departments': *The Times* magazine, 31 May 2003
71. Morrisons' salad bars: visit to Morrisons, Spalding, 22 September 2003
71. Asda pizza 'Freshly Made for You': visit to Asda, The Jewel, Edinburgh, 27 September 2003
71. Safeway's pizzeria: visit to Safeway, Union Street, Aberdeen, 14 September 2003
72. Sainsbury's 'First For Fresh': *The Grocer*, 24 May 2003
72. Apple Bites dipped in vitamin C solution: *Which?*, 14 June 2004
72. Sainsbury's 'Fully Prepared Apple Bites' and Brian Logan: *Guardian* G2, 12 November 2002
73. Vitamin C levels in supermarket-prepared fruit and vegetables: *Which?*, June 2004

11 Permanent global summertime

75. 'Strange Fruit': *Guardian* Weekend, 7 September 2002
76. Fruit and vegetables are a destination category: Dr A. Fearne, 'The Strategic Importance of Market Research', Food Industry Management, Wye College, University of Leeds
76. 'Adams Pearmain . . .': *The Grocer*, 11 January 2003
78. Hugh Fearnley-Whittingstall: 'A Man For All Seasons', *Guardian*, 14 May 2003

78. Sainsbury's Cromwell Road shoppers: *Sainsbury's Magazine*, May 2003
78. Dennis Cotter: *Paradiso Seasons*, Atrium, 2003, page 2
79. Friends of the Earth apple surveys: press releases, 24 November 2002 and 19 November 2003
80. 'Aroma management': *Guardian*, 24 April 1996
81. Lewisham stallholder: Jim Driver, Virgin.net, 26 April 2000

12 Lost at sea

85. William Black: *Fish*, Headline, 1998, page 24
85. Decline in fish consumption: 2001–2002 Expenditure and Food Survey
86. Rick Stein: interview in *The Grocer*, 30 November 2002
87. Safeway's local fish initiative: *The Grocer*, 28 June 2003
88. 70 per cent of fish consumed in the UK originates in foreign waters: *Guardian* 'The Way We Eat Now' special, 18 May 2003
89. Rex Goldsmith: interview 20 February 2003
90. William Black, *Fish*, Headline, 1998, page 24
91. Questions to supermarket fish counters: telephone questionnaire

13 Bright red meat

93. David Lidgate: interview 5 November 2002
94. Julian Barnes: *The Pedant in the Kitchen*, Guardian Books, 2003, page 75
94. Simon Howie: *Herald* Business, 26 February 2003
95. Richard Haddock: interview 2 March 2002
95. David Lidgate: interview 5 November 2002
97. ibid.
98. Sainsbury's reader's letter: *Sainsbury's Magazine*, November 2002
98. Jamie Oliver '21 day Extra Matured Beef': *The Grocer*, 31 May and 28 June 2003
98. ITC ruling on Sainsbury's matured beef: ITC bulletin 22, 15 September 2003
99. Questions to supermarket meat counters: telephone questionnaire

14 Our weekly bread

101. 'The smell of fresh bread . . .': *The Grocer*, 17 May 2003
102. 1,500 instore bakeries: Mintel
103. 'No-time' dough: Warburton's fact sheet 'Commercial bread baking'
103. Visit to Waitrose, Henley-on-Thames: 13 November 2003
105. 85 per cent of bread sold in supermarkets: Warburton's fact sheet 'Commercial bread baking'
105. Industrial baking market: Flour Advisory Bureau statistics, www.fabflour.co.uk/businessinfo.asp
105. 'The largest food retailers . . .': Professor Leigh Sparks and Pamela Bremner,

'The Future of the Bread Retailing Market', Institute of Retail Studies, University of Stirling, 2003
105. 'Advances in enzyme technology . . .': Federation of Bakers Factsheet 20

15 Gastro-gap
106. Sainsbury's Market at Bluebird: press release 29 January 2003 and visit 30 June 2003
112. Iain Mellis: interview 21 May 2003
114. Sainsbury's cheese: *The Grocer*, 14 June and 6 September 2003
114. Tesco's curry-flavoured cheese: *Guardian*, 15 September 2003
114. Fish-and-chip-flavoured cheese: *Sunday Telegraph*, 14 September 2003

16 My big welcome
117. *Sunday Times* 'Best Company to Work For' award: *The Grocer*, 30 August 2003
117. Vacancies in supermarkets: *The Grocer*, 20 September 2003
117. Ten lowest-paid jobs, 2001: Low Pay Unit/New Earnings Survey 2001
118. Asda Big Welcome: 'Welcome to the World of Asda', October 2002, Asda Colleague Relations Guidelines, Asda Colleague Handbook
119. National minimum wage: National Minimum Wage – An Introduction
119. Low Pay Unit minimum wage recommendation: Low Pay Unit, National Minimum Wage Policy Statement 2002
124. Asda staff turnover rate: *The Grocer*, 20 September 2003

17 Life on the checkout
126. TWIST: Tesco Corporate Social Responsibility Review 2002/03
129. Anti-loyalty card T-shirts: www.fatlooby.com and *The Times* Money, 10 January 2004
130. Health and Safety Executive finding: 'Supermarket Checkouts and Musculoskeletal Disorders': Local Authority Circular 58/1
130. Sainsbury's scanning and packing advertisement: *Daily Telegraph*, 24 June 2003
131. Sir Terry Leahy's 2003 pay package: *Guardian* Business, 27 August 2004
131. Low Pay Unit minimum wage recommendation: Low Pay Unit, National Minimum Wage Policy Statement 2002
131. Tesco was one of the ten lowest-paying FTSE companies in 2003 and the average Tesco annual salary: *Guardian* Business, 27 August 2004
131. The GMB union has calculated that workers have to work 94 hours a week to achieve the average British wage: *Guardian* Business, 18 May 2004
132. Phil Hogan: *Observer* Magazine, 30 May 2004
132. Naomi Craft: *Guardian*, 18 May 2004
132. Tesco's annual staff turnover rate: *The Grocer*, 20 September 2003

132. Majority of supermarket staff are women working part-time: Keynote Superstores and Supermarkets Report, 2002

18 Climate of fear

135. Tesco salaries and profits: Tesco Annual Report and Financial Statements 2003
137. Average farming income 2002: DEFRA statistical press release, 30 January 2003
138. Patience Wheatcroft: *The Times* Business, 14 June 2003
139. Charles Secrett: interview 20 February 2003
139. Richard Haddock: interview 2 March 2003
140. Climate of apprehension: Competition Commission Report on Supermarkets, volume 1, page 6, para 1.9
140. Confidentiality and supplier reticence: ibid., volume 3, page 354 and volume 2, page 233, paras 11.21–11.28

19 Extracting the best deal

142. Relationships with suppliers: Tesco's: Tesco Corporate Social Responsibility Review 2002/3; Asda's: Mike Snell, Asda director, *Daily Telegraph* Money, 28 September 2003; Sainsbury's: Felicity Lawrence, *Guardian*, 18 March 2003
143. Carlos Criado-Perez: *The Grocer*, 17 May 2003
144. Booths 'Overall Wine Merchant of the Year': Booths press release, 5 September 2002
145. Tim Atkin: *Observer* Magazine, 5 October 2003
145. 'All he needs to know . . .': *The Grocer*, 2 August 2003
145. 'Multiples switch their buyers around . . .': Competition Commission Report on Supermarkets 2000, volume 3, page 394
145. 'The attitude is . . .': *The Grocer*, 2 August 2003
147. 65 per cent discount on books: *Bookseller*, 21 November 2003
147. 'On the whole, supermarket buyers . . .': Competition Commission Report on Supermarkets 2000, volume 3, pages 393–4
148. Sainsbury axes 200: *The Grocer*, 14 June 2003
148. 100 Sainsbury's buyers face sack: *Guardian*, 24 May 2003
148. Tesco slashes 100 executives: *Observer*, 18 May 2003
149. David Smith: 'Review of UK supermarket code set to bring out complaints', just-food.com, 2 April 2003

20 Pay to play

151. Number of practices: Colin Breed MP, 'Checking Out the Supermarkets', House of Commons, March 2003, volume 1, pages 98–143, volume 3, appendix 11.3, table 1
151. Safeway 'Focus' promotion: ibid., volume 2, page 237, para 11.41
151. Tesco and Ethical Trading Initiative: *The Grocer* 7 and 14 June 2003

152. 'Pay to play': Competition Commission Report on Safeway 2003, volume 1, page 141

152. Tim Atkin: *Observer* Magazine, 22 September 2002

152. 'Substantial number of serious concerns': Competition Commission Report on Supermarkets 2000, volume 1, page 67, para 2.299

152. Supermarket practices: Competition Commission Report on Supermarkets 2000, volume 1, pages 139–143, volume 3, pages 366–87

153. 8 per cent market share: ibid.

153. Supermarket criticisms of Competition Commission's questionnaire: Competition Commission Report on Supermarkets 2000, volume 1, page 99, paras 2.463–2.467

21 Green beans from Kenya

171. Tesco's sugar snap advertisement: *Guardian* Weekend, 9 October 2004

171. 'To explain why carbon levels soar': reader letter, *Guardian*, 12 October 2004

172. Air freight produces nine times more CO_2 emissions: Tully Wakeman, East Anglia Food Link 'Food Miles' 2004 conference, 26 May 2004

172. Tale of Kenyan green bean grower: author interview with anonymous grower, October 2004

176. South African apple picker: Oxfam's *Trading Away Our Rights* report by Kate Raworth, chapter 4, 'Injustice in the Fields'

176. Real export prices for South African apples have fallen 33 per cent since 1994: ibid.

176. Table grape grower: ibid.

176. 'Supermarket shoppers have never had so much low-cost choice': ibid.

22 Get it in writing

177. 'Talk about partnerships . . .': Competition Commission Report on Supermarkets 2000, volume 2, page 234

177. Written contracts: ibid., volume 2 page 239, volume 3 page 372

178. Tesco's producer clubs: www.tescofarming.com/ct1.php

180. Unreliability of sales forecasts, etc.: Competition Commission Report on Supermarkets 2000, volume 3, page 372

23 You've been category managed

187. By 2004, Asda was sourcing its milk from only one supplier: just-food.com, 26 May 2004

187. 250 potato growers by 2005: *The Grocer*, 8 February 2003

187. 90 per cent of herbs in pots grown by one company: 'Fruit and vegetables industry ripe for consolidation': just-food.com, 18 May 2002

187. Half Sainsbury's sales from 100 suppliers: www.j.sainsbury.co.uk/csr/suppliers.htm

187. 800–80 fresh produce suppliers: Catherine Dolan, School of Development Studies, University of East Anglia, John Humphrey, Institute of Development Studies, Brighton, 'Changing Governance Patterns in the Trade in Fresh Vegetables between Africa and the UK'

187. 'The major supermarkets now deal with just a handful of suppliers . . .': Dr A. Fearne, 'The Strategic Importance of Market Research', Food Industry Management, Wye College, University of Leeds

189. 'The major retailers' policy . . .': Seth and Randall, *The Grocers*, Kogan Page, 1999, page 281

189. Consequences of category management: Competition Commission Report on Supermarkets 2000, volume 3, pages 385–7

191. 'They stand between manufacturers and the public . . .': Competition Commission Report on Supermarkets 2000, volume 3, page 394 (726)

24 Business as usual

193. Competition Commission's recommendation for a code of practice: Competition Commission Report on Supermarkets 2000, volume 1, page 7, para 1.12

194. Clive Beddall: *The Grocer*, 19 October 2002

194. Supplier letter re Safeway and cash demands: *The Grocer*, 15 February 2003

195. Safeway's vigorous denial: ibid.

195. Supermarket code of practice: Schedule 2 Code of practice on supermarkets' dealings with suppliers, Office of Fair Trading, 17 March 2002

195. Friends of the Earth and 'close liaison': 'Farmers and the supermarket code of practice', press briefing, 17 March 2003

195. 'None of the critical points made by the NFU . . .': 'Supermarket code of practice dismally fails to deliver', press release, 31 October 2001

196. 'Vulnerable group': ibid.

196. 'If you are a small supplier . . .': *The Grocer*, 7 September 2002

196. Waitrose's view of the code of practice: Competition Commission Report on Safeway 2003, page 348, para 8.162

196. Senior executive poll: *The Grocer*, 3 May 2003

196. Competition Commission confirms poll had had no effect on buyer behaviour: Safeway Merger Inquiries, Remedies Statement, 24 June 2003

196. House of Commons on code of practice: 'Gangmasters', House of Commons Environment, Food and Rural Affairs Committee, Fourteenth report of session 2002–03, page 12

197. 'The code of practice has not been working . . .': Competition Commission Report on Safeway 2003, page 63, para 2.253

197. 'A waste of space': *The Grocer*, 25 October 2003

197. Poll of suppliers on code: *The Grocer*, 29 November 2003

25 Pruning horticulture
202. Interview with Charles Secrett: 20 February 2003
204. Celeriac: Tesco recipe magazine, October 2003
205. Statistics for brassicas: Basic Horticultural Statistics, DEFRA, table 27
205. GM crop trials in Lincolnshire: *Guardian*, 2 October 2003
208. Supermarkets' demands and effect on local labour supply: 'Gangmasters', House of Commons Environment, Food and Rural Affairs Committee, Fourteenth report of session 2002–03, page 6, paras 3–6
208. John Hayes MP: *Hansard*, 24 May 2002, columns 536–7
209. Geest PLC letter to Competition Commission: Competition Commission Report on Safeway 2003, page 352, paras 8.198–8.203
209. Bar codes debut in Spalding: BBC *News*, 16 February 2002

26 Market grab
213. Horticultural produce trading statistics: Changing governance patterns in the trade in fresh vegetables between Africa and the UK: Catherine Dolan, School of Development Studies, University of East Anglia, and John Humphrey, Institute of Development Studies, Brighton 'Changing Governance Patterns in the Trade in Fresh Vegetables between Africa and the UK' and Competition Commission Report on Safeway, page 361, para 8.280
213. Peter Jacobs: interview January 2003
214. New Covent Garden turnover: Covent Garden Market Authority 40th report 2000/2001

27 A perfect world
222. Project to extend shelf life of broccoli: *The Grocer*, 14 December 2002
222. 'They were rock hard . . .': letter from Mrs M. Cullen, 7 September 2002
223. Friends of the Earth apple and pear survey: 21 October 2002
223. 'With Flavorino vine tomatoes . . .': *Observer Food Monthly*, July 2003
224. Ginny Mayall: *BBC Good Food*, October 2003

28 Variety is not the spice of life
226. Apple varieties statistics: from Common Ground 01747 850821
227. 80 per cent of UK strawberries are Elsanta: National Summer Fruits 2002
227. 'We work with our growers . . .': www.tescofarming.com/qs.php
228. Spanish orange varieties: interview with Peter Jacobs, January 2003
230. Tesco's Supasweet onion: *Herald*, 1 August 2003

29 First stop Europe
232. Tesco in central Europe: Tesco Annual Review 2003, pages 12–17
233. Tesco's international growth strategy: 'State of the Art in Food', Cap Gemini/Ernst & Young, 2002

237. Tesco own-label in Poland: ibid., page 13
238. Tesco online auctions in Europe: *The Grocer*, 8 March 2003
238. Online auctions and hefty 'listing fees': *The Grocer*, 22 March 2003

30 Next stop the world

241. Statistics on supermarkets in Africa, Asia and Latin America and supermarket development: Thomas Reardon, C. Peter Timmer, Christopher B. Barrett and Julio Berdegue, 'The Rise of Supermarkets in Africa, Asia and Latin America', *American Journal of Agricultural Economics*, December 2003
241. Croatia: Thomas Reardon, Goran Vrabec, Damir Karakas and Conrad Fritsch, 'The Rapid Rise of Supermarkets in Croatia', 2003
242. Tesco's strategy: 'State of the Art in Food', Cap Gemini/Ernst & Young 2002
242. Tesco's depot in Korea: Tesco PLC Interim Report 2003
242. Tesco is market leader in six countries: Tesco PLC Annual Review 2003
242. 18.2 per cent of Tesco's sales are outside UK: Top 50 Grocery Retailers, M+M Planet Retail/CIES 2003
242. Tesco's £140 million China stake: *Guardian* Business, 15 July 2004
242. Tesco's acquisition of C Two-Network: Tesco PLC Interim Report 2003
242. Wal-Mart and Supermercados Amigo: M+M Planet Retail M&A database
242. Global market attractiveness: Institute of Grocery Development's Market Index 2002
243. Carrefour in thirty-one countries: M+M Planet Retail M&A database
243. Carrefour's higher margins in Argentina: Thomas Reardon, C. Peter Timmer, Christopher B. Barrett and Julio Berdegue, 'The Rise of Supermarkets in Africa, Asia and Latin America', *American Journal of Agricultural Economics*, December 2003
244. David Simons: *The Grocer*, 15 February 2003
244. Asda/Wal-Mart's buying advantage: *Daily Telegraph*, 15 January 2003
245. Tesco's sourcing of Value lines: Tesco PLC Interim Report 2003
245. Tesco sourcing from India and former USSR satellites: *The Grocer*, 7 December 2002
245. Albert Heijn's boycott of Unilever products: *The Grocer*, 12 October 2002
245. Tesco's blacklist: ibid.
245. 'Bigger multiple grocery retailers obtained lower prices ...': Competition Commission Report on Safeway 2003, page 248, para 6.65
245. Tesco is the fourth biggest retailer worldwide: Mintel European Retail Rankings 2004 and just-food.com, 15 September 2004
246. Thirty grocers account for 33 per cent of global food sales: Siam Futures, Top 30 grocery retailers

31 The new community

249. Asda wedding: *Instore Marketing Magazine*, January 2003
249. Somerfield and Asda Valentine's Day: *Herald*, 8 February 2003

250. Somerfield and psychologist: ibid.

252. Bill Grimsey: *Independent* Business, 8 May 2003

252. Wal-Mart size and sales: Magnus Linklater, *The Times*, 15 January 2003

252. Asda Neighborhood Centers and Home Town stores: Seth and Randall, *The Grocers*, Kogan Page, 1999, pages 204–5

252. Asda greeters: BBC *News*, 21 June 2001, and *Sunday Herald*, 14 September 2003

253. Asda's community services: *Instore Marketing Magazine*, January 2003

253. Terence Blacker: *Independent*, 20 January 2003

254. Suppliers' donations to supermarket charities: Competition Commission Report on Supermarkets 2000, volume 3, pages 401, 424

254. Louise Redknapp's single and Asda: *Independent on Sunday*, 28 September 2003

254. Tesco Computers For Schools scheme: Tesco Annual Report 2003

254. *Which?* Investigation: *Which?*, December 2001

255. 273 million Tesco vouchers: Tesco Annual Report 2003

255. Asda student gift card terms: Student Survival Guide mailing, September 2003

256. 'Promiscuity cards' and Waitrose's view of loyalty cards: *The Grocer*, 21 September 2002

256. Tesco on Clubcard: Tesco PLC Interim Report 2003

257. Geodemographic profiling: Tony Kent and Ogenyi Omar, *Retailing*, Palgrave Macmillan, 2003, pages 234–5

257. Supermarkets' social demographic profiles: compiled from various catchment area profiles prepared for *The Grocer* using CACI's impact analysis software and Provision supermarket catchment modelling

32 That's supermarket price

259. 'Our purpose is to make goods and services more affordable . . .': Welcome to the World of Asda, February 2002, Asda Colleague Relations Guidelines, Asda Colleague Handbook

259. UK spending on food 1958 and 1998: ONS, 1999

259. Richard Ali: letter to *The Times*, 25 January 2003

260. UK spends less on food than transport or recreation: Expenditure and Food Survey, Office for National Statistics, 23 January 2003

261. Survey of British consumers – 'I trust UK stores . . .': talk by retail director, Research International, 9 June 1999

261. Price perceptions about supermarkets: Keynote Supermarkets and Superstores Report 2002

261. Farmers' markets and supermarkets price comparison: *Which?*, July 2002

261. Dominic Prince's price check: *Spectator*, 12 June 2004

262. The 'bulk penalty' on supermarket food: *Sunday Times* Business, 27 June 2004

262. Prices of Tesco's half-price raspberries and strawberries: Tesco Value mailshot, 26 July 2004

262. Tesco's 'phoney' price war: *Sunday Times* Business, 19 September 2004

263. Spanish lettuce co-operatives complain about prices: *The Grocer*, 30 November 2002

263. NFU price survey: *Guardian*, 9 September 2002, and *Observer*, 29 September 2002

263. Lib Dem statistics on retail and farmgate price rises: Lib Dem news release, 7 August 2003

264. The mystery of milk prices: *The Grocer*, 12 September 2004

265. Post-BSE additional costs in meat processing: *The Field*, December 2002

265. Bananas are number-one contributor to British supermarket profits: Banana Link

265. The Banana Split: ibid.

265. Zimbabwean mangetouts: Institute of Development Studies, Percentage of retail value of mangetouts

265. Kenyan fresh vegetables: ibid.

265. UK top fruit grower return/retail margin: Alastair Robertson, Worldwide Fruit, presentation to Parliamentary British fruit industry group

265. Supermarket price reduction and consequences for suppliers: Competition Commission Report on Supermarkets 2000, volume 3, page 394, para 721

266. Patrick Holden: *The Grocer*, 8 November 2003

266. Sainsbury's asks suppliers to cut costs: *Financial Times*, 16 November 2002

267. Big brands complain about supermarkets (Proctor & Gamble): *The Grocer*, 9 November 2002

267. 'A competitively priced non-food provides a halo . . .': HSBC Food and Drug Retailers Report, 2001, page 14

267. Massive discounts from publishers: *Bookseller*, 21 November 2003

268. KVIs: Competition Commission Report on Safeway 2003, page 40, para 2.135–6

268. Traffic generators and cross-subsidising: Professor Paul Dobson, 'The Economic Effects of Constant Below Cost Selling Practices by Retailers', Loughborough University, 2002

268. Windward Islands bananas and price wars: Competition Commission Report on Safeway 2003, page 358, paras 8.249–8.252

268. Consequences of banana price war: Banana Link from industry sources, 2003

268. Price co-ordination: Competition Commission Report on Safeway 2003, pages 40–41, paras 2.136–2.137

269. 7-pence loaf: FARM Briefing, 'Where the money goes in the food chain – fresh bread supermarket discounting on bread and "predatory pricing" in 1996', *Financial Times*, 15 May 1996

270. Instore bakeries' share of market and impact on high-street bakers: Flour Advisory Bureau, www.fabflour.co.uk/businessinfo.asp

270. Baked beans price cutting: Competition Commission Report on Super-markets 2000, volume 2, page 246, para 11.100

270. 'Gangmasters told us . . .': 'Gangmasters', House of Commons Environment, Food and Rural Affairs Committee, Fourteenth report of session 2002–03, page 10

33 Take our word for it

272. Puffin and Classic Cola: Seth and Randall, *The Grocers*, Kogan Page, 1999, pages 283–4

272. Survey of 100 brand managers: P. Dobson, 'The Competition Effect of Own-label Goods', School of Management and Finance Discussion Papers V111, University of Nottingham 1998

273. 'In grocery products . . .': Seth and Randall, *The Grocers*, Kogan Page, 1999, page 281

274. Dave Hammond: interview 6 October 2003

274. Proportion of own-label sales in UK and abroad: Seth and Randall, *The Grocers*, Kogan Page, 1999, page 280

275. E-auctions: *The Grocer*, 29 March 2002

276. Supplier abandoning own-label: *The Grocer*, 21 June 2003

277. Confectionery suppliers: *The Grocer*, 21 June 2003

277. Sainsbury's 'taking quality out': *The Grocer*, 23 August 2003

278. Value engineering: *Financial Mail*, 23 November 2003

34 Safety in numbers

279. Tesco's 'technical and quality standards . . .': www.tescofarming.com/quality standards

279. 'Food safety is paramount to Sainsbury's . . .': www.j-sainsbury.co.uk/ Consumer FAQs What is Sainsbury's food safety policy?

279. 'The multiples must be seen as keepers of food safety . . .': Keynote Super-markets and Superstores Report 2002

279. ICM poll: *Guardian* 'The Way We Eat Now' special, 10 May 2003

280. Exploding soup recall: *Guardian*, 4 March 2003

280. Asda making amends: just-food.com, 4 March 2003

280. Asda's French set yogurt recall: Asda press notice, 10 February 2003

281. Asda's nut cookie recall: Asda press notice, 28 January 2003

281. Tesco's fruit muesli recall: Oxfordshire County Council, Trading Standards, 19 May 2003

281. Asda's and Lidl's hot dog recall: Food Standards Agency press release, 21 December 2001

281. Tinned gooseberries recall: Trading Standards News, Wigan Council, Issue 6, July 2001

281. Morrisons' salad cream recall: adverts in national press/www.ukrecallnotice/ co.uk 29 August 2003

281. Tesco's vegetarian nut cutlet recall: Watchdog product recalls, BBC *News*, 8 January 2003

281. Morrisons' soup recall: Food Standards Agency press release, 19 September 2003

282. Nitrofuran in prawns and shrimps: Food Standards Agency press release, 18 March 2002

282. Sudan 1: Food Standards Agency advice

282. Sudan 1 product recalls: Food Standards Agency press release, 29 October 2003

283. Denby Poultry Products case: Food Standards Agency press release 29 August 2003; just-food.com press release, 27 August 2003; *Guardian*, 30 August 2003

283. BBC1 *Food Police*: 12 November 2003

35 Meet the locals

285. Visit to Waitrose, Twyford: 20 October 2003

285. Visit to Marks & Spencer, Edinburgh: 21 October 2003

286. Sainsbury's photos of organic farmers on packaging: Sainsbury's press release, 12 December 2003

286. Safeway's regional produce: Safeway statement, 16 October 2003

287. Asda's Best of Wales and Best of the Lakes range: *The Grocer*, 5 July 2003

287. Somerfield's local/regional food lines: Somerfield statement, 21 October 2003

287. Waitrose's Long Crichel bread: *Financial Mail on Sunday*, 18 May 2003

287. Sainsbury's supplier development programmes: *The Grocer*, 3 May and 14 June 2003

287. Tesco's regional buying offices: Tesco farming press release, 19 March 2003

287. Mintel survey: Competition Commission Report on Safeway, page 371, para 8.350

288. Waitrose 30-mile criterion: author questionnaire 2003 (see below)

288. Booths wins Radio 4 Food and Farming Award: Booths press release, November 2003

288. Supermarket responses to author questionnaire: collected between 13 and 31 October 2003

289. Local foods in Waitrose, Marlow: visit 3 November 2003

289. Marks & Spencer 'Meet the Farmer and Grower' events: Marks & Spencer press release, 9 September 2003

290. Average number of food lines in UK supermarkets: 'State of the Art in Food', Cap Gemini/Ernst & Young, 2002

290. Visits to Co-op and Sainsbury's Local, Edinburgh: 1 November 2003

292. Soil Association Supermarket Survey: Living Earth, Spring 2004

292. Opportunities for local jewels: 'State of the Art in Food', Cap Gemini/Ernst & Young, 2002

36 Race to the bottom

293. Sainsbury's traceability website: Sainsbury's press release, 16 July 2003

293. Sainsbury's lack of response to questions: author questionnaire, responses sought between 13 and 31 October 2003

294. Co-op switches own-label coffee to Fairtrade: *Daily Telegraph*, 13 November 2003

294. Tesco selling illegally logged hardwoods: *Independent on Sunday*, 13 July 2003

295. Race to the Top: www.racetothetop.org

298. 'Billy Bunter of food retail': *Sunday Times* Sharewatch: 16 November 2003

298. Sir Peter Davis and Sainsbury's performance: *Guardian* Business, 19 November 2003, and *Financial Times*, 20 November 2003

298. Carlos Criado-Perez: *The Grocer*, 17 May 2003

37 Retail domination

303. Tesco's share of every £100 spent on the UK high street and groceries: *Guardian*, 17 September 2003

303. Asda overtakes Sainsbury's: Taylor Nelson Sofres press release 31 July 2003

304. 2007 forecasts for non-food sales: Richard Hyman, 'Verdict Research', *Observer*, 28 September 2003

305. Supermarket chains looking for larger stores: Competition Commission Report on Safeway 2003, page 18, para 2.25

305. David Reid: *Guardian*, 17 September 2003

305. Asda's George clothing line: *The Grocer*, 13 September 2003

306. Tesco 'eyeing up Matalan': *Daily Telegraph*, 27 September 2003 and *Financial Mail*, 21 September 2003

306. 'Things are really changing fast...': *Sunday Herald* Fashion Issue, 28 September 2003

306. Tesco Finest clothing range: *Sunday Times*, 23 November 2003

306. One in every five music albums is bought in a supermarket: *The Grocer*, 4 October 2003

306. Supermarkets' share of book market: *Bookseller*, 21 November 2003

306. Asda and optical retailing: Keynote Supermarkets and Superstores Report, 2002

306. Tesco's market leadership in news: *The Grocer*, 1 February 2003

306. Tesco sells more than Boots, Superdrug, HMV and WHSmith, and leader in airtime sales: *Guardian*, 17 September 2003

306. Tesco Mobile venture: *Guardian*, 23 September 2003

306. Tesco teams up with Lastminute.com: *Sunday Times*, 10 August 2003

306. Oddbins' advertisement: *Observer Food Monthly*, August 2003

307. Thresher's anxiety: Competition Commission Report on Safeway 2003, page 346, paras 8.150–8.154

307. Supermarkets control 65 per cent of UK wine sales: *Independent*, 4 December 2003

307. Tesco sells one in five bottles of wine: Tim Atkins, *The Observer* Magazine, 5 October 2003

307. Marks & Spencer suffers 6 per cent plunge in share of schoolwear: *The Times*, 24 September 2003

307. M & S loses its crown to Asda: *Independent* Business, 23 August 2004

307. BHS concern: *Observer* Business, 28 September 2003

308. WHSmith and Boots on the decline: *Guardian*, 15 October 2004

308. 'There is high demand . . .' and Asda insurance and call-centre staff: *Herald*, 27 September 2003

308. Asda's altered checkouts: *The Grocer*, 27 September 2003

308. Tesco, Sainsbury's and legal services: *The Grocer*, 2 August 2003

308. Tesco divorce finalising and wills: just-food.com, 21 January 2002

308. 'Tesco law' and the Lord Chancellor: *The Times*, 25 July 2003

308. One-stop legal shops: *The Times*, 16 September 2003

38 Big day out

311. *Crap Towns*: Sam Jordison, Dan Kieran and *Idler* magazine, *Crap Towns*, Boxtree Pan Macmillan, 2003

311. Sainsbury's Hazel Grove: J. Sainsbury PLC news release, 6 June 2002, and *The Times* Magazine, 31 May 2003

313. 'Splurchases': *Guardian*, 24 April 1996

313. Consultants visualising the store of the future (Kinneir Dufort/Appliance Studio): *The Grocer*, 3 May 2003

314. RFIDs: *Independent* Review, 22 September 2003

315. Metro's Future Store: ibid.

315. Aktiv Markt's '50-plus' stores: *The Times*, 18 November 2003

315. Federal Statistics Office prediction: ibid.

315. Research on purchase decisions: POPAI UK 1998

316. Andrew Harrison: *The Grocer*, 9 November 2002

316. Marks & Spencer's 'chillovator': *The Grocer*, 2 November 2002

316. Tesco TV: *The Grocer*, 26 July 2003

316. Sainsbury's digital pilots: ibid.

316. Safeway tracker trolleys: *The Grocer*, 9 November 2002

317. The Greenery salad 'octagon': UK salad market report 2003

39 You've been Tescoed

320. 'We have worked hard at developing a business model where "everyone is welcome" ': *www.tesco.com/talkingtesco/How we compete*

320. Prunella Scales: 'Tesco Prunella champions small stores': *Daily Mail*, 13 November 2006

321. 'At least 75 active campaigns in Britain opposing Tesco's plans': *www.tescopoly.org/local campaigns*

321. 'Tescoization' of the internet: *www.socialaffairsunit.org.uk/blog/archives/001156.php*

321. Iain Duncan Smith: speech at Third Sector's Award Ceremony, reported in *The Times*, 8 November 2005

321. Sean O'Grady: 'Happy to be the supermarket that ate Britain', *Independent*, 9 April 2005

322. Jonathan Glancey: 'Coming to a high street near you . . .', *Guardian*, 22 November 2004

322. Julia Finch: 'Where to avoid Tesco': *Guardian*, 11 October 2006

322. 'Tesco is rampaging through Hove like Attila the Hun': 'Anger at the Tescoisation of the nation', *Argus*, 4 October 2005

322. 'Almost 32 per cent of the nation's food spend . . .': *BBC News*, 30 August 2006

322. 'One out of every eight pounds spent in shops in Britain . . .': *BBC News*, 7 January 2007

322. '94% of the population has access': *www.tesco.com/talkingtesco/How we compete*

323. 'Locations that have been well and truly "Tescoed" include . . .': Julia Finch, 'Where to avoid Tesco', *Guardian*, 11 October 2006

323. Tesco was the dominant supermarket in 81 out of Britain's 121 postcode areas: ibid.

323. 'From small beginnings': *www.tesco.com/talkingtesco/How we compete*

323. 'There is a political-correctness bandwagon': Richard Hyman, MD Verdict Research, *Sunday Times*, 31 December 2006

324. Tesco's plans for Purley: *Natural Product News*, January 2007

324. 'Sales outside the UK now account for nearly a quarter of the chain's total revenues': *BBC News*, 25 April 2006

324. 'Over half of Tesco's selling space is now outside the UK': *Tesco Annual Review*, 2006

324. 'Tesco's inexorable progress': Richard Hyman, MD Verdict Research, *BBC News*, 30 August 2006

324. Sainsbury's warned the Competition Commission: *Guardian*, 21 October 2006

325. William Sitwell: interview in *Metro*, 19 December 2006

325. Lucy Neville-Rolfe: oral evidence to All Party Parliamentary Small Shops Group Committee, 3 November 2005

325. The proportion of Tesco's floor space taken up by these hypermarkets more than tripled between 2003 and 2006: figures taken from Tesco financial information

325. Friends of the Earth calculates: Friends of the Earth briefing, 'Calling the Shots', January 2006

325. Tesco has stated that it anticipates 'opening a further 20 Tesco Extras a year': 2005 Tesco annual report

325. It says that it will 'only proceed . . .': letter from Tesco to Friends of the Earth, 30 June 2006

326. Bridgnorth: *Shropshire Star*, 1 December 2005

326. 'Tesco wrote a letter to members of the planning committee at their home addresses': Carlisle City Council, Minutes of Development Control Committee Special Meeting, 5 August 2005

326. Eric Martlew: 'Tesco store delay anger', *News & Star*, 28 June 2005

326. 'These guys are professionals': Friends of the Earth, *The Tesco Takeover*, January 2006, page 11

327. 'Tactics include . . .': 'Tesco store delay anger', *News & Star*, 28 June 2005

327. The *Daily Telegraph* has reported seeing a 'battle plan': *Business Telegraph*, 7 November 2005

327. Allerton: Liverpool City Council Planning Committee minutes, 25 October 2005, *Liverpool Daily Post*, 12 October 2005

327. 'Tesco owned 58 per cent of the unbuilt-supermarket sites in the UK . . .': *Independent*, 12 March 2006

327. 'Preferring to refer to it as a "pipeline"': *BBC News*, 7 January 2007

327. 'We build stores of different sizes': ibid.

328. Sainsbury's, for instance, has complained: *Independent*, 21 October 2006

328. Barker Review: *Guardian*, 6 December 2006

328. 'Britain is changing': *www.tesco.com/talkingtesco/*

Index